# Canmore & Kananaskis
## Best Hikes • Best Activities

### by Ward Cameron
### An Altitude SuperGuide

# Publication Information

**Altitude Publishing Canada Ltd.**
1500 Railway Ave.
Canmore, Alberta
T1W 1P6
1-800-957-6888
www.altitudepublishing.com

Extreme care has been taken to ensure that all information presented in this book is accurate and up-to-date, and neither the author nor the publisher can be held responsible for any errors.

**Canadian Cataloguing in Publication Data**
Cameron, Ward, 1961-
Canmore and Kananaskis

(SuperGuide)
Includes index.
ISBN 1-55153-623-4

1. Kananaskis Country (Alta.)--Guidebooks.
2. Natural history--Alberta--Kananaskis Country--Guidebooks. 3. Outdoor recreation--Alberta--Kananaskis Country--Guidebooks. I. Title.
II. Series.
FC3695.K36C35 2001  917.123'32043  C96-910289-5
F1079.K36C35 2001

9  8  7  6  5  4  3  2

We acknowledge the financial support of the Government of Canada through the Book Publishing Industry Development Program (BPIDP) for our publishing activities.

**Front cover photo:** The Three Sisters
**Inset front cover:** The Bow Valley from Ha Ling Peak
**Frontispiece:** Mt. Birdwood reflected in Mud Lake
**Back cover photo:** Upper Kananaskis Lake

Made in Western Canada
Printed and bound in Canada
by Friesen Printers, Altona, Manitoba

Altitude GreenTree Program
Altitude Publishing will plant in Canada twice as many trees as were used in the manufacturing of this product.

## Project Development

| | |
|---|---|
| Concept/ Art Direction | Stephen Hutchings |
| Design/Layout | Scott Manktelow |
| Design Assistant | Andy Stanton |
| Editing | Andrea Murphy |
| | Penny E. Grey |
| | Jennifer Groundwater |
| Index | Elizabeth Bell |
| Maps | Scott Manktelow |
| | Andy Stanton |
| | Mark Higenbottam |
| Financial Management | Laurie Smith |

## A Note from the Publisher

The world described in Altitude SuperGuides is a unique and fascinating place. It is a world filled with surprise and discovery, beauty and enjoyment, questions and answers. It is a world of people, cities, landscape, animals, and wilderness as seen through the eyes of those who live in, work with, and care for this world. The process of describing this world is also a means of defining ourselves.

It is also a world of relationship, where people derive their meaning from a deep and abiding contact with the land–as well as from each other. And it is this sense of relationship that guides all of us at Altitude to ensure that these places continue to survive and evolve in the decades ahead.

Altitude SuperGuides are books intended to be used, as much as read. Like the world they describe, Altitude SuperGuides are evolving, adapting and growing. Please write to us with your comments and observations, and we will do our best to incorporate your ideas into future editions of these books.

Stephen Hutchings
Publisher

# Contents

## Canmore & Kananaskis Hiking Trails

| Hike | Rating | Length | Elev. Gain | Features |
|---|---|---|---|---|
| 1 Benchlands Trail System | Moderate | 9.0 km loop | 240 m | |
| 2 Mount Lady Macdonald | Strenuous | 3.5 km one way | 890 m | |
| 3 Cougar Creek Trail | Moderate | 3.0 km one way | 30 m | |
| 4 Townsite Trail Network | Easy | Varies | 0 m | |
| 5 Canmore Canalside | Easy | 4.6 km one way | drops 30 m | |
| 6 Canmore Nordic Centre Provincial Park | All Ratings | Varies | Varies | |
| 7 Georgetown Trail | Moderate | 5.8 km loop | 70 m | |
| 8 Rundle Riverside Trail | Moderate | 14.1 km one way | 30 m | |
| 9 Grassi Lakes Trail | Easy | 3.1 km loop | 95 m | |
| 10 Prairie View | Moderate | 16.1 km loop | 576 m | |
| 11 Stoney Trail | Easy | 16.6 km one way | 76 m | |
| 12 Baldy Pass | Strenuous | 17 km one way | 460 m | |
| 13 Kananaskis Village Trail System | Easy | 6.0 km one way | 150 m | |
| 14 Terrace Trail | Easy | 9.0 km one way | 45 m | |
| 15a Ribbon Creek to Ribbon Falls | Easy | 11.0 km one way | 400 m | |
| 15b Ribbon Creek to Ribbon Lake | Strenuous | 12.8 km one way | 600 m | |
| 16 Galatea Creek Trail | Moderate | 7.2 km one way | 630 m | |
| 17 Centennial Ridge Trail | Strenuous | 16.8 km one way | 1319 m | |
| 18 Skogan Pass Trail | Strenuous | 20.9 km one way | 763 m | |
| 19 Evan-Thomas Bicycle Path | Easy | 11.0 km one way | 75 m | |
| 20 Ptarmigan Cirque | Easy | 4.5 km loop | 219 m | |
| 21 Mist Creek | Strenuous | 11.9 km one way | 563 m | |
| 22 Cataract Creek | Moderate | 14.1 km one way | 642 m | |
| 23 Etherington Creek | Moderate | 11.2 km one way | 753 m | |
| 24 Paved Trail | Easy | 10.4 km one way | 75 m | |
| 25 Pocaterra to Kananaskis Fire Lookout | Strenuous | 12.1 km one way | 480 km | |
| 26 Whiskey Jack Trail | Moderate | 3.7 km one way | 225 m | |
| 27 Elk Lakes | Strenuous | 8.2 km one way | 215 m | |
| 28 Mount Indefatigable | Strenuous | 2.2 km one way | 500 m | |
| 29 Upper Kananaskis Lake Circuit | Moderate | 14.9 km loop | 70 m | |
| 30a Three-isle Lake | Strenuous | 11.6 km one way | 610 m | |
| 30b Turbine Canyon | Strenuous | 16.5 km one way | 668 m | |
| 31 Lower Lake Trail | Easy | 3.5 km one way | 30 m | |
| 32 Elbow Lake | Easy | 1.3 km one way | 120 m | |
| 33 Goat Creek | Easy | 19.8 km one way | 291 m | |
| 34 Buller Pass | Strenuous | 6.5 km one way | 670 m | |

## Canmore & Kananaskis Hiking Trails

| # | Hike | Rating | Length | Elev. Gain | Features |
|---|------|--------|--------|-----------|----------|
| 35 | Mount Shark to Mount Assiniboine | Strenuous | 25.5 km one way | 417 m | Scenic views, Wildflowers, Fall colours, Equestrian-use allowed |
| 36 | Burstall Pass | Moderate | 7.1 km one way | 460 m | Scenic views, Wildflowers, Fall colours, Bicycle-use allowed |
| 37 | Chester Lake | Easy | 3.9 km one way | 320 m | Families, Scenic views, Wildflowers, Fall colours |
| 38 | Sawmill Trail System | Moderate | 18.4 km loop | 185 m | Bicycle-use allowed |
| 39 | Black Prince Cirque | Easy | 4.0 km loop | 70 m | Families, Scenic views, Wildflowers |
| 40 | Many Springs Trail | Easy | 1.5 km loop | nil | Families, Scenic views, Wildflowers, Fall colours |
| 41 | Flowing Water Interpretive Trail | Easy | 2.0 km loop | nil | Families, Scenic views, Wildflowers, Fall colours |
| 42 | Montane Trail | Easy | 2.2 km loop | nil | Families, Wildflowers, Fall colours |
| 43 | Bow Valley Bicycle Path | Easy | 4.1 km one way | nil | Families, Fall colours, Bicycle-use allowed |
| 44 | Middle Lake Trail | Easy | 2.5 km loop | nil | Families, Scenic views, Wildflowers, Fall colours |
| 45 | Jumpingpound Loop | Easy | 9.0 km loop | 100 m | Families, Scenic views, Wildflowers, Fall colours, Equestrian-use allowed |
| 46 | Eagle Hill | Moderate | 5.0 km one way | 222 m | Scenic views, Fall colours, Equestrian-use allowed |
| 47 | Tom Snow Trail | Moderate | 15.6 km one way | 150 m | Fall colours, Equestrian-use allowed, Bicycle-use allowed |
| 48 | Jumpingpound Ridge to Cox Hill | Strenuous | 19.3 km one way | 680 m | Scenic views, Wildflowers, Fall colours, Equestrian-use allowed |
| 49 | Telephone Trail | Moderate | 16.0 km one way | 25 m | Fall colours, Equestrian-use allowed, Bicycle-use allowed |
| 50 | Alder Trail | Easy | 1.0 km loop | nil | Families, Wildflowers, Fall colours |
| 51 | Fullerton Loop Trail | Easy | 6.1 km loop | 155 m | Families, Fall colours, Equestrian-use allowed, Bicycle-use allowed |
| 52 | Diamond T Loop | Easy | 3.7 km loop | 125 m | Families, Fall colours, Equestrian-use allowed, Bicycle-use allowed |
| 53 | Elbow Valley and Sulphur Springs Loop | Moderate | 13.0 km loop | 150 m | Scenic views, Wildflowers, Fall colours, Equestrian-use allowed, Bicycle-use allowed |
| 54 | Moose Mountain Ridge Road | Strenuous | 7.1 km one way | 477 m | Scenic views, Wildflowers, Fall colours, Bicycle-use allowed |
| 55 | River View Trail | Easy | 4.0 km loop | nil | Families, Scenic views, Wildflowers, Fall colours, Equestrian-use allowed, Bicycle-use allowed |
| 56 | Powderface Creek Trail | Moderate | 9.1 km one way | 500 m | Equestrian-use allowed, Bicycle-use allowed |
| 57 | Prairie Creek Trail | Moderate | 10.4 km one way | 225 m | Equestrian-use allowed, Bicycle-use allowed |
| 58 | Powderface Ridge Trail | Strenuous | 4.5 km one way | 590 m | Scenic views, Wildflowers, Equestrian-use allowed, Bicycle-use allowed |
| 59 | Nihahi Ridge Trail | Moderate | 3.8 km one way | 510 m | Families, Scenic views, Wildflowers |
| 60 | Nihahi Creek | Moderate | 2.6 km one way | 50 m | Families, Scenic views |
| 61 | Big Elbow/Little Elbow Loop | Strenuous | 44.2 km loop | 625 m | Scenic views, Wildflowers, Fall colours, Equestrian-use allowed, Bicycle-use allowed |
| 62 | Forgetmenot Rounder | Strenuous | 46.4 km loop | 450 m | Scenic views, Wildflowers, Equestrian-use allowed, Bicycle-use allowed |
| 63 | Junction Mountain Fire Lookout | Strenuous | 14.2 km one way | 682 m | Scenic views, Wildflowers, Fall colours, Equestrian-use allowed, Bicycle-use allowed |
| 64 | Sandy McNabb Interpretive Trail | Easy | 1.8 km loop | nil | Families, Scenic views, Wildflowers, Fall colours |
| 65 | Death Valley Trail | Moderate | 11.9 km one way | 60 m | Fall colours, Equestrian-use allowed, Bicycle-use allowed |
| 66 | Missinglink Trail | Moderate | 7.4 km one way | 25 m | Fall colours, Equestrian-use allowed, Bicycle-use allowed |
| 67 | Gorge Creek Trail | Moderate | 11.8 km one way | 360 m | Scenic views, Wildflowers, Fall colours, Equestrian-use allowed, Bicycle-use allowed |
| 68 | Wolf Creek Trail | Moderate | 11.0 km one way | 145 m | Fall colours, Equestrian-use allowed, Bicycle-use allowed |
| 69 | Sheep Trail | Moderate | 42.2 km one way | 355 m | Wildflowers, Fall colours, Equestrian-use allowed, Bicycle-use allowed |

Legend: Appropriate for families · Scenic views · Wildflowers · Fall colours · Equestrian-use allowed · Bicycle-use allowed

# Introduction

*Mount Baldy towers above Highway 40*

**W**elcome to Alberta's best kept secret. The town of Canmore is more than just the gateway to Banff National Park; it's also one of the key entry points to the fabulous wilderness of Kananaskis Country to the south. This 4,000 sq. km (1,544 sq. mi.) recreation area contains the highest driveable point in Canada, along with the highest maintained hiking trail in the Canadian Rockies. Other highlights include a Robert Trent Jones golf course, five-star hotels, horseback, mountain bike and four-wheel drive trails, and even a former prisoner-of-war camp.

Canmore began as a railroad siding and evolved to become a major supplier of coal for the Canadian Pacific Railway. When the mines closed in 1979, Canmore risked slowly disappearing like so many other small towns when the mines closed up. Within a very few years tourism began to pick up and Canmore became attractive for its beautiful scenery and inexpensive real estate. In time, the prices rose with the towns popularity, but the casual character and quiet charm remain. In 2001, Harrowsmith Country Life Magazine ranked it as one of the "Ten Prettiest Small Towns in Canada".

Kananaskis Country, established in 1977, is a virtual newborn compared to hundred year-old of Banff National Park. Despite its recent designation, Kananaskis has become famous for its fabulous scenery and unparalleled alpine recreation. It was Alberta's Premier, Peter Lougheed, who set aside 4,000 sq. km (1,544 sq. mi.) of Alberta's eastern slopes as Kananaskis Country Provincial Recreation Area. At the same time, an area of 304 sq. km (117 sq. mi.) around the Kananaskis Lakes was preserved within the newly established Kananaskis Provincial Park (now Peter Lougheed Provincial Park). Geographically, Kananaskis Country is west of Calgary and borders Banff National Park and the continental divide on its western margin. Since 1977,

*Opposite: Mt. Kidd reflected in Wedge Pond*

*A hiker surveys the Goat Range from Ha Ling Peak*

Peter Lougheed Provincial Park has been joined by numerous other park designations within Kananaskis Country's boundary. Since the first edition of this book, the Alberta Government has established the Elbow-Sheep Wildland Park, Bow Valley Wildland Park, Spray Valley Provincial Park, and Canmore Nordic Centre Provincial Park.

While not technically a park, Kananaskis Country is a Provincial Recreation Area within which there are seven Provincial Parks. The area is managed under a multiple-use concept, allowing it to support a wide variety of activities. As planners were unleashed on this new area, they divided it based on sensitivity to impact. Delicate areas were classed as "prime protection", while others were zoned to allow development. Kananaskis Country straddles the transition from foothill to Rocky Mountain. This provides a dramatic landscape, with a varied plant and animal population. From the white-tail deer of the plains, to the alpine-dwelling mountain goat, all manner of wildlife can be viewed from within its boundaries.

Over the years, the Kananaskis has seen many visitors. In its early days, it was used as a travel corridor for the early settlers en route to the Oregon Territory. Later, during the Great Depression, a camp provided work for the multitudes of unemployed. Like residents of many such camps across North America, these workers built some of the earliest recreational developments in this area. As the Depression ended, and war approached, the camp was taken over as an internment camp for German nationals. It was later converted into a full-fledged prisoner-of-war camp. Once the prisoners were repatriated, the valley returned to a quiet existence until its formal designation in 1977. Even then, things remained relatively peaceful, as marketing outside the province was virtually nonexistent. This all changed in 1988 with the Calgary Winter Olympics. Since both the downhill and Nordic events were held within the boundaries of Kananaskis Country, millions of people were introduced to this area. Subsequently, Kananaskis has been the focus of media attention and endless numbers of development proposals. At the same time, it provides some of the most spectacular scenery and extensive outdoor recreation in the Rockies.

## How to Use this Book

Canmore and Kananaskis Country, along with their well developed roads and facilities, offer picturesque panoramas, quiet campgrounds and scenic Sunday drives. They can satisfy every kind of outdoor passion, whether that encompasses technical rock climbing or more passive pursuits. This book is designed to provide a general introduction to the

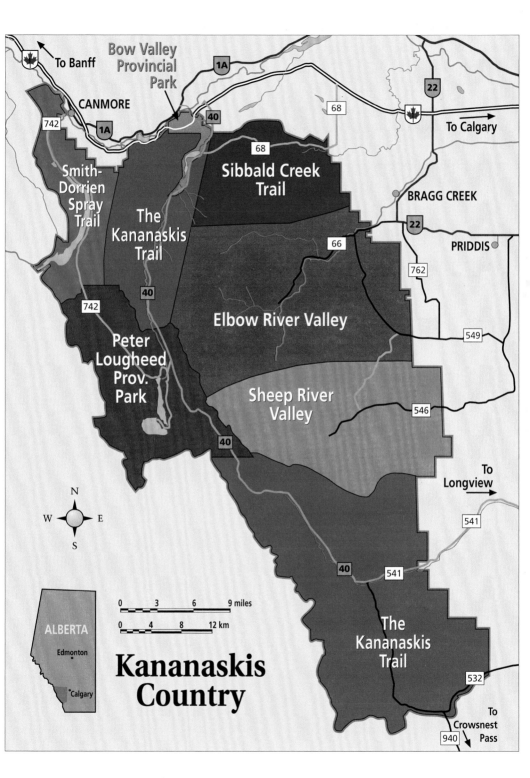

To Banff

Bow Valley Provincial Park

1A

CANMORE

742

1A

40

68

22

To Calgary

BRAGG CREEK

PRIDDIS

Smith-Dorrien Spray Trail

The Kananaskis Trail

Sibbald Creek Trail

68

66

22

762

742

40

Elbow River Valley

549

Peter Lougheed Prov. Park

Sheep River Valley

546

To Longview

541

40

541

N

W ← ⬤ → E

S

0   3   6   9 miles
0   4   8   12 km

The Kananaskis Trail

532

To Crowsnest Pass

940

ALBERTA

Edmonton

Calgary

# Kananaskis Country

*King Creek in the Opal Range*

area, its recreational potential and scenic highlights. At the same time, it is designed to facilitate browsing, and allow serendipity to take over.

To maintain some semblance of order, it has been divided into sections. Beginning with a general description of the natural and human history, we've tried to place the area into the proper context. The mountains are a unique area with features and processes that aren't found elsewhere. In addition, the plants and animals must also be capable of surviving in this harsh environment.

While the plants and animals have had hundreds of generations to adapt to the harsh realities of mountain life, the area's non-native residents have had only a few. In the Rockies, the history is short, but there's no shortage of history! The short timespan of European involvement provides a surprising number of anecdotes and examples of struggle and exploration.

The mountains beg to be explored and personally experienced. Kananaskis is a unique playground with opportunities for just about any wilderness activity. There are places for quiet hikes, or screaming dirt bikes. The camping facilities are endless, and the backcountry beckons. The fourth section describes some of the opportunities for recreation. It is merely a primer on some of the options available, and will help you to make more of your trip to the Kananaskis.

After these introductory chapters, we've divided the book based on region. The colour bar at the top of each page is can be used to locate yourself within the book. Every colour bar corresponds to a region within Canmore/Kananaskis (identified on the map on the previous page). We begin with a thorough description of the town of Canmore. This is followed by a region by region breakdown of the facilities and highlights of Kananaskis Country. Since the western region of Kananaskis is the most highly visited, and extensively explored, we've started here. From the western region, we move on to other areas, including Bow Valley Provincial Park, the Elbow and finally the Sheep River Valleys. One challenge of writing a book on the Kananaskis comes from its habit of naming roads 'Trails'. Roads like the Powderface Trail, are often confused with true trail names like Powderface Ridge Trail, or Powderface Creek Trail. When necessary, We have added the word 'road' to the names of highways to avoid confusion.

Finally, we've greatly expanded the trail section in this new edition. We've moved them to the second half of the book to allow us to focus specifically on the trails, their descriptions and maps. We hope this makes it easy to find the information you need. The pages are colour coded to help you quickly navigate through the various sections of the book.

As you explore Kananaskis Country, you will undoubtedly find the area's diversity and rugged nature, in addition to its spectacular beauty, will continue to draw you back again and again.

*Opposite: Snow-covered field in Peter Lougheed Provincial Park*

# Highlights of Nature

*View from Nihahi Ridge*

Kananaskis Country's landscape is a unique combination of prairie, foothill, and mountain. Plains give way to the jagged peaks of the Rocky Mountains, and the plants and animals reflect this diversity. The eastern part of Kananaskis Country exhibits the rolling character of the foothills, with a gentle transition from valley to ridgetop. Primarily sandstone and shale, these low, tree-covered slopes support a diverse plant and animal life. They also form an ideal terrain for recreational pursuits like mountain biking and horseback riding. The valleys are normally composed of soft shale surrounded by resistant ridges of sandstone. The youngest of the Kananaskis rock structures, they range in age from 135–75 million years.

The western ends of the Elbow and Sheep river valleys mark the official start of the Front Ranges of the Rocky Mountains. Particularly evident along Highway 66, the rolling face of Powderface Ridge stands in stark contrast to the jagged knife-blade appearance of Nihahi Ridge. Climbing Nihahi Ridge, you see only jagged peaks to the west and rolling foothills to the east.

The Front Ranges are characterized by steeply angled slopes with extensive folding. Good places to see these slopes are along the Opal, Highwood, and Kananaskis ranges.

Further west, the jagged peaks of the Front Ranges give way to the higher, more castellate summits of the Main Ranges. These resistant slopes are made of ancient limestones and dolomites, the oldest rocks in the Kananaskis area.

Kananaskis' combination of plains mixed with foothills and mountains makes it an ideal place to study natural history. By following the transition of aspen parkland to rocky alpine ridges, you find a larger variety of plants and animals than by travelling either east to the plains or deeper into the mountains.

The mountain climate also has an effect on the plants and animals. When the steep,

## Life Before the Mountains

*Mounts Sarrail, Foch, and Fox above the Upper Kananaskis Lake*

**The mountains didn't** always exist as they do today; 345 million years ago, much of western Canada was submerged beneath the waves of a large inland sea. Within these waters, thick beds of limestone were deposited. Today this limestone is a major component of the Rocky Mountains. We can see stark limestone formations in the cliffs above the Kananaskis Lakes and Mount Birdwood along the Smith–Dorrien/Spray Trail.

By 156 million years ago, the seas had receded and been replaced by a swampy lowland. To the southwest was a large sea, whose shoreline changed over time. In the shallow waters, limestone, siltstone, and sandstone formed. In the deeper waters farther from shore, fine clays settled to the bottom, forming extensive layers of shale.

In time, the oceans receded, and by 65 million years ago, warm temperate conditions prevailed, with large rivers meandering across the plains, bringing sediments from low mountains to the west. Daily, across Alberta, the age-old struggle for survival

continued as it had for eons. Huge meat-eating dinosaurs, like *Albertasaurus,* were patrolling the edges of marshes and rivers, looking for potential prey. Many left their remains behind, to be dug up as fossils in Alberta's dinosaur country. Most of the fine-grained sandstone, siltstone, and shale, created over wide areas of land, were later removed by erosion, and none remain within Kananaskis.

To understand the formation of the Rockies, we need to examine a theory known as Plate Tectonics. According to this theory, the surface of the Earth is made up of a series of plates, each moving relative to the others. At one time, all the continents were joined into one large land mass. Slowly this supercontinent began to break apart into numerous plates, and the continents began to drift.

Periods of mountain building are known as Orogenys, and in this area two have been responsible for the mountains we see today. Prior to these, the North American Plate had been moving in a westerly direction, and the

neighbouring Pacific Plate trending northward.

As the two plates collided, shock waves moved inland, compressing and piling up the rocks to the east of the impact. The first shock wave initiated the Columbia Orogeny (forming the Columbia Mountains, made up of the Caribous, Selkirks, Purcells, and Monashees), and occurred about 175 million years ago. As the shock wave moved eastward, it forced huge masses of rock to crack and slide up over their neighbours. This thrust faulting was instrumental in the formation of the Rockies. The shock wave began pushing up the western ranges, and then the Main Ranges, about 120 million years ago.

The second shock wave moved inland about 85 million years ago, and touched off the Laramide Orogeny. The force behind this second collision formed the Front Ranges and the foothills, but died out as it approached present-day Calgary, and so the prairies were left undisturbed.

rocky mountains are mixed with a dry, continental climate, we find an environment where only the strong survive. Under difficult conditions, plants and animals become uniquely adapted, and luck is often a key to survival.

## Weathering and Erosion

One of the amazing things about mountains is that they are always changing. No sooner had their heads emerged above the waves, when nature began to slowly tear them down. Erosion has taken the original peaks of the Rockies and created a "work in progress," a landscape of ever changing, slowly shrinking peaks.

When the Front Ranges were formed about 75–85 million years ago, they were quite a bit larger than they are today—almost twice the size. A variety of forces are at work.

Water is the biggest agent of erosion, flowing down the

## Glacier Cooled

*Glaciers changed the landscape*

**Glaciers are the** most recognizable force helping to shape the mountains. During the ice age, the entire landscape of Alberta changed. Across the prairies huge sheets of ice made their way towards the mountain front, while upslope, rivers of ice were sculpting and scouring the landscape.

Glaciers are a special type of ice. Unlike the brittle ice we are familiar with, glacial ice acts more like a very thick liquid. As glacial ice accumulates into huge masses, pressure on the lower layers allows the ice to flow, slowly, under the force of gravity. The ice

on the surface of the glacier isn't under pressure and so remains brittle, and huge crevasses, or cracks, form as it moves over obstacles.

Contrary to popular belief, glaciers are always moving—even during the hottest days of summer—however, they may melt back from the "toe" faster than they move forward. If a glacier moves forward 18 m in a year, but melts backward 23 m during the summer, then the net movement is 5 m up the valley. We call this a receding glacier, and this is the situation for most glaciers in

Alberta today.

Glaciers themselves do very little eroding. It's the material carried within the ice that acts as an abrasive, carving away at the valley. Glaciers pick up rocks and debris along their margins, and this material is carried down the valley, forming a powerful abrasive. As you might imagine, these rocks are quickly ground into a fine powder, known as rock flour, which then makes its way into our streams and lakes, giving them the incredible colours known the world over.

## Mountain Types

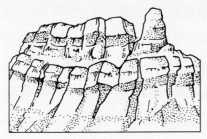

### Castellate Mountain
Typically found in the Main Ranges, this type of mountain shows towers composed of horizontal layers of resistant limestone, dolomite, and quartzite, and ledges of softer shale. Mount Kidd is a classic example.

### Horn Mountain
Carved by glaciers on several sides, horn mountains are remnant peaks left behind when the glaciers melted.

### Sawtooth Mountain
Common in the Front Ranges, sawtooth mountains are formed when steeply angled slopes are carved by the action of wind and water to create jagged ridges similar to the blade of a saw.

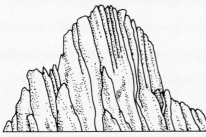

### Dogtooth Mountain
Another Front Range mountain, the dogtooth occurs when the layers of a peak are thrust almost straight up leaving a resistant spire appearance. Mount Birdwood is a classic example of such a peak.

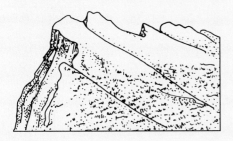

### Overthrust Mountain
Often described as a "writing desk" type of mountain, overthrust mountains are a classic Front Range peak. Formerly horizontal layers of rock are thrust up, at steep angles, over younger rocks. Mount Rundle is a classic example, as is Nihahi Ridge in the Elbow Valley of Kananaskis Country.

*Big Elbow River and Forgetmenot Mountain*

mountain as runoff. As it flows, it picks up material, and these sediments in turn act as abrasives that wear away at the rock. Water has a dramatic impact on the landforms we see. Each mountain is being slowly dissected by flowing water. As rivulets give way to rivers, mountain ranges are cut into peaks.

Further downstream, the river may carve intricate canyons and create roaring waterfalls, depending on geological conditions. Water is the chisel with which the mountains are being sculpted.

Constant freezing and thawing works to chip away the mountains. Water expands as it freezes, and when it flows into small cracks and subsequently freezes, it acts as a powerful wedge. When you look at the large, loose-rock, or scree, slopes found at the base of most cliffs in the area, you're looking at the results of millions of years of freezing and thawing.

Much of the scree that makes up these slopes was formed near the end of the last ice age, as areas adjacent to the receding glaciers experienced climatic conditions similar to permafrost areas. This periglacial, or "near glacial" climate resulted in significantly more frost-wedging than today. So for a short time, geologically speaking, the mountains were being worn down at a more rapid rate than they are now.

Chemical erosion is another process acting on the mountains. Water and carbon dioxide in the atmosphere react to form a weak carbonic acid, which easily dissolves the limestone and washes it away.

Plants also help to wear the mountains down. Some, like the orange lichens coating many of the local rocks, can slowly dissolve the rock and help in the creation of soil. Other plants force their roots down the smallest of cracks and cause results similar to those of frost wedging.

By understanding the processes that have helped to shape the mountains, we can more easily interpret the landforms themselves. Each process has distinctive impacts, and helps us to see the process of change, even though we may not notice the mountains visibly shrinking.

## Climate

Living in the mountains has its ups and downs—literally. It has the advantage of some of the most dramatic scenery in the world; however, it also requires dealing with weather patterns that vary as dramatically.

The variation in temperature is difficult for most newcomers to comprehend. Sun and shade can vary by as much as 50°F, while daily fluctuations can be even larger. One July day, the high at the Kananaskis Ranger Station was 32.8°C (91.8°F), while the average for July is a more moderate 22.7°C (72.9°F). Temperatures can easily drop below freezing when sudden

**17**

*Sheep River Valley*

storms come through. It is normal for it to snow at high elevations at least once in July each year. In January, the temperature can vary between a frigid -45°C (-49°F) and a balmy 10 (50°F) or 15°C (59°F).

The prevailing winds are generally from the west, and greatly influence the weather. Heading inland from the Pacific coast, they begin as moisture-laden clouds that cool rapidly as they are forced to climb over the mountains. This drop in temperature forces them to release much of their moisture as snow and rain, long before they reach the eastern side of the Divide. Kananaskis would be much wetter were it not for our mountain wall. For instance, Revelstoke has an annual precipitation of around 1,064 mm (43 in.) compared to the 400–600-mm (16–24-in.) average in Kananaskis.

Not to be outdone, the prairies also influence our weather. Despite our normally western winds, we often feel the sting of easterlies during early summer or in the midst of cold winters. Since these clouds are still moisture laden upon reaching the mountains, and cool as they head west, we find ourselves digging out the rain gear. This "upslope weather" can last several weeks at a time, and is characterized by the presence of clear weather on the western side of the Divide. Head west and you may be able to escape the grasp of an upslope storm.

During winter upslope conditions, the weather is usually very dry, and is influenced by the large arctic fronts so well known in the north. We are often left with little precipitation and very cold temperatures. You may also notice ice crystals in the air for extended periods during a cold upslope pattern.

These same slope weather patterns can also occur more locally. Called orographic lifting, water droplets that evaporate during the day, rise and rapidly cool. As the water condenses with increased altitude, you may notice clouds around high summits on otherwise cloudless days.

Along with orographic lifting comes orographic weather. As the air warms during the heat of day, it rises and slowly condenses around the mountain tops. By mid to late afternoon, enough moisture has condensed to cause a sudden, torrential downpour. These storms are usually short lived, and very localized in nature, but can be extremely violent and prone to lightning. It's important to be on the look-out for this type of weather when hiking on hot summer evenings. There have been numerous fatalities caused by lightning. Make sure you drop down off exposed ridges when bad weather comes in. Since the patterns vary with the local geography, moving from one side of a valley to another can mean a huge change in weather.

## Chinooks–the "perfect hurricane"

**Of the many** weather patterns characterizing the Rockies, none are more steeped in mystery and folklore than the Chinook wind. These hot, dry winds are famous for bringing a welcome respite to winter, and for leaving Calgary free of snow in January. The temperature changes can be dramatic. On Jan. 11, 1983, the temperature in Calgary rose 30°C (54°F) (from -17°C to 13°C) in four hours, and on February 7, 1964, the humidity dropped by 43 percent, while the temperature rose 28°C (50.4°F).

To the local Indians, it was known as the "Snow Eater," for it could literally eat a foot of snow per hour. With rapid rises in temperature, snow has little time to melt, so instead, quickly evaporates. To local natives living on the plains during frigid winters, the Chinook was seen as a welcome break from the cold.

The journals of early explorers are filled with details on the Chinook. Alexander MacKenzie referred to a Chinook as a "perfect hurricane." In 1787, David Thompson wrote that the rise in temperature experienced by travelling to the mountains was similar to travelling south. Even at the turn of the century, the *Calgary Herald* was writing about these warm winds.

*"Those who have not the warm, invigorating Chinook winds of this country, cannot well comprehend what a blessing they are. The icy*

*The famous Chinook arch*

*clutch of winter is lessened, the earth throws off its winding sheet of snow. Humanity ventures forth to inhale the balmy spring like air. Animated nature rejoices." (1900– Calgary weekly Herald)*

How does a Chinook form? Its creation requires a mountain range that runs perpendicular to the prevailing winds. As the winds blow inland from the coast, they rise to climb over the

mountain summits. With increased altitude the temperature drops, and before long, clouds become saturated as the moisture within condenses. These wet clouds cool as they rise, and release their moisture as rain and snow along the western slopes of the Rocky Mountains. By the time they crest the summit of the Continental Divide, they are largely devoid of moisture, and rapidly descend the eastern slopes. Dry air changes temperature with decreasing altitude at almost twice the rate of saturated air. Simply stated, it warms up more coming down the Alberta side than it cools climbing up the western slopes. The end result is a warm, dry wind blowing off the mountains.

## What to Wear?

**In the mountains,** having the proper clothing can make the difference between a pleasant experience and misery. This is the land of the synthetics. Products like polypropylene and fleece rule the roost. Unlike cotton, which holds moisture and keeps you cold, these materials cannot absorb water, and will continue to keep you warm even when wet.

The motto "Be Prepared" provides words to live by. With weather changing in minutes, having extra clothes to put on, or rain gear to stay dry, can be

critical. It can still rain, even on a cloudless day. During winter outings, having warm clothes can be a life saver, especially in the case of unexpected injury.

Dressing in layers allows you to add layers as you cool down, and remove them as you warm up. Heavy layers cause you to sweat as you begin working, and sweating is never good during winter. Suddenly your clothes are wet, and their insulating capacity compromised, especially if you're wearing a cotton T-shirt.

*Western anemone*

*Yarrow*

*Yellow hedysarum*

*Cow parsnip*

*Bunchberry*

## Plants

In mountainous areas, plants must adapt to the harsh environment in order to survive. Large variations in temperature over a short period of time, mixed with short growing seasons, means only the most versatile plants are found in the mountains.

Many things may determine whether a plant is able to survive in a particular area. In terms of nutrients, if even one critical component is in short supply, the distribution of the plant may be curtailed. A plant's survival is also dependent on less predictable factors. If a particular animal takes a liking to a plant, this may limit its distribution, though the plant may otherwise thrive. Fire may also affect distribution. Other limiting factors include altitude, exposure to sun, temperature, moisture, and wind. If successful, the end result is a delicate, yet vibrant community of plants that are well-adapted to their environment.

## Wildflowers
### White Flowers
**Western Anemone** *(Anemone occidentalis)*
Often the first flower to bloom in the alpine, it has five whitish petals and a fuzzy stem and leaves. The flower quickly gives way to a shaggy seed head, earning it the nickname "hippie on a stick."
**Yarrow** *(Achillea millefolium)*
This umbrella-like flower is widely distributed across Canada. The leaves are finely dissected and look almost fern-like. This plant was used to heal Achilles' soldiers during the Battle of Troy in Greek mythology.
**Yellow Hedysarum** *(Hedysarum sulphurescens)*
A favourite food of grizzlies, this member of the pea plant is common in spring and early summer. The distinctive pea-like flower heads tend to grow on one side of the tall stem. The leaves grow in groups of 9–17 leaflets, forming a typical compound leaf.
**Cow Parsnip** *(Heracleum lanatum)*
This giant of a plant may be

*Early yellow locoweed*

*Yellow mountain avens*

*Shrubby cinquefoil*

*Brown-eyed Susan*

*Heartleaf arnica*

upward of 2 m (7 ft.) in height. Its large umbrella-shaped flower head and huge rhubarb-like leaves make it unmistakable. Another favourite of grizzlies, it is common along moist avalanche slopes. It may also be found along rivers and other wet areas.

## Bunchberry *(Cornus canadensis)*

Part of the dogwood family, bunchberry gets its name from the clump of red berries it produces each year. The leaves consist of a rosette of 4–6 leaves. The veins in the leaves clearly run parallel to the outer margin of the leaf, in typical dogwood style. Four whitish bracts that appear as petals form what most people view as the flower.

## Yellow Flowers

### Early Yellow Locoweed *(Oxytropus sericea)*

Locoweed, like other members of the pea family, is easy to identify. The compound leaves and flower head grow from a common base. The flower is a cream colour, forming a clump of pea-like flowers at the top of a hairy stem. It is poisonous to cattle, and earned its name from its effect on unwary cows.

### Yellow Mountain Avens *(Dryas drummondii)*

One of the toughest mountain plants, it forms a carpet along river washes, roadsides, and other inhospitable, dry spots. It has serrated leaves set off by small, nodding yellow flowers. The seed stage resembles a blond ponytail, which opens to form a fluffy seed head.

### Shrubby Cinquefoil *(Potentilla fruticosa)*

This common shrub grows as both an ornamental and native plant. Usually a few feet high, it has leaves that grow in groups of 3–7 (usually 5). The flowers are yellow, with five petals, and resemble a buttercup in appearance.

### Brown-eyed Susan *(Gaillardia aristata)*

These yellow daisy-like flowers have a chocolate-coloured centre. They are common in the foothills, and their long stalks (30–80 cm, or 12–32 in.) sway in the breeze. The leaves at the base are long and thin, but become heavily toothed along the stem.

*Indian paintbrush*

*Common vetch*

*Pink wintergreen*

*Calypso orchid or fairy slipper*

*Common fireweed*

**Heartleaf Arnica** *(Arnica cordifolia)*
Looking like a yellow daisy, the heartleaf arnica is one of the easiest flowers to identify, and one of the more common. Its green leaves are serrated and heart-shaped. They are also quite large. The flower is common in lodgepole pine forests, and brightens the sparse vegetation.

## Pink and Red Flowers

**Indian Paintbrush** *(Castilleja miniata)*
This versatile flower can vary dramatically in colour, from deep purple to red, yellow or white. The "petals" are really a series of coloured bracts surrounding the small tubular flowers. The top of the plant looks like it has been dipped in paint, hence the name.

**Common Vetch** *(Vicia americana)*
This trailing vine is common in the lower montane forest. Typical of pea plants, the leaves are in pairs and the flowers are purple in colour. Unlike the Hedysarum, it doesn't stand tall, but uses other plants as an anchor.

**Pink Wintergreen** *(Pyrola asarifolia)*
This pleasant pink flower is common in lodgepole pine forests during the spring. Waxy in nature, it has a basal rosette of dark leaves. The reddish and cup-shaped flower rises above. The flower is unique and easy to identify.

**Calypso Orchid or Fairy Slipper** *(Calypso bulbosa)*
This pleasant orchid also brightens up a lodgepole pine forest during June. Unmistakable, this delicate, lady-slipper orchid has pinkish petals above and a large scoop-like lip below—the slipper. There is usually a single basal leaf with the veins running parallel to the leaf margin.

**Common Fireweed** *(Epilobium angustifolium)*
Often the first flower to colonize a fire site, this plant is aptly named. Forming large fields of pink, its tall stem can be upwards of 2 m (7 ft.) in height. The stem has narrow green leaves growing along it, until it gives way to a pink spike of flowers on the upper portion of the stem.

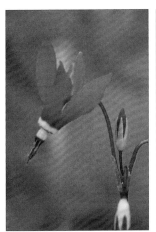

*Shooting star*

*Prairie crocus or pasque flower*

*Alpine forget-me-not*

**Shooting Star** *(Dodecatheon radicatum)*
This nodding flower easily lives up to its name. Its reverse petals point upward like the tail of a shooting star, and the flower points toward the ground. The light-green, oblong leaves form a simple rosette at the base of this wonderful flower.

## Purple Blue Flowers
**Prairie Crocus or Pasque Flower** *(Anemone patens)*
This harbinger of spring is a welcome sign each year. Its densely hairy stem hosts a six-petal, purple flower, even before the leaves fully develop. The feathery seed stalk that soon replaces the purple head is also a common sight. It is the provincial flower of Manitoba.

**Alpine Forget-me-not** *(Myosotis alpestris)*
High in the alpine, the forget-me-not really is unforgettable. Often growing amidst rugged scree slopes, its five blue petals and yellow centre eye are easily identified. The leaves are lance-shaped, covered with soft hairs, and alternate along the length of the stem. The for-

get-me-not rarely grows more than 20 cm (8 in.) high.
**Common Harebell** *(Campanula rotundifolia)*
The harebell, also known as the bluebell, is one of the most common flowers. The bell-shaped flowers have five petals and form a cup-like bell. Some are nodding in nature, and the stem may be 15–40 cm (6–16 in.) tall. The leaves are generally basal in nature and somewhat round.

**Early Blue Violet** *(Viola adunca)*
Another sign of spring, the early blue violet is a pleasant, if tiny, flower. It rarely grows above 10 cm (4 in.) high. The leaves are heart- or kidney-shaped, and the flower distinctive in its appearance.

# Animals
Kananaskis Country hosts a diversity of wildlife. Unlike Banff, its boundaries incorporate the transition from plains to foothills to mountains, and contains, therefore, animals and birds from many different habitats.

Viewing wildlife requires the proper mix of knowledge

*Common harebell*

*Early blue violet*

Golden eagle

Red-tailed hawk

Red-naped sapsucker

Black-billed magpie

Canada jay

and luck. I've spoken to people that have visited the Kananaskis once and seen cougars. I've spent 10 years in the area and never had such good fortune. On the other hand, the fact animals are not leaping out from behind every tree has a lot to do with our excitement in being treated to a rare sighting. In places like Banff, where elk are sometimes as prevalent as the cameras surrounding them, it doesn't take long before visitors become jaded. This has never been a problem in Kananaskis. With hunting still a part of the annual cycle, the animals have a healthy fear of man, and tend to keep their distance.

The best way to improve your odds is to learn as much as you can about the area's animals—their habitats, diets, and annual cycles. Often, finding the signs of animals—their droppings, markings or nests—can be as enjoyable as spotting the real thing. Sure, nothing beats seeing a bear from the safety of your vehicle, but finding a tree that has been climbed by a black bear,

or the berry-blackened droppings of a grizzly, can also get the blood flowing.

This section will help you identify some of the common birds and animals within Kananaskis Country. It is by no means a definitive list, but is meant to get you started in your Kananaskis wildlife hunt.

## Common Wildlife

### Birds

#### Golden Eagle

This relatively common eagle is easily identified by its large size and dark profile. The bald eagle, also fairly common, has a white head and tail. Recently, a migration route for golden eagles was discovered in the Kananaskis area. It nests in the area, and may be seen soaring overhead.

#### Red-tailed Hawk

Our most common large hawk, the red tail is the key feature for identifying this aerial hunter. It is often seen soaring above open areas looking for ground squirrels. It is also commonly seen perched atop fence posts. The distinctive call is a long whistle.

*Raven*

*Black-capped chickadee*

*Red-breasted nuthatch*

*Mountain bluebird*

*Cedar waxwing*

### Red-naped Sapsucker

This common woodpecker can be identified by its black and white back, buff breast, and red throat and head patches. It also has two white stripes, one above and one below the eye. Like most woodpeckers, it is usually heard pecking before it's observed. It makes parallel rows of holes in trees, and then returns later to eat the insects and sap that has collected.

### Black-billed Magpie

This common member of the jay family is notable for its long tail and iridescent colours. It has a black head and beak, with white patches on the side and breast. The tail and lower wings seem to vary from a green to a bluish tint. No other bird has a similarly long tail.

### Canada Jay

This common jay is variously known as Gray Jay, Camp Robber, or Whiskey Jack. It is gray in colour, with a short beak and dark patch on the top of the head. Its short beak distinguishes it from the Clark's Nutcracker, for whom it is often mistaken.

### Raven

The raven has been maligned through the ages. It is a very large scavenger and our largest songbird. Its heavy beak, large size, and wedge-shaped tail distinguish it from the common crow. Its call is a hoarse croak.

### Black-capped Chickadee

The distinctive call of the chickadee, "chick-a-dee-dee-dee," gives this bird its name. Common throughout the area, it has an easily recognized black cap and throat patch. Its breast is buff-coloured. There are two other chickadees in the area: the Boreal Chickadee has a brown cap, and the Mountain Chickadee has a white eye stripe.

### Red-breasted Nuthatch

This wonderful bird is another common visitor throughout the area. It has a bluish back and a distinctive rust-coloured breast. It also has a black cap on its head and a white eye stripe. It generally moves down a tree, collecting insects from behind the bark.

*Mule deer*

*Elk*

*Moose*

*Bighorn sheep*

*Mountain goat*

## Mountain Bluebird

Almost wiped out by competition from introduced cavity nesters like the starling, the mountain bluebird has made a comeback with the help of a large program of nestboxes. It is easily identified as the only bird in the area that is entirely blue in colour. The males are dark blue above, and lighter below. The females are more gray than blue, helping them blend into their surroundings.

**Other common birds**

• Mallard
• Spruce, Blue, and Ruffed Grouse
• Common Snipe
• Great Horned Owl
• American Dipper
• Nighthawk
• Tree, Cliff, and Barn Swallows
• Clark's Nutcracker
• Bohemian and Cedar Waxwings
• Brown-headed Cowbird
• Dark-eyed Junco

## Mammals

The elusive cougar, the ferocious grizzly, the proud mountain goat: these are what people think of when they think of the mountains. The large game provide the impetus for many people to head out onto the backroads and away from the crowds. While Banff is more famous for its wildlife, Kananaskis has the same selection, with some added benefits. Watching a bighorn sheep begging for handouts along the highway may be a novelty, but it's hardly "wild" life. In Kananaskis, when you see a stag elk, you can see the fire in his eye and feel the wildness in his heart. This makes even a common sighting exciting.

Dawn and dusk are your best opportunities for spotting animals. Most animals are more active at these times, and also more visible. While you travel through Kananaskis Country, keep your eyes open for the large animals, but don't forget the smaller, less sensational residents. Animals like the pika can add as much excitement to a child's visit as a grizzly.

## Ungulates

### Mule Deer

This is our true mountain deer. It is easily identified by

*Grizzly bear*

*Black bear*

*Cougar*

its large mule-like ears, and its black-tipped tail. In the male, the antlers form Y-shaped junctions. It weighs in at about 100 kg (220 lbs.), and stands 100 cm (3 ft.) at the shoulders. It is a browser, eating mainly grasses and flowers, moving on to leaves as the flowers disappear in the latter part of the season. During winter it chews on buds and twigs.

## White-tailed Deer

More common in the eastern portions of Kananaskis, the white-tailed deer is a low-elevation animal. Unlike the mule deer, which is common in the mountains, the white-tail tends to be seen along the foothills and plains. It is becoming increasingly popular, in particular along the Bow Valley. It has a brown tail, and when it senses danger, it lifts its tail, revealing the white underside. This flagging warns others of potential harm, and they head for cover. Lighter than the mule deer, it weighs in at about 90 kg (200 lbs.), but stands about the same height at the shoulder.

## Elk

These dark, stocky animals are one of the premier game animals in the mountains. The Shawnee Indians called it "Wapiti," which literally translates to "white rump." This is an apt description, as the rump is indeed white, whereas the rest of the animal is brown, the head and shoulders being significantly darker. Elk are heavier than deer, and weigh about 315 kg (694 lbs.). The antlers of the stags can be as long as 150 cm (5 ft.).

## Moose

This is the largest member of the deer family. Its large size, dark colour, and magnificent antlers make it distinctive. It weighs about 450 kg (992 lbs.), and its height averages 180 cm (6 ft.) at the shoulder. The word "moose" means "twig eater" in the Algonkian language, and that is exactly what it does. In winter, it browses on the twigs and branches of willows and other local species. In spring, it is often seen feeding in deep marshes.

## Bighorn Sheep

Bighorn sheep are often confused with mountain goats. This is largely because the females have short goat-like horns. Only the males get the full curl horns that are so distinctive of this animal. In Kananaskis, if it's not snow-white in colour, it's a sheep. It is common on grassy hillsides, where it feeds, but may come down to the roadsides to lick mineral-rich gravels. It weighs about 125 kg (275 lbs.), and is just under 100 cm (3 ft.) tall at the shoulders.

## Mountain Goat

This white goat is not really a goat at all. It is more closely re-

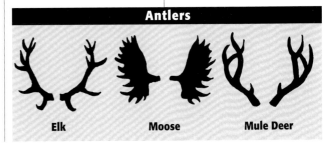

**Antlers**

Elk  Moose  Mule Deer

*Gray wolf*

*Porcupine*

*Red squirrel*

lated to the mountain antelopes of Asia. Its white coat and dark horns are distinctive. It weighs about 85 kg (187 lbs.), and stands just over 100 cm (3 ft.) at the shoulder. It prefers the true high country, and rarely appears along the roadsides within Kananaskis Country.

## Bears

### Grizzly Bear

The grizzly seems to epitomize the wilderness. It is large, powerful, and potentially dangerous. It weighs 250–350 kg (550–770 lbs.), and it averages 130 cm (4 ft.), at the shoulders. It has a prominent hump on the shoulders, and a "dished-in" appearance to the face. The claws can be up to 7.5 cm (3 in.) in length, and leave distinctive marks in the footprints.

### Black Bear

Our most common bear, the black bear is easily identified by its lack of a shoulder hump, and its dog-like face. It may be black, but it can also be cinnamon-coloured. It tends to weigh about 170 kg (375 lbs.) and stand 95 cm (3 ft.) at the shoulders.

## Other predators

### Cougar

Rarely seen, the cougar is the largest cat in Kananaskis. It may weigh 70 kg (154 lbs.), and be 150 cm (5 ft.) long (not counting the tail). It hunts the area's large game animals, like moose, elk, deer, and bighorn sheep. After eating their fill, cougars cover the remainder of their prey with leaves and other material, and return later.

### Gray Wolf

The wolf is finally returning to the mountains. Wolf studies in Banff National Park show a strong and growing population. It is occasionally seen along roadways, crossing to move to new territories. It weighs about 50 kg (110 lbs.), and varies in colour from gray to almost black.

## Other small animals

### Porcupine

This prickly rodent is easily recognized by its long hair-like spines. Often its handiwork—plywood signs chewed to splinters or pack straps munched for the salt in the hiker's sweat—makes it less than welcome. It is fairly com-

mon in the Kananaskis area, and is an agile climber. It weighs an average of 6.5 kg (14 lbs.), and measures about 77 cm (3 ft.) long.

### Red Squirrel

This noisy resident needs little introduction. With its distinctive reddish colour and bushy tail, it is known far and wide. It forms the early warning system in the forest, announcing your presence to the other forest dwellers. It spends the summers collecting cones, and then stores them to provide a winter food supply. It creates large piles of cone fragments, called middens, and nests beneath them.

### Columbian Ground Squirrel

Incorrectly called "gophers," the Columbian ground squirrel is our most common underground resident. Its coat has a "salt-and-pepper" appearance to it, and this is offset by a reddish belly. It lives in large colonies, and you'll often see it standing tall, performing sentry duty. It falls prey to eagles and hawks, and grizzlies like to dig up colonies for a protein fix.

*Columbian ground squirrel*

*Golden-mantled ground squirrel*

*Pika*

**Golden-mantled Ground Squirrel**

As you climb above the valley bottom, the golden-mantled ground squirrel becomes common. It is similar to, but larger than, a chipmunk, and the stripes stop at the shoulder. On a chipmunk, the stripes continue through the eyes.

They quickly become "spoiled," and end up begging for handouts at viewpoints and attractions. Please don't give in. Let them find their own natural foods.

**Pika**

The rock rabbit, as the pika is also known, is more closely related to rabbits than rodents.

It lives high in the mountains, usually above 2,000 m (6,560 ft.), and prefers the barren landscape of loose-boulder slopes. It uses the rocks as sentry posts, and the spaces between the rocks as tunnels.

## Trees

**Trembling Aspen**
- small paddle-shaped leaves, long leaf stalk
- most common leafed tree
- bark greenish-white, becoming furrowed with age

**Lodgepole Pine**
- needles 2.5–7 cm (1–3 in.) long, in groups of two
- cones hard and waxy
- few branches on the lower trunk

**White Spruce**
- needles square in shape, not in pairs
- cones 5 cm (2 in.) long, and stiff
- often grows under lodgepole pine

**Subalpine Fir**
- flat needles 2.5–4.5 cm (1–2 in.)
- bark may be smooth with resin blisters
- usually grows above elevations of 1,540 m (5,082 ft.)

**Alpine Larch**
- soft needles, in groups of 30–40
- loses its needles every year
- oval cones 3–5 cm (1–2 in.) in length

*Fall colours at Barrier Lake*

## Ecology

In any environment, the inter-action between a diverse set of landscapes, varying climatic conditions, and plants and animals makes for unique, yet delicate ecosystems. The study of ecology looks at the whole—the connection between the parts. The more we understand about the landscapes of the Rockies, the more we realize that the rocks are as important as any of the other components making up this diverse ecosystem.

Within Kananaskis Country, each ecological community is known as an ecoregion. These have unique collections of plants and animals adapted to a specific set of geological and climatic conditions. Kananaskis Country includes numerous ecoregions. In the lower valley we find the Montane. Further to the east, on the edge of plain and foothill, lies the Aspen Parkland.

The parkland is characterized by forests of trembling aspen mixed with open grassland. Warm, south-facing slopes are often devoid of trees, and cooler, wetter, north-facing slopes are darkened by white spruce. Animals like the coyote, white-tailed deer, elk, and ruffed grouse call the parkland home.

As you move westward, the altitude increases and the Montane forest becomes dominant. This forest community is characterized by Douglas fir and limber pine. Often the lower slopes of the Rockies are improperly identified as Montane when they are actually Boreal Foothills, or Boreal Uplands. Douglas fir and lim-ber pine thrive in the dry, Chinook-blasted valleys of the lower eastern slopes. Located between 1,200 (3,960) and 1,500–1,650 m (4,950–5,445 ft.), the Montane forest comprises most of the valley of the Bow River, as well as parts of the Elbow and Sheep river valleys. This is prime elk habitat, along with white-tailed and mule deer, black bear, spruce grouse, and snowshoe hare.

More common than the Montane is the Boreal Foothills ecoregion. Typically comprising dense forests of lodgepole pine, white spruce, trembling aspen, and balsam poplar, it is the third-largest ecoregion in the province. The Boreal Foothills begins at approximately 1,340 m (4,422 ft.), and may be interspersed with various Montane species. With increasing altitude, it gives way to the Boreal Uplands. This is identified by a noticeable lack of aspen and poplar, and normally borders the subalpine, at approximately 1,540 m (5,082 ft.). Common wildlife include ruffed grouse, snowshoe hare, lynx, black bear, and white-tailed and mule deer.

The Subalpine is a zone of transition. It begins as the trees of the Montane and Boreal Uplands give way to subalpine fir and Engelmann spruce. Alpine larch may also be present in this zone. Climbing upwards through the subalpine, the trees get progressively more stunted in appearance, until they exhibit a growth form known as "krummholz." German for "crooked wood," krummholz are small clumps of stunted trees that provide protection for each other. Often only a metre (a few feet tall), the trees may be several hundred years old. Eventually, by approximately 2,300 m (7,590 ft.), the trees begin to disappear, and we enter the true Alpine. Like its plant community, the animals of the subalpine tend to be a mixture of those preferring higher or lower locales. You may see a ptarmigan picking at willow buds or a red squirrel scurrying through the trees. Animals like the marten prefer the dense forests, while bighorn sheep prefer the open slopes near the margin of alpine and subalpine.

The alpine is a rugged place. It's an area where even the toughest trees cannot survive. Biologists studying treelines have found that the cutoff for most species will occur at the point where the average July temperature is 10°C (50°F). This tends to hold true from Alaska to California. With the lack of tree growth, the alpine blooms in July and supports plants capable of living in harsh climates. Low-lying flowers, many of which reproduce vegetatively due to the short growing season, make up the majority of the plant life in the alpine. Animals like the mountain goat, the tiny pika, and the ptarmigan make the alpine their home. They have learned to prosper where other animals may have floundered. For some alpine animals, the unique collection of hardy plants mixed with the high winds, have combined to create a wind-blown world where forage is available year round. In the open habitats, grizzly bears and bighorn sheep forage, while the pika rules the rocks.

## Yellowstone to Yukon Conservation Initiative

**With increased** development along North America's Rocky Mountain ridge, critical habitat has been eroded as townsites have expanded, new roads have been built and more recreational developments have been created. Increasing development serves to dissect critical wildlife ranges and reduce the ability of animals to move freely, decades of development have taken their toll on native wildlife populations. Researchers have proposed a unique way to ensure long term survival of viable populations of large carnivores. A close examination of wildlife habitat shows that it is composed of areas of prime habitat linked to adjacent core refuge areas by movement corridors. Without viable movement corridors, these islands of habitat become isolated from each other, preventing the influx of new individuals to adjacent core refuge areas.

The Yellowstone to Yukon Conservation Initiative (Y2Y) was born in 1993 as a way to preserve and restore a viable network of connecting corridors that will stretch from the Yukon in the north to Yellowstone National Park in the south. The initiative now involves a network of 270 organizations, individuals, and conservation groups in both the United States and Canada.

## Multiple-Use in Theory and Practice

Kananaskis Country is like few other areas in the world. From its earliest inception, it was designed to accommodate a multitude of recreational users, limited resource extraction, and traditional uses such as free ranging cattle. This was an intimidating task, but it began long before the official designation of Kananaskis Country.

By 1900, the eastern slopes of the Rocky Mountains began seeing increasing pressure on their resources. Ranchers had moved cattle up the valleys of the foothills, forests were falling under the axe, rivers were being diverted for irrigation, and coal was being mined in numerous areas. The government realized that a program of controlled conservation might be necessary to ensure the future of this area. Even though Alberta gained provincial status in 1905, the federal government maintained control on the province's natural resources until 1930.

In 1906, the Forest Reserve Act placed restrictions on the sale of most of the eastern slopes. This prohibited homesteading, and numerous settlers were moved out of the area. There were provisions in the act to allow mining, logging, resource extraction, and limited grazing. During this period, the forest rangers were responsible for the management of the forest reserves, along with all the fish and game in the area.

In 1911, the Forest Reserve Act was supplemented by the Dominion Forest Reserves and Parks Act. This controlled logging through the issuance of permits.

With increased ranching pressure, a permit system was implemented in 1914. This promoted the formation of cattle associations, and limited grazing to specific allotments. This was the foundation of the system of grazing distribution units still used today. Range inventories over the years have provided data on carrying capacities, and this has been used in the issuance of permits.

In 1930, the Alberta government took control of its natural resources for the first time. The Alberta Department of Lands and Mines assumed control, and was subdivided into five branches: Forestry, Mines, Lands, Fisheries, and Water Power. Unfortunately the Alberta gov-

ernment gained control just as the Great Depression set in. This was followed by several years of extensive forest fires. By the early 1940's, the provincial government was feeling the strain, and in 1947, a joint federal-provincial body was organized to take over management of the eastern slopes.

The Eastern Rockies Forest Conservation Board (ERFCB) had a 25 year mandate, and immediately passed the Eastern Rockies Forest Conservation Act. The mandate included the construction of facilities, the protection of forests, and the conservation, maintenance and development of the forest resources, all with a focus on water flow management.

The capital period, between 1947-1955, saw a flurry of development. Facilities were upgraded, new roads built, and equipment modernized. It was during this period that the forestry trunk road from Nordegg to Coleman was built. This includes present day Highway 40.

The ERFCB also set about to collect watershed and climatic data on the area, and began recording temperature, wind, humidity, and cloud cover information. This was done in conjunction with stream flow gauges to measure and predict river flows. This research helped them to modify and update the grazing allotment system within the foothills.

While the mandate of the ERFCB expired in 1968, it continued to act as an advisory council until it was disbanded in 1973. The Alberta Forest Service (AFS), once again, took control of the province's wilderness. The AFS continued many of the programs initiated by the ERFCB.

In 1977, the Alberta government published "A Policy for Resource Management of the Eastern Slopes". This document used the concept of carrying capacity as a basis for zoning within the eastern slopes. Areas were zoned based on the types of impact they could sustain.

Also in 1977, Kananaskis Country was officially established, and began its own period of capital development. For the next 15 years, ten's of millions of dollars were spent on the upgrading of roads and campgrounds, the building of a golf course, Olympic ski hill and cross-country ski

site, the development of a hotel complex, and numerous other projects.

In 1983, when Kananaskis Country announced its "Kananaskis Resource Management Policy", it followed the recommendations of the 1977 Eastern Slopes Policies. Since then, it has provided resource protection while still attempting to provide facilities for as wide a variety of users as possible. There are 4x4 and snowmobile areas, some oil and gas exploration and limited logging, as well as hiking, biking, horseback riding, hunting, and fishing. This list is by no means exhaustive.

Kananaskis Country is undergoing a period of change yet again. As budgets become increasingly tight, the government has moved to a program of privatization and private sector partnerships. Over the past few years, most of the campgrounds have been turned over to private operators, and many other facilities and services may be likewise transferred in the future.

With increased pressure on the limited mountain landscape, Kananaskis Country is now finding itself under pressure to re-evaluate its

management strategies. Historically, its multiple-use mandate as outlined in the Kananaskis Integrated Resource Plan (IRP) has been the underlying foundation upon which management decisions were made. Today, certain uses, in particular oil and gas exploration, logging and free-ranging cattle are becoming more and more controversial. Since the IRP was published more than a decade ago, Kananaskis is finding its wilderness under attack. As the public becomes more aware of the finite nature of our wilderness, it is also becoming increasingly opposed to anything that might reduce the inventory of wilderness.

Organizations like the Kananaskis Coalition and the Canadian Parks and Wilderness Society have brought increasing pressure on Kananaskis to reduce development, and to re-evaluate current management policies. The next decade will see more focus on protection, and perhaps a movement away from the policies of multiple-use upon which Kananaskis was originally created.

# Highlights of History

*Filling barrels with oil at Discovery Well, Turner Valley, 1914*

The Kananaskis has seen many travellers over the years. Beginning with early bands of nomadic hunters, the valley has evolved into an internationally recognized destination. Through its history, Kananaskis Country has reflected the history of southern Alberta. It witnessed the railway surveyors, the origin of ranching, the beginnings of the oil and gas industry, prisoner-of-war camps, and even an Olympics.

**11,000 BP** – Following a pathway formed by an ice-free corridor between the winding mountain glaciers and the expansive continental ice sheet, small bands of nomadic hunters made their way into the area by following wandering herds of animals. They crossed from Siberia to Alaska along a land bridge formed by lower ocean levels during the ice age. As they passed, they left evidence of their presence.

**1787** – Fur trader David Thompson made his first trip into the mountains. Thompson spent his life mapping the west and learning native languages and stories.

**1792** – Peter Fiddler entered the foothills and mapped some areas of Kananaskis Country, including the Sheep River.

**1800** – David Thompson passed through the area a second time when he travelled past present-day High River on his return from Rocky Mountain House. The next 30 years would not see much white travel in this area, as the Peigan Indians avoided contact with the Hudson's Bay Company.

**1841** – James Sinclair of the Hudson's Bay Company passed present-day Canmore, continuing through the Spray Valley on his way to the newly opened Oregon territory. He was taking Scottish settlers from the Red River Settlement, then located near present-day Winnipeg.

**1845** – Father Jean de Smet passed by present-day Canmore on his way east from British Columbia

**1854** – James Sinclair was sent by George Simpson to take a second group of British settlers to the Oregon territory. They brought along with them

250 horses and oxen, 15 white families, and approximately 100 Cree to protect the group from possible Blackfoot attacks. This time, he travelled via the Kananaskis valley.

**1858** – The British and Canadian Governments sent John Palliser to undertake the first in-depth surveys of what is now Western Canada.

**1860s** – The life of the plains Indian began to change rapidly as the bison began to disappear and whiskey traders began to test the waters of southern Alberta.

In the late 1960s, a man known as One Spot Samples opened a short-lived Whiskey Fort on the Sheep River. He probably only operated one season before clearing out.

**1870** – The Hudson's Bay Company relinquished its control over its vast western land holdings. Suddenly the west was without formal pro-tection, as the fledgling country of Canada had no official representatives in the wilderness. Whiskey traders quickly moved north from Montana and began to sell whiskey to the local Indians.

Along the Elbow River, two such forts were erected. In 1871, a part-time sheriff from Montana—Fred Kanouse—opened a post. During his first season, he was lucky to escape with his life after a long siege attempt by the Bloods. Despite this, he did return for a second season of trading.

A second fort trying to compete with him was opened by Dick Berry in 1872. Berry was later killed by one of his customers, a Blood Indian.

**1881** – George Dawson surveyed the Kananaskis valley between 1881 and 1884, and was later followed-up by his assistant, R.C. McConnell.

**1882** – John Ware arrived. He

*Eau Claire and Bow River Lumber Company logging camp*

was a former slave who became Alberta's most famous black cowboy. He was also one of the Sheep River valley's first settlers in 1891. His brand "9999" became well known in the area.

**1883–84** – The vast forests in the Bow and Kananaskis valleys came under the scrutiny of L.B. Stewart, a Dominion

## The Palliser Expedition

**During the early** to mid-19th century, the Hudson's Bay Company ruled the Canadian west. Very secretive, it allowed little information on the west to make its way back to either Upper Canada or Britain. It realized that information was power, and the Bay Men didn't want to relinquish any of their lands. They worried about settlers scaring away the animals, and that was bad for business. As a result, they kept everything tightly locked away.

John Palliser was commissioned to do the first in-depth surveys of the west and to report his findings back to London. Along with him came Dr. James Hector (physician and geologist), Eugene Bourgeau (botanist), and Lieutenant Thomas Blakiston (magnetical observer). The group split up to cover more territory and, as a result, each individual was responsible for a variety of discoveries in these different areas.

Palliser travelled into the Kananaskis and bestowed its name. He heard a legend of an Indian by the same name, who apparently had been hit in the head with a battle axe and survived. Since this was a tough valley, and that was one tough Indian, the valley was given his name. His subsequent report on this valley led to the Vermilion Pass being chosen over the Kananaskis Valley as the future route for a highway.

The expedition completed detailed surveys of most of Alberta, and was the first to describe the valuable coal reserves in this province. It also detailed the prairies, and marked off the famed Palliser Triangle as worthless farmland. Palliser felt the possibility of a railroad remote, and even a wagon road far premature. His expedition was an important part of this areas early non-native history.

Hector also travelled through part of Kananaskis. He followed Swift Water Creek (now the Elbow River), and caught 36 trout in less than two hours.

**Prisoners at Kananaskis Valley Internment Camp**

surveyor, who divided the area into timber limits. Soon after, Kutusoff MacFee, along with the Eau Claire and Bow River Lumber Company, began exploiting these deposits. By 1886, their mill in Calgary was producing more than three million board feet annually.

**1884** – Canmore became the first divisional point 68 miles west of Calgary. It was composed of a boxcar structure built near the present west crossing. Charles Compton was the agent and recorded the first train passing through Canmore at noon on May 11, 1884.

**1888** – NWMP records list this as the year the first offical Canmore post was set up. Before this, Canmore was part of the Banff detachment. The policeman was Constable Harris.

**1880s** – T.K. Fullerton made numerous attempts to start a timber operation in the Elbow Valley, with little success. Later, around 1905, his son, T.W. Fullerton, would be successful. The Fullertons are still a dominant name in the Bragg Creek area today.

**1888** – H.W. McNeil & Co took control of Canmore mines, operating under the name Canadian Anthracite Coal Co. McNeil was given two consecutive 10 year leases to operate the mines.

**1903** – The coal seams of Ribbon Creek were assessed for their commercial value by D.B. Dowling. The results of this assessment were published in 1909, sparking increasing interest in the area's rich deposits.

**1908** – The No.2 Mine of the Canmore Coal Company opened. With this, a new settlement of company houses was built east of No.1 Mine.

**1914** – Oil was discovered at Turner Valley when Dingman #9 blew out. This same year, a small well near present-day Bragg Creek Provincial Park was opened. The Mowbray–Berkley well was a poor performer and only operated for a few years.

**1932–3** – Construction on the hydro projects on the Kananaskis Lakes began. Ten

years later, the original dam was replaced, and it was again modified between 1947 and 1955.

**1936** – Depression workers built the first road down the Kananaskis Valley. Little more than a narrow cart track, access to the valley remained difficult.

**1939** – With war in Europe, the former Relief Camp became an internment camp for German and Italian nationals. This lasted only a short time, until the detainees were released or moved to other camps. The camp was then converted to a prisoner-of-war-camp and used for the duration of hostilities.

**1945** – Development of the Barrier Lake Reservoir began with German prisoners-of-war clearing the forests.

**1951** – The Spray Lakes Reservoir opened, along with its original power-generating structures.

**1952** – The Forestry Trunk Road was opened and passed south through the Kananaskis Valley, all the way to Coleman. This finally allowed easy access to this remote area.

**1977** – The Alberta government, under Premier Peter Lougheed, set aside 4,000 sq. km (1,600 sq. mi.) of Alberta's eastern slopes as Kananaskis Country. This mixture of prairie, foothill, and Rocky Mountain includes four Provincial Parks: Bragg Creek, Bow Valley, and Kananaskis (now Peter Lougheed Provincial Park), and the newly established Elbow–Sheep Wildland Park.

**1979** – On July 13, 1979, the final whistle blew, marking the closure of the Canmore mines.

# Life in the Mountains

*The Bow Valley from Ha Ling Peak*

K ananaskis Country is not a park—it is a recreation area that contains a number of provincial parks. This structure allows it to support more varied recreational pursuits than the vast majority of "parks." Through its multiple-use mandate, it accommodates many types of users, but keeps them separate whenever possible. For instance, the McLean Creek Off-Highway Vehicle Zone provides a large area specifically for dirt bikes, four-wheel-drive vehicles, and, in winter, snowmobiles. Since these activities are incompatible with hiking, the facilities have been separated from non-motorized recreation. In the past, many of the routes followed by today's hiking trails were open to off-highway traffic. The Big Elbow, Little Elbow, and Sheep trails are examples of former vehicle-access roads that have been converted to non-motorized use only. Although the closure of these areas to vehicles was controversial, the provision of high-quality facilities elsewhere helped to ease the change.

Since Kananaskis Country's inception, an almost limitless number of facilities, campgrounds, and trails have been created to facilitate increased access to the area. Today there are thousands of campsites, along with hundreds of kilometres of trails. Dirt bikes are able to coexist with horseback riders. Mountain bikers maintain a relatively peaceful relationship with horse and hiking traffic. Kananaskis is more than a few highways providing access to magnificent scenery—it's a place to play!

## Frontcountry Camping

Perhaps more than any other activity, camping is something that brings families into the area and allows them to become intimate with the many riches that Kananaskis has to offer. Most of the campgrounds offer basic services, including drinkable water, washroom facilities, firepits, and picnic tables. A few sites require you to boil water before using, but they tend to be remote areas, and the water

*Opposite: Backcountry skiing to Burstall Pass*

sources are posted unsafe for drinking.

Camping in western Kananaskis is extremely popular. You'll travel Highway 40 for 23 km (13.8 mi.) before encountering your first campground. Uniquely designed, Sundance Lodges offers a completely different camping experience. Instead of tents or camper trailers, you can stay in an authentic Sioux-designed, hand-painted teepee. Also included are hot showers, washrooms, coin laundry, pay phone, and small grocery store. Facilities for traditional trailers and tents are also available—some of them adjacent to teepees. Reservations can be made by calling (403) 591-7122.

Mount Kidd R.V. Park provides deluxe camping, with everything you could ever want. Just a few minutes from the Kananaskis Golf Course, it includes such options as electricity, satellite TV, laundry facilities, showers, flush toilets, snack bar, convenience store, games room, sauna, and Jacuzzi tub. Reservations are essential for this perpetually busy campsite. Call (403) 591-7700 to ensure a site for your stay.

Farther south, within Peter Lougheed Provincial Park, there are seven campgrounds, designed to accommodate more traditional camping. There are no satellite hookups, in fact no electrical hookups at all. What they do offer is location! The 16 km (10 mi.) Kananaskis Lakes Trail accesses some of the area's premier hiking, mountain biking, cross-country skiing, and fishing. Of the six campsites, the

*Mount Kidd R.V. Park*

most popular are Boulton and Elkwood. These two offer the advantage of showers, as well as amphitheatres for interpretive programs. Boulton also has a small store and restaurant.

Beyond the junction to the Kananaskis Lakes, the campgrounds are much more primitive. There are no summer campsites until beyond Highwood Junction. However, during the hunting season, Strawberry campground, just north of the Junction, is opened. South of the Junction, Etherington and Cataract Creek campgrounds offer basic services only.

Along the Trans Canada Highway, in Bow Valley

## What to Bring

Camping is the sort of activity that takes you far from the luxury of home and makes you choose those items that you simply can't live without. It's amazing to see the choices made by some campers—hairdryers make their way to campgrounds without electrical hookups. It's important to keep in mind certain items that should be included in any camper's list of essentials. Here is a list of suggested supplies:
- flashlight with extra batteries
- barbecue or Coleman stove
- matches—lots of them
- camera, film, and extra

batteries
- tent if not travelling with a larger unit
- tarp to shelter picnic table
- at least one complete change of clothes, including shoes
- warm jacket for the evening
- hat and gloves, even in summer
- rain gear
- good footwear
- axe—not a hatchet
- toiletries and towel
- first aid kit
- mosquito repellent
- sunscreen

## Kananaskis Country Vehicle Access Campgrounds

| Area | Campground | Open Dates | Total # of Sites | Reservation # |
|------|------------|------------|------------------|---------------|
| Bow Valley | Bow River | May 1-Oct 13 | 32 | |
| | Three Sisters | Apr 15-Oct 31 | 36 | |
| | Lac Des Arcs | May 1-Sept 30 | 28 | |
| | Bow Valley | May 1-Oct 31 | 169 | (403) 673-2163 |
| | Willow Rock | Apr 1-Oct 31 | 124 | (403) 673-2163 |
| | Sundances Lodges | May 19-Oct 1 | 30 | (403) 591-7122 |
| Kananaskis Valley | Mt. Kidd R.V. Park | Year round | 229 | (403) 591-7700 |
| | Eau Claire | May 18-Oct 9 | 51 | |
| | Sundance Lodges | May 16-Sept 30 | 30 | (403) 591-7122 |
| Sibbald | Sibbald Lake | May 1-Oct 14 | 134 | |
| | Dawson Equestrian | Year round | 17 | |
| Peter Lougheed Provincial Park | Canyon | June 19-Sept 1 | 52 | |
| | Elkwood | May 15-Sept 1 | 130 | (403) 591-7226 |
| | Boulton Creek | May 1-Oct 19 | 118 | (403) 591-7226 |
| | Lower Lake | May 15-Oct 13 | 104 | |
| | Mt. Sarrail | June 19-Sept 1 | 44 | |
| | Interlakes | May 15-Oct 13 | 48 | |
| Spray | Spray Lake West | May 18 to snow | 50 | |
| | Buller Mountain | Winter Only | 12 | |
| Elbow Valley | Beaver Flat | May 15-Sept 5 | 55 | (403) 949-3132 |
| | Fisher Creek | Year round | 30 | |
| | Gooseberry | Apr 28-Oct 10 | 83 | |
| | Little Elbow | May 15-Nov 1 | 94 | (403) 949-3132 |
| | Little Elbow Equest | May 15-Nov 1 | 46 | (403) 949-3132 |
| | McLean Creek | Year round | 170 | (403) 949-3132 |
| | Paddy's Flat | May 5-Oct 10 | 98 | |
| | Mesa Butte Equest | May 1-Oct 15 | 15 | |
| | North Fork | May 5-Oct 10 | 24 | |
| Sheep River Valley | Blue Rock | May 15-Oct 15 | 66 | |
| | Blue Rock Equest | May 15-Oct 15 | 17 | |
| | Sandy McNabb | May 1-Oct 15 | 98 | |
| | Sandy McNabb Eq. | Year round | 21 | |
| Highwood Cataract Creek | Cataract Creek | May 15-Sept 3 | 102 | |
| | Etherington Creek | May 1-Oct 15 | 61 | |
| | Etherington Creek Eq | May 1-Oct 15 | 10 | |
| | Green Ford | May 1-Oct 15 | 13 | |
| | Indian Graves | May 15-Sept 15 | 40 | (403) 601-3051 |
| | Strawberry Equest | May 15-Sept 15 | 24 | |

## World-famous Golf

*World-famous Kananaskis Country Golf Course*

**Sitting beneath the** imposing slopes of Mount Kidd, and along the winding course of the Kananaskis River, the Kananaskis Golf Course provides one of the most dramatic golf courses in North America. Its 36 holes will challenge even the most accomplished player.

The course was designed by Robert Trent Jones, a man famous for designing difficult, but spectacular, courses. With over 400 courses to his credit, Jones picked the location after flying over the valley in a helicopter. He described the site as, "The finest location I have ever seen for a golf course." Into his design he integrated white sands imported from British Columbia, along with vast amounts of water, extensive fairways, and undulating greens.

When it comes to sand, this course spared no expense. In order to provide the best sand possible, $345,000 was spent importing large-particle white silica from Golden, B.C. The silica was almost double the cost of regular sand, but had several benefits that justified its cost. Primary among these was a large grain size, which makes it heavy and resistant to the high winds in the valley. The silica, unlike sand, has a tendency to remain fluffy, rather than to pack down like normal sand, and, visually, the white colour of the silica complements the glacial landscapes of the Rockies.

**Mount Glasgow from Nihahi Creek Trail**

Provincial Park, Bow Valley Campground provides basic services, whereas Willow Rock offers the advantage of electrical hookups on some sites. Some sites at Bow Valley Campground can be reserved by calling (403) 673-2163. In addition to basic services, both offer showers, a dumping station, and a playground. Two other campgrounds, Lac Des Arcs and Bow River, are located along the Trans Canada Highway, and offer basic services only.

Sibbald Creek Trail provides more rustic accommodation. Sibbald Lake Campground provides basic ser-

vices, while Dawson Equestrian, at the head of the dusty Powderface Trail, provides limited facilities for those camping with their horses.

The Elbow Valley is less hectic, yet it provides numerous camping opportunities. It has five campgrounds along Highway 66, and two farther south, at the end of McLean Creek Trail. All provide basic facilities, with McLean Creek, Paddy's Flat, and the Little Elbow adding amphitheatres for evening naturalist shows. McLean Creek offers some sites for off-highway vehicle users, while the Little Elbow offers corrals for horses. Some sites at McLean Creek and Little Elbow campgrounds can be reserved by calling (403) 949-3132.

Last, but not least, the Sheep River Valley, west of Turner Valley, provides two basic campgrounds: Sandy McNabb and Bluerock. Both have traditional and equestrian camping, and provide only basic facilities.

## Backcountry Camping

For those hikers that prefer the solitude of the backcountry, Kananaskis provides numerous opportunities to explore, and you will still enjoy the luxury of a well-designed campground. In the past, backcountry campers chose their own sites, and tented wherever the spirit moved them. Today, with increasing numbers of people heading into the wilderness, this practice leads to excessive impact and unnecessary hardship. Kananaskis Country has developed backcountry campsites designed to assist you in tak-

## Summer Theatre

**Kananaskis Country** is famous for its interpretive theatre programs. They run throughout the summer in many of the campgrounds, and are designed to provide an entertaining way to learn about the area's natural and human history. These programs include traditional nature hikes, as well as entertaining evening amphitheatre programs. During these plays, comedy is used to help ease the educational message. If the audience is laughing at a clever presentation, they may not realize they are learning something. It also helps keep

**The stage is set**

the kids attention for the length of the program.

The programs in Kananaskis have become a yardstick against which similar programs elsewhere are compared. Stop in at any of the visitor centres for information on summer programming.

## Bear Encounters

**Camping and hiking** in bear country requires caution and respect. Some people are so concerned about encountering bears that they avoid camping and hiking altogether. The mountains beg to be explored, and bears are an integral part of this wilderness. Without their proud presence, we would all be poorer.

In years of mountain camping, hiking, and biking, you can meet many bears and never have a negative encounter. George Field, one of Kananaskis' Alpine Rescue Specialists, could not recall in 1995 a single bear injury in Kananaskis Country, and he has been involved since 1982. Knowledge is a powerful weapon against fear. By learning about bears, their habits and habitats, you can minimize unwanted encounters on the trail. When camping, a clean site is the best insurance against visits by master bruin. Bears are lazy, they tend to take the most easily available food. If your site is pristine, and someone else has left a cooler out, it's not hard to guess where the bear will head. Avoid bringing anything into the tent that has a strong odour. Bears see better with their nose than their eyes. Don't use sweet-smelling soaps or deodorants, and never bring food or toothpaste into the tent. In Kananaskis, with its bear-proof garbage cans, extensive public education, and ever vigilant rangers, the problem of campground bears is minimized.

When hiking, make sure the bears know you're coming. Groups of hikers generally make

*Black bear*

noise by talking, and the bear is warned of their approach. Lone hikers need to make a point of making noise. Give out a holler every once and awhile, and don't trust bear bells. They don't make a very loud noise, and tend to create a false sense of security.

The most dangerous situation occurs when the wind is in your face as you pass a loud stream. The bear may not hear or smell you approaching. Make an extra effort to ensure it knows you are

*Grizzly bear*

in the area, and be especially vigilant.

If you suddenly find yourself eye to eye with a bear, don't panic. In most cases the bear will defer to your authority and leave without delay. If you are very close, and he feels threatened, he may try a bluff charge. This straight-legged charge is a good time to show him that you are indeed harmless. Move slowly away, don't make any sudden moves, and do not run.

Look around you for any suitable tree to climb, should the situation continue to deteriorate. Although grizzlies can climb trees, they rarely do so. Black bears may follow you up, but normally use the opportunity to retreat.

As a final resort, in a defensive attack, you can play dead. Keep your backpack on your back to provide some additional protection. Drop to the ground and curl up into a tight ball. Use your hands to protect your neck, and if possible, pull your pack up to provide some added protection for this vulnerable area. Remember, it is highly unlikely you will ever need to resort to playing dead. NEVER play dead if you believe that a bear has been following or stalking you. This indicates a predatory encounter and you'll need to fight back. While you won't likely injure the bear, you may convince it that you are more trouble than you're worth. Always be vigilant.

*Cresting one more hill*

ing advantage of the wilderness, while still providing a little comfort. In keeping with this philosophy, they discourage random camping. These backcountry sites provide the convenience of a privy toilet, fire pits, moderately level sites, and a place to hang your food.

Most of the backcountry sites along the Kananaskis valley are designed for backpackers. Most of the campsites are along hiking-only trails, which means they are great for those people that prefer a quieter experience. Elbow Lake campsite, west of Highway 40, is the only one in Peter Lougheed Provincial Park that allows horse access. It is also accessible by mountain bike.

Several of the campgrounds provide loop options, in particular the campsites of Ribbon Falls, Ribbon Lake, and Lillian Lake. This loop can keep the backcountry fishermen busy for several days, as these regularly stocked lakes challenge your skills. The loop is easiest in the order listed above, as a rock wall above Ribbon Falls is easier to negotiate in the uphill direction.

Within Peter Lougheed Provincial Park's facility zone, there are four backcountry

sites: Point, Forks, Three Isle Lake, and Turbine Canyon. They're all located west of the Kananaskis Lakes, and provide access towards the north and south Kananaskis passes.

Quaite Valley campground, operated by Bow Valley Provincial Park, is located along the trail of the same name, between Jewell Pass and the Trans Canada Highway.

The eastern portions of Kananaskis Country really shine when it comes to backcountry camping. Part of this lies in the area's popularity with equestrian users, and the system of campsites reflects this. Most are used primarily by horseback campers, and all are in fairly remote areas. They are however, accessible by hikers and bikers as well, adding to their popularity.

Between the Elbow and Sheep River valleys there are numerous sites. These include Big Elbow, Tombstone, and Mount Romulus along the popular Elbow Loop trail system. Spur trails from this provide access to Threepoint Mountain and Wildhorse campgrounds. South of the Sheep River Trail (Highway 546), Wolf Creek Campground

provides the sole backcountry site.

## Hiking

If there's one activity that brings more people to Kananaskis Country than any other, with the exception of sightseeing, it's got to be hiking. There's something magical about getting off the beaten path and wandering along a wilderness trail. Most of the trails are well maintained, and important junctions are signed. The trails run the entire spectrum, from tender strolls to rugged subalpine slogs. With 1,360 km (845 mi.) of trails, there's more than enough to keep the avid hiker busy for season after season. Other trails tend to beckon you back, like an old friend, welcoming you to its varying seasons and moods.

Hiking, like any alpine activity, requires caution and common sense. Many hikers in Kananaskis have problems because they don't plan for contingencies or don't want to carry too much weight. Never head off the highway without a well-stocked daypack, and always plan for the unexpected.

The trails within the Kananaskis area are as diverse as the landscape. Along the main valley, some popular trails include Prairie View, Centennial Ridge, Ribbon Creek, Galatea, and Ptarmigan Cirque. Many offer the hiker panoramic views of the surrounding peaks and valleys, although there is a price—plenty of elevation gain. Others follow the meandering streams towards pleasant lakes and waterfalls.

One hazard within

Kananaskis Country relates to the fact that many hiker-defined routes are described in trail guides without specifying their rough character. These are not formally designated hiking routes. There are no signs, maps, or markers of any kind. They require the hiker to be familiar with route-finding and confident in travelling off the beaten path. For this reason, such routes are not described in this book.

Some trails require you to ford streams, which may be high during spring runoff. Fording can be dangerous business. Take the time to move slowly, place each foot firmly before continuing, and use a walking stick, if possible, for balance. Never take a seemingly simple ford for granted. Most accidents occur when we let our guard down.

Water is a powerful force and needs to be treated accordingly.

Speaking of water, make sure you bring lots of it with you. With increased travel into the backcountry, the danger of bringing more than the water home with you gets greater. Giardiasis, also known as beaver fever, is becoming more common, and all water sources must be suspect. Avoid drinking from streams. Make sure you boil water for at least five minutes before drinking. Normal chlorine tablets don't kill *Giardia* cysts. Filters need to be capable of filtering organisms measuring as small as .4 microns. To reduce the spread of this malady, make sure you don't void within 50 m (165 ft.) of a water source, and bury all solid wastes.

Another scourge of hikers are wood ticks. These tough little critters are more common during spring, and often find their way into tender areas to steal a blood meal. They are not to be feared, but respected. A good tick check is a necessary addition to any spring hiking activities.

## Mountain Biking

Mountain biking is a relative newcomer to the mountain recreation scene. Over the past ten years, the quality of equipment has improved and bikers have extended their reach into more and more remote areas. Kananaskis, with its multiple-use mandate, is one of the few areas that looks at mountain biking as an appropriate activity. With this in mind, the mountain biker in Kananaskis has endless opportunity for

## Tips for the Trail

**Ah, hiking!** The freedom of the hills…the call of the wild…uh oh, I've got a blister and I've still got 9 km to go. We've all lived it. We begin the day with great intentions, and then some simple oversight, or some not-so-simple oversight, ends up ruining the trip. We crawl back to the trailhead wondering why we put ourselves through such agony. Hiking, like any outdoor pursuit, requires planning and proper technique. There is method to this madness. Here are some hints to help ensure your hike is enjoyable.

- Don't try to go too far, especially on the first hike of the season.
- Keep a steady pace. Too fast or too slow can be tiring, as can an erratic pace.

- When walking uphill, shorten the stride and place your hands on your thighs to help provide a little extra push.
- On the downhill, bend the knees slightly to reduce the strain and constant pounding on these vulnerable joints. This also reduces the likelihood of falling face-first, as it puts your weight a little lower to the ground.
- Good footwear is worth its weight in gold. Don't head out on a long hike with new boots.
- Make sure your first aid kit has plenty of moleskin for treating blisters.
- When loading your daypack, place the heaviest objects close to your back, and high. This places them at the opti-

mum point for hiking, and provides for a more stable load.
- Always bring along extra clothing, rain gear, gloves, and a hat, even on nice days.
- Take time to enjoy the destination. Don't plan a trip that is so ambitious that you're too rushed and can't enjoy the views you've worked so hard to see.

**Essential First Aid Kit**
Before tossing it in your pack, make sure your first aid kit includes the following essentials:
- plenty of adhesive bandages
- a moleskin and scissors
- gauze pads
- triangular bandages
- a tensor bandage

*Fording a river on the Forgetmenot Rounder trail*

excitement.

The Kananaskis valley has numerous trails that are ideal for riding a bike. It is important, however, particularly in this area, that cyclists are courteous and make sure that hikers are aware of their approach. Get off your bike and allow hikers to pass. With increased animosity between hikers and mountain bikers, more and more trails are being closed to cyclists. Some of the trails in the area may be ideal for riding, but their popularity with hikers makes cycling them inappropriate and, in some cases, dangerous.

Within Peter Lougheed Provincial Park there are numerous trails that provide the length that cyclists want and the opportunity to attain some lofty viewpoints. The Kananaskis Fire Lookout is a particularly good example. With clear views high above the Kananaskis Lakes, this trail is worth experiencing. Most of the best cycling routes are used less by hikers due to their long length and, in some cases, lack of scenery. On the other hand, hikers can attain views inaccessible to fat tires.

Further south, into the Highwood area, there are numerous trails radiating out from the highway. Some of these are non-maintained, former fire roads, so be prepared for many natural hazards and obstacles. The main network of signed trails in this area radiates west from the area of Etherington Creek and Cataract Creek campgrounds.

The premier areas for mountain biking within Kananaskis Country are centered around the Sibbald, Elbow, and Sheep river areas. The intensive equestrian use through these corridors has resulted in a well-developed series of trails designed with horses in mind. However, the two activities are not all that different: both try to cover similar distances and both prefer some solid surface on which to ride.

Since mountain bikes can reach far into the wilderness in a very short time, it's important to be prepared for any contingency. Proper repair kits are essential. Some vital inclusions are: spare tube and patch kit, chain tool and extra links, air pump, spoke and Allan wrenches, and the ever necessary duct tape.

While riding, always ride at a controlled speed. Many accidents are caused by riding too fast. Make sure you stay on

## Friends of Kananaskis

**The Friends of Kananaskis** is a non-profit organization dedicated to the preservation and protection of Kananaskis Country. They work with Kananaskis Country to help produce and sponsor environmental education programs, enhance displays and interpretive trails, help purchase equipment for amphitheatres, encourage public safety and wildlife studies, perform volunteer trail maintenance, and also help fund environmental research.

The Friends of Kananaskis have produced a video entitled Think Big—Protecting Natural Systems in the Rocky Mountains, designed to help school children understand conservation. They are also sponsoring a new display featuring bear ecology and its role in the mountain environment. Edu-Kits have been designed to teach school children about wolves and birds of prey. These are available for school groups to use in the classroom. The Friends also funded a study of Brown Trout ecology.

As less and less money is made available for park operations, it becomes even more critical that associations like the Friends of Kananaskis receive support. For more information, or to become a member, contact the Friends of Kananaskis, Suite 201, 800 Railway Ave., Canmore, AB, T1W 1P1. Phone: (403) 678-5508.

designated trails, and avoid riding muddy trails and trampling native vegetation. Make sure you always wear a helmet, and never head out without letting someone know of your destination. With the ability to cycle in one day what would take a hiker three days, there is a potential for getting caught out overnight. With this in mind, make sure you bring enough extra clothes and food to make it through the night, just in case.

## Cross-Country Skiing

Cross-country skiing is one of the fastest growing winter activities, and cross-country skiers seem to be heading into the mountains in increasing numbers. Kananaskis Country has anticipated this increased use, and provides a huge number of properly track-set and maintained cross-country trails. Centered primarily in the western parts of Kananaskis, simply because the eastern valleys don't tend to hold enough snow, these trails can keep you busy for season after season.

Travelling south in the Kananaskis valley, the Ribbon Creek Trail system is the first network encountered. It includes 17 different trails, all radiating out of the Ribbon Creek/Kananaskis Village area. You can make your way 5 km (3 mi.) down Ribbon Creek before turning around, or you can climb high above the valley towards Skogan Pass or the Sunburst Lookout. Numerous trails provide loop options out from and around the Kananaskis Village. Another trail of note, the Evan–Thomas

*Cycling the Evan-Thomas bicycle path*

Trail, follows the route of the paved summer trail, and trends south from Ribbon Creek all the way to Wedge Pond.

Beyond Ribbon Creek, the Kananaskis Lakes area of Peter Lougheed Provincial Park provides the most popular network of trails. Not only is this network larger than the Ribbon Creek system, but it provides the option of skiing some longer trails. Loops in excess of 30 km (18 mi.) can be created by linking many of the trails together. Some climb toward panoramic viewpoints. In particular, the Kananaskis Fire Lookout, for expert skiers, has the best skiable view in the area. Blueberry Hill provides another good view of the Kananaskis Lakes. Beginner trails, like Pocaterra or Lionel,

make sure that skiers of all abilities find something to challenge them.

Along the Smith–Dorrien/ Spray Trail, there are two trail systems. The Smith–Dorrien Trail System provides a variety of loop options of varying difficulties. Each loop is colour-coded, and the trail map provides good details on gradients and level. Further north, the Mount Shark Trail system gives racers a place to put in some miles. It is used primarily for early- and late-season races, when the Canmore Nordic Centre is not at its best.

Designed for the 1988 Winter Olympics, the Canmore Nordic Centre provides an intricate series of trails designed to test the skills of the world's best skiers. The Banff Trail provides the single beginner-

*Kananaskis has 825 km (513 mi.) of horseback trails*

of the Elbow and Sheep rivers. As such, it is used mainly as a staging area for multiple-day excursions.

Throughout the Sibbald, Elbow, Sheep, and Highwood regions, horseback riding is a popular way to traverse the trails and to access remote areas. Most of the day rides are focused around the numerous equestrian campgrounds and trailheads. Places like Etherington Creek in the Highwood area, Dawson in the Sibbald area, Little Elbow along Highway 66, Mesa Butte along the McLean Creek Trail, and Sandy McNabb and Bluerock in the Sheep Valley provide facilities for overnight camping with horses.

When riding in the Elbow Valley, particularly south of Highway 66, be aware that wild horses also roam the area, and mares have been stolen by wild studs. Avoid bringing mares in heat to this area.

While riding, make sure you bring basic farrier tools, a plastic removable hoof boot, tack repair kit, horse bell, fly wipe, horse brushes, and equine first aid kit. At night, hobble horses that tend to wander, as they can cover quite some distance overnight. Bring your own feed when possible, and take advantage of tie posts, when available, rather than trees. Use a portable bucket and look for rocky areas to water your horses. This will help reduce erosion around streambanks.

There are a few equestrian group campgrounds available by reservation only. They can be booked by calling the Canmore office of Kananaskis Country at (403) 678-5508.

trail option. The remainder are one-way racing trails designed for intermediate and expert skiers.

## Horseback Riding

Horses have been travelling the trails of Kananaskis for over 100 years. Long before there was a recreational attraction to this valley, ranchers ranged their cattle through its isolated valleys. Range riders kept a constant vigil on the stock, and forest rangers patrolled the valleys.

As time passed, and southern Alberta saw more and more settlement, horses began to take on the dual role of work animal and recreational animal. In time, trails were developed, and today several areas of Kananaskis have been specifically adapted to offer equestrian users the ultimate in backcountry riding. At present, there are 825 km (513 mi.) of trails within Kananaskis Country that are open to horse travel.

Horses are forbidden within Peter Lougheed Provincial Park, with one exception. The trail to Elbow Lake provides ideal access to the valleys

## Off-Highway Vehicles

Prefer to have several hundred horses underneath you, rather than just one? In that case, the McLean Creek off-highway vehicle zone may the place for you. With approximately 200 sq. km (77 sq. mi.), and several hundred kilometres of formal and informal trails, the McLean Creek area provides options for every type of equipment and all of your moods. There are staging areas at the McLean Creek Campground, at the north end of the zone, and a second one at Fisher Creek on the south boundary.

Large four-wheel-drive units will do better on the major trails, and these tend to traverse the area from corner to corner. Options include the Elbow River, Silvester, Fisher, Fish Creek, Priddis Creek, McLean, Quirk, and Quirk Ridge trails. Most of these routes are passable, though deep mud holes are often a part of the experience. These trails may also include river fords, but they are generally passable in a 4x4. Remember, the condition varies dramatically, so be prepared for anything.

For dirt bikes and quadrunners, there are numerous trails that are narrower and more challenging and provide an opportunity to leave the gas guzzlers behind. The steep faces of Mount Barwell are the sole domain of these more agile vehicles. Although helmets are not legally required, they are an essential part of any rider's safety kit. Helmets, sturdy gloves, a kidney belt, good boots, and water- and

*McLean Creek off-highway zone*

mud-resistant clothing are recommended.

Within the McLean Creek zone, vehicles are allowed on all cutlines and trails. Trail users are asked to stay on main routes whenever possible, to minimize damage to surrounding areas. Between the signed trails and unsigned cutlines there is an almost endless potential for exploration. Before heading off on a trail, make sure you have a map, in addition to first aid, emergency, and repair kits. A minimum repair kit should include a screwdriver set, duct tape, a wrench set, spark plugs and wrench, a tire repair kit, vice grips, and a spare chain or belt.

## Legal Requirements

When planning a trip to the McLean Creek area, please be aware that rangers regularly patrol the area and regulations are enforced. Off-highway vehicles are governed by the Alberta Off-Highway Vehicle (OHV) Act.

- All vehicles must be

licensed as an off-highway vehicle, and must have proper insurance and registration.
- All vehicles must have a stock muffler, exhaust pipes, a spark arrestor, a headlight, and a tail-light.
- Moto-cross bikes are only allowed if they comply with the OHV Act.
- Any vehicle used on public roadways must have a highway license plate, insurance and registration, a horn, signal lights, mirrors, a speedometer, and brake lights.

## Snowmobiling

Winter is an amazing time in Kananaskis. Families pack into their cars, head to the mountains, and take advantage of a plentiful supply of snow. Cross-country skiing and downhill skiing seem to be the primary activities, but hot on their tails is snowmobiling. Snowmobiling is ideally suited to the mountains. It's a great family pastime and provides the opportunity to see the mountains while they're covered in a blanket of fresh

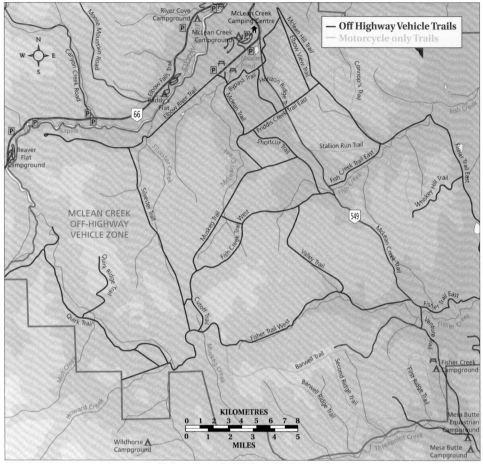

*McLean Creek Off-Highway Vehicle Area*

snow. It also enables the rider to cover large distances through fairly remote, pristine winter wilderness. This is both a blessing and a danger. When conditions are perfect, riding the Elbow Loop Trail in a snowmobile provides the vision of a winter wonderland. As the machine crests the summit of Elbow Pass, with Tombstone Mountain to the west and Mount Cornwall and Banded Peak to the east, there are few places as wondrous.

There can be a dark side, however, to snowmobiling. The ability of a snowmobile to

transport people to remote areas with a minimum of fuss can mean an easy ride to tragedy. Suffering through a break-down, far from the nearest road and without the likelihood of passers-by, can be a lonely experience. See the discussion on snowmobile safety for suggestions on how to ensure your trip is a pleasant one.

There are three main areas open to winter snow vehicles. The McLean Creek area, with its diverse trail system, is the best known. Unfortunately, it often suffers from a lack of

snow. Also subject to poor snow is the Sibbald Flat snow vehicle zone. Located adjacent to the Sibbald Creek Trail (Highway 68) at the north end of Powderface Trail, it provides a limited snowmobile area, even in good snow. Its real advantage is its access to the Powderface Trail. This summer road is open to snow vehicles in winter, and can be used to access the Elbow Loop Trail. This loop can also be reached from the McLean Creek area.

In the Highwood area, the Cataract Creek snowmobile

area provides an additional 100 km (62 mi.) of trails. This network tends to see more predictable snow and, consequently, plenty of snowmobile traffic. The trails in this network are well marked, although some of the signs are confusing. One of the routes allows access all the way into British Columbia over the Fording River Pass. This route passes over a major avalanche slope, so be extremely cautious in this area.

## Snowmobile Safety

It's easy to understand the attraction of snowmobiling, but travelling through remote country during winter weather also brings a touch of danger into the activity. Winter weather can change in a heartbeat, and sudden storms can catch you unaware. Luckily, snowmobiling means heavy snowsuits and sturdy, warm boots. This can be a lifesaver when a break-down occurs or a blizzard blows over the ridge. Here are some additional suggestions to help make your trip pleasant.

- Never head into the backcountry without a good map.
- Always bring a repair kit, which includes a screwdriver set, duct tape, a wrench set, spark plugs and wrench, vice grips, and a spare belt.
- To ease walking out in a serious mechanical breakdown, bring a pair of snowshoes, some extra food, and a warm drink. Don't forget to pack some matches, a blanket, a tarp, and a flashlight when heading into remote country. You could end up

*Whitewater canoeist on the Kananaskis River*

spending the night.
- Learn about avalanche danger. Snow slides are a constant reality in remote mountain valleys. Always check with Kananaskis Country for current avalanche forecasts.
- Watch for the signs of hypothermia. It is characterized by uncontrollable shivering, loss of coordination, slurred speech, and, in severe cases, a desire to sleep. The symptoms come on slowly and can be easily missed.
- In minor cases of frostbite try to warm the area as soon as possible. This will minimize tissue damage. Don't rub the area, and be cautious of burning the injured part by placing it too close to a fire, as the heat may not be felt. If the freezing is severe, do not attempt to thaw the injured part. It will require medical attention and should wait until it can be thawed safely.

## Boating

The Kananaskis and Spray valleys have been modified over the years to provide water storage and hydroelectric power. In the process, the levels of the Upper and Lower Kananaskis Lakes, as well as the Spray Lakes, have been raised significantly. During the same period of development, Barrier Lake was created by flooding the Kananaskis Valley

### Rafting Companies

**Here are a** few of the many companies operating on the Kananaskis River.

**Canadian Rockies Rafting**
Canmore, AB, (403) 678-6535
Toll Free: 1-877-226-7625
www.rafting.ca

**Mirage Adventure Tours**
Box 233, Kananaskis Village, AB
T0L 2H0, (403) 591-7773
Toll Free: 1-888-312-7238
www.miragetours.com

**Rainbow Riders Adventure Tours**
3312-3rd Avenue NW
Calgary, Alberta, T2N 0L9
(403) 678-Raft (7238)
Toll Free: 1-877-717-Raft (7238)
www.rainbowriders.com

*Mirage River Adventures on Kananaskis River*

behind Barrier Dam. When these programs were implemented, they were very controversial. George Pocaterra, an early prospector and trapper in the area, felt hydro development had completely destroyed the character of the valley. Today, people travel from all over the world and marvel at these giant mirrors of the surrounding peaks.

Boats are becoming increasingly common. Families load up the boat, the tent, and the kids and head to the mountains for the weekend.

## River Guide

**Following are short** descriptions of a few of the main river routes in the Kananaskis area. It is not meant to be complete or to be followed as a guide. It is merely designed to highlight some of the principle areas. There are more detailed sources on whitewater paddling available, which will provide the information necessary to safely paddle these rivers.

### Kananaskis River

This is the most popular stretch of water in Kananaskis Country. The main route begins at Widowmaker Day Use, 7.9 km (4.7 mi.) south on Highway 40. The put-in is at the bottom of a short trail, in a large natural eddy in the river. Beneath the put-in, a competition-level, Class 3 course has been built. It runs toward Canoe Meadows, where most take out, though you can continue to Seebe Dam along mostly Class 1 and 2 waters. Because it is dam-controlled, you'll need to check with Barrier Information Centre at (403) 673-3985 for current release times.

### Highwood River

The Highwood is one of the best paddling rivers in the area, but, like most, the water level drops quickly during the season, making this a spring paddle. The top section, putting in at Highwood Group Camp, provides 10 km (6 mi.) of Class 2 and 3 rapids, with a bit of Class 4 near the lower end. Further downstream, a portage to the right takes you around a Class 5 section.

The next 10 km (6 mi.), from Green Ford Campsite, contains a seemingly endless supply of Class 3 and 4 rapids. There are one or two portages near the end of this stretch. The final 11 km (6.6 mi.), to the Highway 22 junction, provides good intermediate-level paddling with Class 2 being the norm along this pleasant stretch. Take out at the Longview Bridge.

### Elbow River

The Elbow can be paddled in numerous sections. The upper stretch from Beaver Flat Campground to Elbow Falls averages Class 1, but don't miss the take-out or you'll end up heading over the lip of Elbow Falls. Lower down, from the put-in at Canyon Creek, the river has numerous rapids of the Class 2 variety along with a Class 3 ledge. The ride is enjoyable and the take-out is at Paddy's Flat Campground.

### Sheep River

In high water, this is a great, expert run. With several deep gorges, this river is not for novice paddlers. From Bluerock Campground there are several portages, with the grade averaging Class 2 mixed with lots of Class 4. It is for expert paddlers only, due to sheer canyon walls and limited access to shore. Make sure you read a more detailed description of this route before attempting it.

The lower stretch, below Gorge Creek, is a little tamer. It still has a canyon to be negotiated, but it's less difficult, with Class 2 and a little Class 3 water. The take-out is at Sandy McNabb Campground..

## Mountain Rescue

*Disaster strikes!*

**Safety is always** a big concern in the mountains. Time and again, seemingly harmless jaunts end up in a rescue situation. With more and more people venturing into the wilderness, the inevitable result is an increase in the number of potential accidents. George Field is one of Kananaskis Country's rescue specialists. When someone gets injured, it's his job to make sure that systems are in place to ensure a quick and appropriate response. "What's really important in my area is the training, that we have a staff and we know what their standards are, so that we can put them into rescue situations that they are comfortable in." The training is diverse. It includes training in wilderness first aid, mountain climbing, organized rope and cable rescue, ski mountaineering, avalanche and snow study, search management, and moving-water rescue.

Kananaskis Country has taken over the search and rescue component of the Royal Canadian Mounted Police (RCMP) mandate. Field has been part of the Rescue Program since 1982, and a certified mountain guide since 1985. In the summer of 1986, three planes went down in eight days in Kananaskis. On June 6, a small plane carrying biologist Orval Pall and his pilot disappeared. A second plane, searching for Pall, crashed into the side of Mount Lougheed. On June 14, a military twin otter, also engaged in the search for Pall, crashed and burned, killing all eight on board. Eleven people had died looking for two. As luck would have it, Pall's plane had also been destroyed, killing both him and his pilot. The carnage included 13, but would reach 22 by the end of summer. That was one of the worst years in the short history of Kananaskis.

Although the rescues vary dramatically, no one group seems to stand out when it comes to incidents of rescue. However, scrambling—climbing without ropes—has become increasingly popular, and this has led to an increased number of rescues. It's not only climbers being rescued. In fact a very small number of climber rescues take place. Despite more than a thou-sand climbers on Mount Yamnuska this summer, there was only one rescue on that sheer face. An average would be two or three per year. Sport climbers, like those commonly seen along Highway 40, tend to self rescue. They get back to the highway and do their own evacuations, so exact statistics are difficult to compile.

Kananaskis Country has a voluntary backcountry registration system. This ensures that park staff know your planned route, and when you will be back. You do need to check back upon return. Unfortunately, a very small number of people use the voluntary system. In 1994, there were over 500 documented occurrences (anything officially dealt with) in Kananaskis, but only about 10% involved rescues. Though media attention usually focuses on those involving mountaineers, according to Field the costs of all the minor rescues combined far outweigh those of the large rescues.

*Mountain climbers*

There are not many large lakes on the eastern slopes that allow boats. Kananaskis Country provides a welcome spot to launch boats and ply the waters of numerous mountain lakes.

Since the lakes were artificially raised, the levels tend to fluctuate dramatically. Beneath the waters, the stumps of ancient forests still defiantly hold their ground. As levels drop, the danger of hitting these roots with your boat's propeller increases. For most large boats it's a hard paddle if things go wrong, so prepare for contingencies. Keep your speeds low and watch for signs. In posted areas the speed is limited to 12 km/hr (7 mi./hr). You won't water-ski at those speeds, but not many people have wanted to ski in these frigid waters.

## Canoeing and Kayaking

When the fur traders first made their way westward they used the water. Paddling huge freighter canoes they moved inland. Across most of the plains it was easier to travel overland than by boat. Once you reached the mountains, forget it! This was the land of the pack train. Once into British Columbia, the horses were traded in for boats, and the traders followed the Columbia River to its source on the Pacific. Today, the mountains see an increasing number of whitewater paddlers testing their skills along many of the local rivers.

In the 1950s, canoeists began to test the waters and found many of the rivers passable. As time passed and technology improved, kayaks became more prevalent. Well-designed for raging water, they have allowed paddlers to push the limits, and they are now a more common sight in many of the larger rivers.

The rivers along the eastern slopes are often shallow. Boats tend to bounce their way down many watercourses, and fiberglass crafts are rarely up to the task. Modern plastics technology has spawned virtually indestructible materials, and these have become the mainstay for whitewater kayaks and canoes.

Any experienced paddler is quick to admit the power of water. It moves fast and has a force far beyond that of a paddler. This power deserves respect. Learn proper techniques on flat water before attempting swift currents. Always wear a helmet and life jacket, and bring a throw bag for emergencies. A seemingly gentle stream can quickly turn deadly when a log jam appears. Sweepers, which are trees or branches overhanging the stream, are a serious hazard on many local rivers. Stay vigilant, and never paddle alone.

## Rafting

Whitewater rafting is becoming more popular every year. As tourism continues to grow, so does our hunger for adventure. Rafting provides an excellent combination of thrill, balanced by the security of professionally trained and certified guides. The Kananaskis River is a great place for the rafting initiate. It isn't a float like the Bow River, yet it's not a heart-stopper like the Kicking Horse. With Class 1 to 3 rapids, it has enough white water to ensure some excitement and the added benefit of the great scenery that has made Kananaskis Country so famous.

## Fishing

Fishing is an excellent way to appreciate some of the areas backcountry lakes, or simply relax at one of the local fishing holes. The options are wide open, as long as you pack your fishing license, and your patience.

According to the Alberta Guide to Sport Fishing, Kananaskis Country lies within Zone 1 Eastern Slopes (ES1). Here are some important points to remember when fishing in Kananaskis.

- The general sport fishing season runs the entire year, except where specifically stated.
- Everyone 16–64 needs to have a valid fishing license.
- Within the boundaries of Kananaskis Country, the possession limit for bull trout and Arctic grayling is zero in order to help populations of these declining species rebound.
- The general possession limit for other trout is a total of 5 trout, of which only only 3 may be lake trout, and none may be Arctic Grayling.

## Stocked Lakes within Kananaskis Country

**Numerous lakes** in the Kananaskis area are stocked annually, most with cutthroat or rainbow trout. According to representatives with Alberta Fish and Wildlife, this list varies annually. Be sure to check the most recent copy of the Sport Fishing Guide for more current stocking estimates.

| Name of Lake | Month Stocked | Amount | Type of Fish | Length (cm) |
|---|---|---|---|---|
| Allen Bill Pond | May | 2,800 | Rainbow trout | 25.0 |
| | June | 1,200 | Rainbow trout | 21.0 |
| | June | 1,900 | Rainbow trout | 27.0 |
| Grotto Mountain Pond | May | 1,600 | Rainbow trout | 19.0 |
| | June | 1,600 | Rainbow trout | 21.0 |
| Kananaskis Village Pond | July | 100 | Rainbow trout | 26.0 |
| McLean Pond | May | 3,800 | Rainbow trout | 19.0 |
| | June | 3,500 | Rainbow trout | 21.0 |
| Mount Lorette Ponds | May | 2,400 | Rainbow trout | 25.0 |
| | June | 2,600 | Rainbow trout | 24.0 |
| Sibbald Lake | May | 1,700 | Rainbow trout | 19.0 |
| Sibbald Meadows Pond | May | 2,000 | Cutthroat trout | 16.0 |
| | June | 2,000 | Cutthroat trout | 19.0 |
| Upper Kananaskis Lake | June | 25,400 | Bull trout | 5.0 |

*Beginner's luck*

- The general limit for mountain whitefish is 5.
- Live fish and live fish eggs cannot be placed in any water except those from which they were taken, and live fish cannot be used as bait.
- All rainbow trout smaller than 30 cm, taken from flowing water, must be released

The Upper and Lower Lakes provide excellent big water fishing. Spray Lake supplies many a frying pan with lake trout—summer and winter. Some of the backcountry lakes can quickly make the walk worth while, and the main rivers have many quiet eddies where the fish bite.

It is beyond the scope of this book to cover all of the many regulations that apply to Kananaskis Country. Before heading out, be sure to spend time with the Alberta Guide to Sportfishing Regulations. Each year the regulations get more complex and a few hours spent perusing this guide with a trusty highlighter may prevent you from accidentally running afoul of the regulations.

## Mountain Climbing

Rock climbing is very popular. Each year more than a thousand climbers ascend the steep face of Mount Yamnuska, and, with the increased popularity of the Kananaskis region, the number of climbers is expected to increase.

Sport climbing involves shorter routes, with fixed anchors. An experienced climber leads or climbs the route first. He then can safely belay for the climbers below. Belaying involves progressively taking up the slack in the rope as climbers ascend. That way, if they fall, they only drop a short distance. The lead climbers run the risk of longer falls, as they must be belayed from the base of the cliff. If they place a small wedge to hold their rope into a crack, and then climb 3 m, they risk falling a total of 6 m before the slack is taken up by the chock. Since most of the sport-climbing routes—

## Poaching

**Several years ago** a hunter had his photo, along with his trophy sheep, published in a local newspaper. According to the article, he had taken the sheep more than 100 km (60 mi.) from the Sheep River Valley. To local biologists studying the sheep within the Sheep River Wildlife Sanctuary, something seemed very wrong indeed. They knew that sheep. They had become intimately acquainted with all the sheep in the sanctuary, and, had learned to recognize each from a distance. This helped them keep "tabs" on the various individuals. When they insisted that animal could not have been taken at the location listed in the article, Fish and Wildlife Officers and Park Rangers began to investigate.

During hunting season, Park Rangers routinely keep records of the license plates of vehicles parked at the various recreation areas adjacent to the Sheep Sanctuary and sure enough, when this hunter claimed to be at some distant location, his car was parked within the Sanctuary boundaries. Strike one for the anti-poaching patrol.

The vast majority of hunters are honest sportsmen. Their fees help pay for many of the province's conservation programs. Unfortunately, some hunters prefer to follow their own rules, and poaching is always a concern. If you suspect poaching, immediately call Alberta's toll-free poaching line at 1-800-642-3800. If your phone call results in charges being filed, you may even be eligible to receive a reward.

places like Barrier Bluffs, Wasootch Tower, and Grotto Canyon—are near main roadways, they are popular for quick afternoon forays.

Mountains like Yamnuska involve multiple pitches and thus high potential dangers. There is a seemingly endless number of routes to the summit, including a hiking trail up the rear of the mountain. There are options for novices and experts. Since this is a major climb, it tends to see the largest number of documented accidents. Beware of sudden storms that can catch you unaware and expose you to the dangers of lightning.

Scrambling is becoming more popular. This involves climbing without ropes. Many summits can be ascended without ropes, but require extensive experience and a much higher skill level. This is one area where the Rangers have experienced a rapid increase in rescues, and they highly discourage this form of climbing.

The most important thing to keep in mind is safety. Too many people head out with little or no training, and risk their lives. Climbing requires very specific knowledge. Don't let your friends teach you—take a course.

*Ice climbing in the Canadian Rockies*

## Hunting

Each autumn, hunters descend on the Kananaskis and head into the backcountry in hopes of bagging the big one. Within certain areas, such as Provincial Parks, hunting is prohibited, and it is important to know these exclusions. The equestrian parking lots become extra busy at these times, as hunters head into the backcountry on multi–day excursions for elk, mule and white–tail deer, trophy sheep, moose, black bear, and even cougar. Black bears are also hunted during April and May. Game birds taken throughout Kananaskis include ruffed, blue, and spruce grouse, Ptarmigan, Ducks, and Geese. The seasons open near the beginning of September, and run through to the end of November. Ducks and geese are hunted until mid-December.

The hunting regulations for Alberta run in excess of 75 pages. It's critical that hunters familiarize themselves with the rules relevant to this area.

Hunters may also choose to donate the hides of their animals to the Alberta Fish and Game Association. This non–profit organization uses the money raised from selling the hides to help acquire critical wildlife habitat within the province. It's one more way that hunters are helping to preserve the resource they enjoy. For information call (403) 437–2342.

*Opposite: Fly fishing at First Picklejar Lake*

# Canmore

*Downtown Canmore*

The rapidly growing community of Canmore has become Canada's gateway to the Rocky Mountains. Nestled in the Bow River Valley, Canmore sits in the shadow of Mount Rundle to the west, Ha Ling Peak, Mount Lawrence Grassi and the famous Three Sisters to the south, and

Mounts Charles Stewart and Lady Macdonald of the Fairholme Range to the north. First-time visitors are struck by the majesty of the mountain landscape rising above this former coal mining community. Over the years, Canmore's role has changed. Once a seasonal campsite and travel route for native Indians moving to and from British Columbia the community evolved into a coal mining town, Olympic host city, and its present incarnation as a mountain playground.

Canmore welcomes visitors from every corner of the planet. Historically, tourists rushing towards Canmore's better-known neighbour, Banff, often bypassed Canmore. Most had no idea of the abundant opportunities available within this small mountain community. Canmore no longer plays second fiddle to the name recognition of Banff. It boasts more than 1,700 hotel rooms, dozens of bed and breakfasts and a diversity of shops and restaurants. Add to this the endless opportunity for outdoor recreation, and you have a community that now serves as the primary destination of many travellers.

Canmore sits at a crossroads. To the south, the rugged landscape of Alberta's Kananaskis Country attracts several million visitors each year, and to the west, Banff National Park lies only a few kilometres along the Trans-Canada Highway.

Canmorites are very active in developing unique events and festivals. Annual highlights include the Heritage Day Folk Festival, the Highland Games, the Festival of Eagles, the Winter Festival and the Alberta International Sled Dog Classic. Athletic events, including World Cup mountain

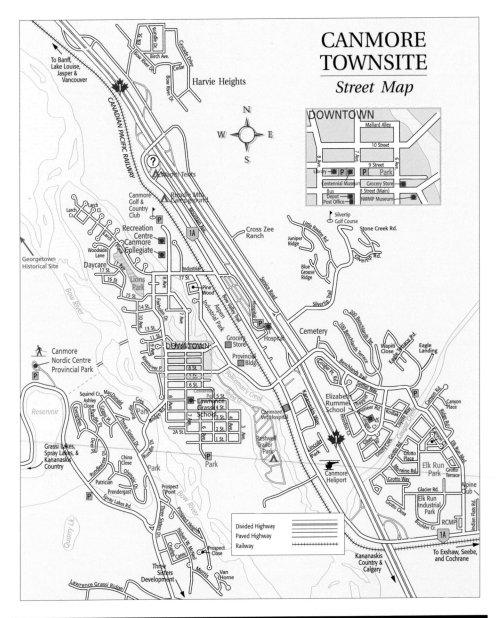

# CANMORE TOWNSITE
## Street Map

**Altitude SuperGuide Recommendations**

- Hike **Grassi Lakes Trail**
- Visit the **Canmore Centennial Museum/Geoscience Centre**
- enjoy a cup of coffee at **The Rocky Mountain Bagel Co.** or **The Coffee Mine**
- Check out the local galleries (see page 80)
- Have a swim at the **Recreation Centre**

- Winter: rent skis at the **Canmore Nordic Centre** and glide along the trails of the 1988 Olympics
- Summer: rent bikes for a ride at the **Nordic Centre**
- Paint some pottery at **Great Bowls Afire!** When you are finished, the owners will fire it for you. You can pick it up after a few days.
- Take a stroll along the Bow River pathways

*Canmore's Three Sisters*

bike and cross-country ski races, have helped to raise the international reputation that was born in 1988 when Canmore hosted the Nordic events of the Winter Olympics. As Canmore has grown, its downtown core has also changed. Today, Main Street is lined with restaurants and shops catering to visitor and local alike.

All of this change has put pressure on the local landscape and wildlife populations. With the population tripling in just over a decade, the town has had to struggle with growth management and the impacts that growth places on wildlife movement. Pressure from residents and environmental groups has had impressive results. Since the first edition of this book was published in 1996, numerous new parks have been established, including Elbow-Sheep Wildland Park, Canmore Nordic Centre Provincial Park, Bow Valley Wildland Park, and most recently, Spray Valley Provincial Park. In addition, the Canmore Flats and Yamnuska Natural Areas have been established. While many conservationists view this as only the first step in ensuring ecological integrity in the area, the progress has been considerable.

## Northwest Mounted Police

**In 1875**, the Northwest Mounted Police arrived in the west and in 1883, following the railway westward, the Mounties began to patrol the Bow Valley. In the beginning, the area was policed from Calgary, then from Banff. By 1888, Banff had begun to grow, and Canmore was rapidly expanding with the railway's desire for a steady supply of coal. Soon, it became apparent that Canmore needed its own NWMP detachment. Canmore was a town of around 50 people, mostly young, single men, and alcohol and rowdiness had become a problem. Macleod Stewart, President of the Canadian Anthracite Coal Company pe-

titioned the Comptroller of the NWMP in Ottawa for more police.

In response, Constable Harris became Canmore's first resident policeman. The detachment grew to two constables and a commissioned officer by 1890. In 1892, the Northwest Mounted Police built a building to be used as a barracks along the shore of what has now become known as Policeman's Creek. The building was a mud-chinked log structure. By 1896, the size of the detachment was reduced to a single officer and one horse, and remained this size until 1929. The barracks were rebuilt in 1909 and have remained virtually unchanged to this date.

## Canmore's Early Days

For thousands of years, natives passed beneath these peaks, camping in the valley bottom as they passed through on their way to seasonal bison hunts on the plains, or to hunt sheep, goats and mountain bison. Recent discoveries show evidence of human occupation as far back as 11,000 to 12,000 years ago. This makes these mountain sites some of the oldest archaeological sites in Alberta.

As Europeans began to ex-

*Coal carts from mining days*

plore the mountains, passing the site of present-day Canmore, they often travelled through Whiteman's Gap (the pass between Ha Ling Peak and Mount Rundle) on their way to points further west. As early as 1841, James Sinclair passed this way with a group of settlers bound for the newly opened Oregon Territory. A few years later, in 1845 Jesuit Missionary Father Pierre J. de Smet returned from the Oregon Territory over this pass. He also became the first man to mention the plentiful coal deposits in the area.

Prior to these visits, fur traders had occasionally passed to the north and east of Canmore. As early as 1807, David Thompson traversed Howse Pass south of the present-day Saskatchewan River Crossing. Travel through the Central Rockies remained sparse until plans for a railway brought surveyors and explorers to the mountains in large numbers. They scoured the valleys and mountain passes looking for a route to the Pacific. In the end, the railway was built along the banks of

the Bow River and over the Kicking Horse Pass into British Columbia. The rails arrived in the Canmore area in 1883 as the crews worked their way westward. Two years later, the last spike was hammered and the mountain barrier had been breached. Also in 1885, surveyor George Dawson, head of the Geologic Survey of

Canada, described extensive coal seams running from Cascade Mountain to south of present day Canmore. Dawson also gave the Three Sisters the name that has stuck. Previously, they had been known as the "Three Nuns" because under a heavy snowfall they looked like nuns in white veils.

## Canmore Centennial Museum Society

**Canmore's rich history** is being preserved though the efforts of volunteers like Royal McKellar of the Canmore Centennial Museum Society. Since the mines closed in 1979, there was a fear that much of the history might be lost. The Centennial Museum opened on its present site in 1988, just in time for the Olympics, and since that time has provided a great showcase for the stories and artifacts of Canmore's past.

The Canmore Museum and Geoscience Centre has become an integral stop for anyone with an interest in the history of Canmore. As you enter the museum, you are greeted by a large collection of mining artifacts and

tools. During the 93 years that the mine operated, the mining equipment changed a great deal, and those changes can be seen in the museum exhibits.

The geological exhibits help to make the complex geology of the area easier to understand. The unique character of the surrounding peaks not only provided endless fodder for artists and photographers, but also resulted in the coal seams upon which Canmore depended for almost a century.

The museum is staffed by volunteers, and is located at 907 – 7th Avenue in Canmore. The phone number is (403) 678-2462.

*Canadian Pacific Railway roundhouse in Canmore (ca. 1886)*

# Humble Beginnings— The Arrival of Coal Miners

Canmore is a town built of coal. With the arrival of the railway in 1883, coal-powered steam engines were hungry for fuel, and the Bow Valley was happy to oblige. George Dawson's surveys had shown good outcrops of coal in the area and entrepreneurs were quick to sense an opportunity.

Canmore began as a divisional point for the railroad and basically consisted of a boxcar-like building that was built near the current west railway crossing. The station's first agent, Charles Compton, recorded the arrival of the first train at noon on May 11, 1884. Soon, railroad bunkhouses were built, and Canmore's first settlers arrived. Mr. and Mrs. James Conroy arrived in Canmore with their daughter Mary and another young woman named Miss Foley. They built and operated a boarding house near the station.

In 1886, a mine was opened up at Anthracite, near the present site of Banff. This small operation began the

## Profile of Malcolm Canmore—killer of Macbeth

**Malcolm III (1031-1093)** ruled Scotland between 1058 and 1093. He earned the nickname Ceann Mor (Canmore), meaning "big head", perhaps for his physical appearance, or for his status as a great leader. His father was Duncan I, who ruled Scotland from 1034-40 when he was murdered by his brother, Macbeth (of Shakespearean fame). Malcolm III avenged his father's death by killing Macbeth in battle in 1057. Macbeth's son, Lulach, who was also killed by Malcolm III a year later, succeeded him.

In 1058, Malcolm III became king of Scotland. During his reign he invaded England five times. He was finally killed in battle at Alnwick Castle on the North Sea coast in 1093. Malcolm's first wife Ingibiorg died after bearing him four heirs. His second wife Margaret was born in Hungary, and brought many European traditions with her to Scotland. Together they had four more sons. Margaret was a devout and well-loved queen, founding the Dunfermline Priory, an 11th century abbey located in Dunfermline, the ancient capital of Scotland. The Priory became the last resting place of Kings Malcolm IV, Alexander I and Robert the Bruce. While the abbey ceased to function in 1560, most of the priory can still be seen today.

## Canmore?

**Canmore was likely named** by Donald A. Smith, railroad financier and the man who hammered the last spike of the Canadian Pacific Railway. Local Stoney Indians referred to the location as "too-wup-chinchin-koodibee" which literally translates to "shooting at young spruce tree." Young Stoney braves would practice their marksmanship by shooting at a young tree when they camped in the Canmore flats area. Surveyors, like Major A.B. Rogers, referred to this area as 'Padmore'.

*No.2 Mine Tipple, built in 1906 on the edge of the Bow River*

mining of coal in the Bow Valley. Nowadays often forgotten, Anthracite was operated by the Canadian Anthracite Coal Company, and the mine was profitable. At the same time, the Cochrane Mine had opened up in Canmore, but lacked any firm commitments to buy its product. In 1891, an American, H. W. McNeill, saw an opportunity here, and leased the holdings of the Canadian Anthracite Coal Company. He was given two consecutive 10-year leases to develop and operate the mines at Anthracite and Canmore. The #1 Mine, located near the current Rundleview subdivision, was worked between 1886 and 1916. Around this mine, a small community known as Mineside grew.

In 1903, the #2 Mine was opened. It was located on the banks of the Bow River along the route of today's Three Sisters Parkway. In 1911, McNeill's lease expired, and the Cana-

## The Canmore Opera House

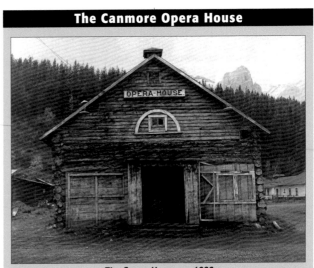

*The Opera House ca.1898*

**In 1898**, Canmore miners built a log building to house social events. The Band Hall was later renamed the Canmore Opera House and was the hub of social activity for the town. All manner of dances, festivals, films, concerts, and plays were hosted. The Canmore Opera House was the first log opera house to be built in Canada. With the opening of the Union Hall in 1913, the Opera House began to lose its prominent position in the community's social life. In 1964, it was sold to Calgary's Heritage Park, where it still remains.

dian Anthracite Coal Company created a subsidiary called the Canmore Coal Company. The #5 Mine was operated briefly under this new name, from 1923 to 1926. It was later reopened between 1944-1951 and again from 1961 to 1974 when it was finally closed.

Adjacent to the mines operated by the Canmore Coal Company, a small mine and townsite arose near the Georgetown Mine. This small mine was operated by the Canmore Navigation & Coal Company, but lasted only a few years, operating from 1913-1916.

Over the years, Canmore Mines, as the Canmore Coal Company was christened in 1938, continued to open new mines, as well as new seams in some of the older mines. The #4 Mine, Number 4 Seam was opened in 1937, the #3 Mine in 1947 and the Wilson Mine, Number 2 Seam in 1961. The final two mines, the #4b Mine (1972) and the Riverside Mine (1976) were still operating when mining finally ceased in 1979.

# From Mining to Tourism

In Canmore, everything changed on July 13, 1979. On this summer's day, the final whistle blew at the Canmore Mines, and at the end of the shift the mine was closed forever. Over the years the market for coal had dwindled, and the railway had long since switched to diesel for its locomotives. It looked like Canmore might follow in the footsteps of neighbouring mine towns that had simply faded off the map. This had been the fate of Anthracite, Bankhead

## Wildlife Road Blocks

**While protecting** wildlife movement corridors in the Bow Valley is one of the key components of development, there is a major roadblock between Canmore Nordic Centre Provincial Park and adjacent ranges such as the Wind Valley—the Rundle Forebay. As the Spray Lakes hydro project drops from Whiteman's Gap, it reaches the bottom of the valley at a large canal known as the Rundle Forebay. Animals trying to move along the base of Mount Rundle towards Wind Valley (or vise versa) are stopped by this canal that acts as a cul-de-sac. They have three options. They can climb onto the steep slopes to the south, head north into residential areas, or they can turn back. Grade 8 students at Canmore's Lawrence Grassi Middle School suggested that a wildlife overpass be built to allow animals to cross over the forebay. This suggestion was selected as one of the legacy projects related to the 2002 G-8 conference (held within Kananaskis Country). This unique crossing structure will span some 30 metres and help reduce the impacts of this un-natural travel barrier.

## Canadian Parks and Wilderness Society

**Since 1975,** the Canadian Parks and Wilderness Society (CPAWS) has been actively involved in the protection and conservation of the wilderness surrounding Canmore, Banff and Kananaskis Country. Currently, as development pressures increase, organizations like CPAWS are finding themselves on the front lines of conservation efforts.

Gareth Thompson is the Education Coordinator for the Calgary-Banff chapter of CPAWS. He has been working with a dedicated group of volunteers to keep pressure on developers to maintain adequate wildlife movement corridors in the Bow Valley, in particular, in the area of proposed development on Three Sisters property. Through the Alberta Special Places designation program, CPAWS played a critical role in helping to establish Bow Valley Wildland Park. This park has recently been dramatically expanded.

As Gareth puts it: "CPAWS is one of the environmental groups in town...we're not a land manager. All we can do really is figure out what's going on, get our antenna up, let people know what is going on, and give them opportunities for influencing the decisions, and see how we do." Gareth is very good at prompting people to action. He has a way of making everyone that will be affected by development feel a responsibility for the impacts of those developments. This, coupled with an excellent communication system, has helped to increase the effectiveness of CPAWS conservation initiatives.

While the Canmore chapter of CPAWS had historically focused on the Bow Valley, Lisa Downing prompted the local chapter to take a closer look at proposed ski hill developments in the Spray Valley. Before long, CPAWS began to work tirelessly to oppose this development. The establishment of Spray Valley Provincial Park shows clear evidence that public involvement can help influence the decision-making process.

and Georgetown. For Canmore, a twist of fate saved the community from oblivion.

In 1977, the Alberta Government announced the creation of Kananaskis Country, a 4,000 square-kilometre recreation area that would border Canmore on the south. In addition, as Calgary won its bid to host the 1988 Winter Olympics, Canmore was chosen to host the cross-country and biathlon events. Slowly, the town's fortunes began to change, and Canmore became a base of operations for painters, sculptors and photographers. In 1982, the population was 3,680, but by the time the Olympics arrived, it had risen to 4,420.

## How the Olympics Affected Canmore

Before 1988, most of the residents of Canmore earned their living in tourism, commuting daily to the bustling mountain mecca of Banff. Most believed Canmore would never be like Banff! People enjoyed the fact that they could leave the madness of tourism behind as they left Banff in the evening and returned to their sleepy little town. Few had any idea about the magnitude of change that was about to take place.

During the Olympics, Canmorites flushed with pride as their town made its international debut. Locals could be seen proudly sporting the Sun Ice jackets given to Olympic volunteers. This was Canmore's finest hour, and few realized how many people were

## Hollywood North

**Hollywood has fallen** in love with Canmore and the adjacent Kananaskis Country. Movies have been filmed in the Canadian Rockies since the silent films of the 1920s, but these early films took advantage of the many panoramas available within Banff and Jasper National Parks. Today, however, those panoramas are far too recognizable. Moviemakers can't pretend that the Bow Falls in Banff townsite is some remote American destination like they did in the Marilyn Monroe film "The River of No Return". Today, Hollywood focuses on the Canmore-Kananaskis region, and since the 1980s, film after film has showcased this area, though it is usually maquerading as an American destination.

In 1980, Charles Bronson filmed "Death Hunt" in the Spray Valley and Canmore area. The 1987 television movie "Gunsmoke: Return to Dodge" was followed in 1988 with the Don Johnson film "Dead Bang". Canmore was showcased in the Tom Berenger film "The Last of the Dogmen".

*Set for "The Edge" at Whiteman's Gap*

More recent films included the Anthony Hopkins film "The Edge", filmed largely in the Spray Valley, which showcased most of the most picturesque views for which this valley has become renowned. During filming, the producers built a wilderness lodge along the shores of the Spray Lakes Reservoir, and crashed a single-engine plane into the pond above Whiteman's Dam. Another film, "Mystery, Alaska", starring Burt Reynolds and Russell Crowe, was filmed right in the town of Canmore. Producers built the entire townsite on the shores of Canmore's Quarry Lake. With the wrap of filming, the townsite came down. The site was resurrected in the winter of 2001, when another Alaska townsite was built for a Disney film starring Cuba Gooding Jr and James Coburn titled "Snow Dogs".

*Main Street, Canmore*

paying attention. Most believed that when the TV cameras moved on to the next story, their town would also return to its previous peacefulness. Nothing could have been further from the truth. Calgary had shown the world that it could throw a party, and Canmore found more and more eyes focused on its valuable real estate. Canmore began to grow at a staggering rate and the town council found itself entwined in debates about growth management strategies, overstressed sewage treatment facilities and environmental impact assessments. Since 1988, the prices of homes have more than doubled.

On the other side, Canmore has become a bustling tourism community with dozens of top-notch hotels attracting millions of visitors annually. Local stores and businesses are picking up on the value of the tourist dollar and reinventing themselves to take advantage of this new bonanza. Main Street and Bow Valley Trail offer an ever-widening array of shops, each with unique treasures for visitor and local alike. More and more stores are extending their hours to take advantage

## Mountain FM

**When locals turn** on their radios, they are usually tuned to 106.5 Mountain FM. This local station provides Canmore and Banff with local and national news, weather and entertainment. It's a great advantage for small communities to have their own radio station and Mountain FM shares the stories of the Bow Valley and its people.

The station began on the AM dial as CFHC, but in 1998 made the switch to its current 24 hour FM location. In rural communities, the newspaper and radio become a kind of glue that holds the people together. It keeps people informed not only about what is happening, but who the local newsmakers are.

## Georgetown Mine

**There have been** numerous mines in and around Canmore over the years. Most, like the Georgetown Mine, were short-lived. The Georgetown Mine opened in 1913 on the lower slopes of Mount Rundle. An English investment company owned the mine and a small community was erected nearby. A trestle tipple lowered the coal to the valley bottom where it could be transported by rail cars.

In 1916, the Bow River flooded and almost washed away the C.P.R. bridge that was used to transfer the coal from the mine to the main line of the railway. The mine workers were put on a 24-hour watch to divert the river and prevent boulders from washing away the bridge. The vigil lasted for three weeks and when it ended, the spirit of the mine owners had been broken. Not only had the work to protect the bridge proven very costly, but the cost of producing and transporting the coal had also become prohibitive. The owners sold out and the remaining buildings were moved into Canmore.

of the average tourists' evening wanderings.

## The Growth Paradox

Canmore is dealing with the challenges that come with increased popularity. With the tourism boom ushered in by the Olympics in 1988, the population began a rapid uphill spiral. By 1990, there were 5,325 residents. By 1995 the population had risen to 7,632 and the town council began plans for managing the rate of growth. The Banff-Bow Valley Report in 1996 also recommended a cap on development within the national park. This resulted in even more pressure on the town of Canmore as developers simply moved their focus from Banff to Canmore. The town's Growth Management Strategy was designed to cap population growth at an annual rate of 6 % or less. In the 1995-96 period the rate maxed out at 9.1 %, but since then the numbers have been dropping.

# Golf

SilverTip Golf Course

Stewart Creek Golf Course

**Each year,** more and more visitors are discovering the expanding opportunities for golf in the Canadian Rockies. Canmore's golf courses are famous for combining dramatic landscapes with challenging fairways and precision greens.

### Canmore Golf and Curling Club:

Operating since 1926, Canmore's oldest golf club lies along the winding course of the Bow River. The 18-hole par 71 course runs 5766 m (6,304 ft.). The plush fairways, bent grass greens and well-placed bunkers make it a popular course. Also available for curling in season.

### SilverTip Golf Course:

SilverTip markets itself as 'extreme mountain golf', and extreme is just what this world-class course delivers. Designed by Les Furber, the course has a 183 m (600 ft.) elevation change along its par 72, 18-hole length. Officially opened on July 1, 1998, the course rolls along the lower slopes of Mount Lady Macdonald. SilverTip runs 6585 m (7,200 ft.) from the back tees and will challenge the most accomplished golfer. Often described as "target golf", each hole requires careful planning and precision execution. The 10th hole alone drops 38 m (125 ft.).

### Stewart Creek Golf Club:

Newly opened in 2000, the Stewart Creek Golf Club is Canmore's newest award winning golf course. The course was designed by local resident Gary Browning, and sits in the shadow of the Three Sisters. Stewart Creek is a par 72, 18-hole course spanning 6540 m (7,150 yards) from the back tee. The course was named after Archibald Stewart, a local coal miner for almost 50 years, and has 35 strategically placed bunkers. Along the course there are restored mine entrances, tumbling streams, and crystal clear ponds.

## Tourism Canmore: From Coal Mines to Mountains of Adventure

*The Three Sisters*

**Canmore's past** may lie in mining, but its future appears to be in tourism. Since the 1988 Winter Olympics, Canmore has embraced this future, and the once sleepy small town has evolved into a year-round mountain playground offering many world-class amenities.

In 1997, the Town of Canmore established a task force to establish a comprehensive plan for future tourism management. The vision that emerged was this:

*In 2015, we will have maintained the natural environment, and as a result will have earned an international reputation as a sustainable tourism destination. Canmore's tourism initiatives will be part of a shared vision and are ecologically and environmentally sustainable. These tourism initiatives...will provide year round visitor experiences that sustain long term economic viability.*

*In 2015 Canmore will continue to be a unique Canadian mountain destination where residents feel comfortable and visitors feel welcome...Activities and special events will express appreciation of our cultural heritage.*

In summary, the tourism industry is community oriented, fostering a sense of pride in our town by effectively managing and sharing our community with all visitors and inhabitants.

Keeping these goals in mind, Tourism Canmore was set up to market Canmore as a holiday destination. Tourism Canmore represents a wide range of local businesses, all of whom benefit either directly or indirectly from tourism.

The easiest way to sell Canmore is to bring someone here. Drop them off for a day, let them go shopping downtown or on Bow Valley Trail, go for a stroll along the paths by the Bow River, and sample some of our excellent restaurants, all amidst our spectacular mountain scenery. It's almost impossible to resist

Canmore's genuine charm.

And for those who love outdoor adventure, Canmore offers almost too much choice: mountain biking or golf? Paragliding or fly-fishing? Skiing or a dog sled tour? Hiking or inflatable kayaking? Snowmobiling or snowshoeing?

These activities are what bring people here, whether it be on holiday or to live. This is what we want to promote and to protect. So we continue to aim our marketing message at travellers who love the outdoors, who revel in a relaxed mountain lifestyle, who want to bring their families here to enjoy the wilderness next door as well as the town.

That's what Tourism Canmore is really selling – the total Canmore experience of spending time outdoors, greeting people when you're out for a walk (the locals say Hi right back- try it!), enjoying life to its fullest while conserving our beautiful surroundings for future generations.

Come and visit us!
www.tourismcanmore.com or call (403) 678-1295 for more info.

## Canmore Characters

*The Three Sisters in the 1920s*

### Lawrence Grassi

Lawrence Grassi was one of Canmore's first trail builders. He emigrated to Canada in 1912, and in 1916 came to Canmore to work as a coal miner. He loved the mountain landscape and, when not working underground, he was an avid hiker, exploring the many valleys and ridges surrounding Canmore. A favourite route led to two small lakes known as the Twin Lakes. During a strike at the Canmore mines, he built a trail to these lakes, and they were subsequently renamed in his honour. The trail to Grassi Lakes is one of the most well known trails in the Canmore area. In 1956, he began to work summers in the Lake O'Hara area of Yoho National Park as an assistant Park Warden. While working, he redesigned many of the trails around these picturesque tarns.

### Lizzie Rummel

Elizabeth von Rummel was born to an aristocratic family in Germany. Her family moved to southern Alberta in the early 1900s and she grew up on a ranch. Lizzie, as she was known to her friends, spent 32 years working at backcountry lodges in the Canadian Rockies. She owned and ran Sunburst Lodge at Lake Assiniboine for many years. Lizzie enhanced the life of many people through her lifelong attachment to the mountains. In 1980, in recognition of her service, the Government of Canada awarded her the Order of Canada. Kananaskis Country's Rummel Lake and Rummel Creek were also named in her honour.

### Bruno Engler

For 60 years, the name of Bruno Engler has been connected with mountain adventure. He was born in Lugano, Switzerland in 1915 and travelled to Banff in 1939 to work as a guide and ski instructor. Over the years, Bruno's resumé expanded to include cinematographer, photographer and storyteller. His photographs record the history of skiing in the Rockies and represent a fabulous legacy. Bruno was also an exceptional storyteller and never missed an opportunity to entertain an audience with his wit and tales of adventure. Bruno passed away on March 23, 2001, but his spirit will forever remain a part of the mountains he loved so much.

## Canmore Nordic Centre Provincial Park

*Nordic ski racer*

*Mountain biker*

**With the 1988** Winter Olympics, Canmore became the host community for the cross-country and biathlon events. Prior to this site being chosen as the official Olympic venue, other sites were also investigated. The old Pigeon Mountain ski area was one potential location for the Nordic events. Other hopeful sites included the Paskapoo Ski area (now Canada Olympic Park) in Calgary, and the community of Bragg Creek. Although Bragg Creek had been used in the original Olympic proposals, concerns over lack of snow resulted in its being removed from final consideration. In the end, it was between the Pigeon Mountain site and Canmore. Although Olympic officials expressed a preference for Pigeon Mountain, it was on private land, and the government wanted to avoid incurring the additional expense of purchasing land. In 1983, Canmore got the nod, and development began in earnest. Three years later, in August of 1986, the trail network was officially approved by Dietrich Martin, the technical representative for the 1988 games.

During the winter of 1987, the site was officially opened, and hosted its first World Cup event. With the coming of the Olympics, the site was fenced in, and security was high. When the athletes descended on Canmore, they were housed in a specially designed residential complex, and quickly made their presence known. International athletes in colourful jerseys jogged along local roadways. Non-athletes found that trading pins with competitors and other visitors was a great way to feel involved.

The events were a great success, and since that time the site has hosted a diverse list of activities. From the Ziggy Gnarly Mountain Bike race, to the annual Alberta International Sled Dog Races, to World Cup cross-country, biathlon, and mountain bike events, there is always something happening at the Nordic Centre.

Following the Games, the site was converted into a year-round training centre. There is now a 2.5 km paved trail to allow skiers to train with roller skis during summer. There is a lit-trail for night skiing during the short days of winter. Snow making is possible on approximately 60% of the trails to ensure a reliable snow supply. There are also facilities for team use, as well as a weight room and meeting facilities. In an attempt to recover some of the operating costs, user fees are charged to winter skiers, while summer access is free to mountain-bikers, disc-golf enthusiasts, picnickers and walkers.

The Canmore Nordic Centre became a Provincial Park in 1998 as part of the announcement of the Bow Valley Wildland Park. Together, these two parks border Banff National Park on the west as well as the newly designated Spray Valley Provincial Park to the south.

**73**

# Donna Jo Massie

*Donna Jo Massie*

*"The Three Sisters"*

**When the mines** closed in 1979, painters, photographers and sculptors discovered the quiet character and (then) reasonable cost of real-estate in this former mine town. Over the years, the reputation of Canmore's artists have grown steadily and today names like Donna Jo Massie, Marilyn Kinsella, Linda Evans, and Ralph Temple have become synonymous with grand mountain images.

Donna Jo Massie was born in Cherokee, North Carolina. She began her career as a teacher, and worked in the field of environmental education in Florida. While there, she worked with Joel Christensen, and when Joel came to Canmore to head up the Visitor Services department of Kananaskis Country in 1977, he recruited Donna Jo to help with the Environmental Education program.

Donna Jo has always sketched and painted, and while working in Canmore, she began to focus on her art. Working part-

time allowed her to focus on her painting, and in 1988, she decided to devote all her energies to her art. She had recently been juried into the Alberta Society of Artists, and it was time to plunge into the unknown. "If you want to do it, you have to either figure out how to do it yourself, and start doing workshops…and then it will happen, or it won't and you'll fall down, but then you'll know." Donna Jo didn't fall down, and her paintings have been acquired by many large collections.

Donna Jo only does original canvases. She loves to paint, and her paintings rarely last long in galleries such as the Stephen Lowe Art Gallery in Calgary, Canada House in Banff and the Sunrise Gallery in Jasper. Over the years, collectors have been drawn to her ability to capture the essence of the Rocky Mountains. With her brush, she reveals the texture of the rocks, and evokes the landscape so you can almost feel the mountain breeze and smell the wildflowers. Her book,

A Rocky Mountain Sketch Book, published by the Alpine Club of Canada, offers a step-by-step approach to painting and drawing mountain landscapes.

Both her recognition as an artist and the popularity of her workshops have grown steadily over the years. Many of her students sign up session after session, some for more than a decade. "For me, it's really about getting people excited about creativity, and enabling them to find that part of themselves, and realize that just because it didn't happen for them in Grade 3, doesn't mean it can't happen for them now…I think people need to do something creative, and I think that when people that can't sing or do music, discover that they can do art on a level that's enjoyable for them…it's really exciting." Perhaps Donna Jo's greatest product is her passion and the way she is able to pass that gift on to others.

**74**

Growth was 6.9 % in 1997, 7.2 % in 1998, 5.2 % in 1999, and only 2.6 % in 2000. The permanent population in the 2000 census was 10,517.

Canmore has also seen enormous growth in the market for weekend homes. For instance, this market increased by a whopping 16.9 percent during 1996-97, and is expected to increase.

Based on estimates of the amount of current developable land in the Canmore area, it is expected that the community will run out of land for housing around the year 2015 at an estimated population of 30,000 people. The growth management strategy attempts to balance development with quality of life and the quality of habitat.

Canmore sits in a delicate landscape, and its footprint (the amount of land the town takes up) has been expanding at an uncomfortable pace.

New parks, like the Canmore Nordic Centre Provincial Park and Bow Valley Wildland Park, have helped provide a finite limit to growth, but we also need to make sure that wildlife populations, including large carnivores, have enough room to continue making the Bow Valley their home. One solutions is wildlife corridors.

## Canmore's Wildlife Corridors

Currently, Three Sisters Developments, along with Stone Creek Properties (SilverTip) are the largest developers in town. Together, they control the vast majority of undeveloped land, and both have found their proposals under intense scrutiny by environmentalists who want to ensure adequate wildlife movement corridors are maintained along the north and south sides of the Bow Valley.

With increased develop-

ment in the Rocky Mountains, prime areas of habitat often become fragmented due to large-scale developments. In essence, one key range becomes separated from adjacent ranges. Wildlife corridors are designed to provide linkages between these core refuge areas so that genetic diversity is maintained, and so that wildlife is able to move between adjacent valleys.

As SilverTip extends up the valley walls on the benchlands to the north, and Three Sisters Resorts sprawls southwards towards the mountains, it becomes difficult to maintain these corridors. Viable corridors cannot be too steep, with inclines in excess of 25° having limited value. In south Canmore, environmental groups like the Canadian Parks and Wilderness Society, the Town of Canmore and Three Sisters Resorts have been actively negotiating to try to ensure the viability of critical corridors running between the pro-

## Canmore Leader

**The Canmore Leader** has been keeping locals informed since 1983. Canmore's weekly newspaper is an important source of news, which forms a communication thread that connects the community. This is where Canmorites learn about everything that is going on within their rapidly growing community— and, as in any small town, it is especially important to keep up on local events. Canmore sits right in the middle of numerous debates pitting development against conservation, and knowing the news allows locals to get involved with the decisions that affect their community.

In 1997, the Canadian Com-

munity Newspaper Association in Canada awarded the Canmore Leader 1st Place in the Better Newspaper Category. Along with this milestone, the paper has won numerous awards for its writing and photography. Shari Bishop Bowes, publisher of the Leader, believes that a lot of the credit goes to "what goes on in this community. It's unlike any other community in Canada. The speed at which things have happened here is phenomenal. The type of people that live here, and the type of things that happen, all create a velocity which doesn't exist in other communities," says Shari.

## Mike...from Canmore

**When Canmorites** leave town, and dare mention that they are from Canmore, chuckles are usually followed by the question: "Canmore, eh, do you know Mike?" Since 1993, John Morgan of CBC television's Royal Canadian Air Farce has been making Canmore famous with his character Mike from Canmore. This dim-witted, monosyllabic character has become one of the most well-known, and well loved, Air Farce characters, much to the chagrin of true locals (especially those unfortunate enough to be named Mike).

**Visitors to Canmore** can get a glimpse into its history by taking a walk through town to view some of its historic buildings and homes. The following is a list of some of its more notable heritage buildings.

## Avramenko House

This house was built in 1910 for James Morris, mine superintendent for the Canadian Anthracite Coal Company from 1894 to 1914. It was converted to a hospital in 1914, and served in this capacity until a new hospital was built in 1937. The Avramenko family then purchased the home, living in it until 1992 when it was sold to the Warwick family.

## Canmore Miner's Union Hall

The Union Hall was built in 1913, and for many years served both as the headquarters for the local miners' union, but also as a social focus of the town. With the closing of the mine in 1979, it continued to play host to numerous events, and recently was converted into "The Hub", a teen community centre.

## Ralph Connor United Church

One of the first Presbyterian missions in southern Alberta, the church was the personal project of Reverend Charles W. Gordon. It opened in 1891 and has operated ever since. Gordon was also a successful author, under the pseudonym Ralph Connor, and in 1942 the church was renamed the Ralph Connor Memorial Church.

## Saint Michael's Anglican Church

Until 1895, Canmore Anglicans worshipped in the local Presbyterian Church, but in 1897 they celebrated the opening of Saint Michael's church. Other than cosmetic upgrades over the years, the church is much as it was originally built.

## North West Mounted Police Barracks

The North West Mounted Police arrived in the west in 1875, and with the expansion westward along the C.P.R. tracks, a small detachment was stationed in Canmore. This barrack was built in 1893 and is the last original N.W.M.P. barracks in western Canada that still sits on its original site. While it was built as a temporary structure, it has lasted over 100 years and today operates as a gift shop and tea room. In summer, the gardens are a delightful place to relax and enjoy the day.

## Canmore Hotel

While not Canmore's first, the Canmore Hotel is its oldest surviving hotel. It was built around 1890 by the Count De Rambouville. It was one of four grand hotels in town, including the Waverly, the Pulman and the Mountainhouse. It is the only one that remains today, making it the second oldest operating hotel in Alberta.

## C.P.R. Trestle Bridge

The C.P.R. built a trestle bridge across the Bow River to provide access to the Cochrane Mine. In 1891, they built another line for the No. 1 Mine and later the No. 2 Mine. This bridge was built on the original site in 1919. It was almost destroyed by a fire in the late 1960's, but was repaired through the use of a steel span. Day after day, coal cars travelled along the railway that linked the mines with the C.P.R. tracks in

*C.P.R. Trestle Bridge*

town. Canmore's last steam locomotive, No. 4 – the Goat, was finally sold to Calgary's Heritage Park in the late 1960's.

## Mine Manager's House

This heritage home was built in 1907 for Walter F. McNeill, the manager of the McNeill Coal Company. For many years, it was the hub of Canmore's social life as the McNeill's were famous for their parties. The Canmore Coal Company purchased the house in 1912, and in 1938 it was transferred to the Canmore Mines. Today, it operates as the McNeill Heritage Inn.

## Mine Shareholder's Cabin

Nestled on the banks of the Bow River, construction of the shareholder's cabin began in 1910, and was completed in 1914. It is made entirely of logs, and each room on the upper floor was built with a private entrance and its own plumbing. The main floor had a large sitting area and a kitchen where the shareholders shared meals. After the mine closed in 1979, the cabin was sold as a private residence.

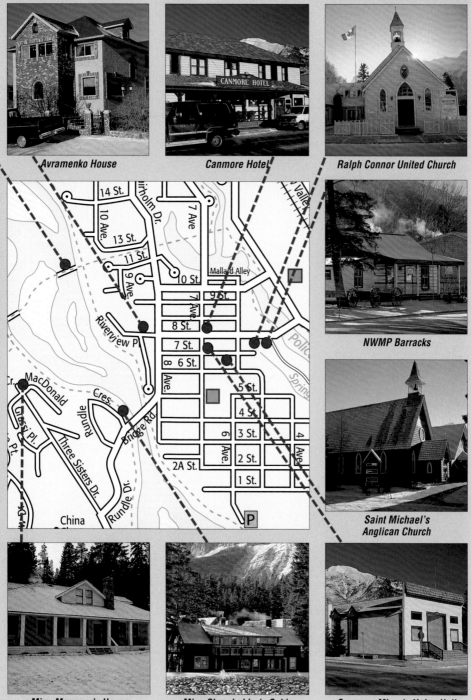

Avramenko House

Canmore Hotel

Ralph Connor United Church

NWMP Barracks

Saint Michael's Anglican Church

Mine Manager's House

Mine Shareholder's Cabin

Canmore Miner's Union Hall

*Ha Ling Peak over the Bow River in winter*

posed developments and the base of the peaks bordering the valley to the south.

Development in resort communities like Canmore is ripe with pitfalls and challenges. How can developers and conservationists find a balance between preservation and growth? Perhaps only time will tell.

take domestic cats and dogs, and more recently cougars have also begun to kill the occasional dog. In January of 2001, a cougar in Banff National Park killed a cross-country skier. This incident served as a wake-up call for mountain residents. It has become all too apparent that living in a mountain landscape, adjacent

to wilderness and wildlife, also comes with responsibility and risks. Since the attack in Banff, there has been an increased focus on making our communities safe, primarily through maintaining viable wildlife corridors and reducing the attractiveness of residential neighbourhoods to predators. By keeping our yards clear of

## Living with Wildlife (Cats Eating Dogs)

There are changes taking place in the mountains. As communities expand towards the mountains on either side of the valley bottom, residential areas begin to encroach upon wildlife corridors and the animals that use them. This has not been without conflicts. Black and grizzly bears, cougars, wolves and coyotes travelling adjacent to outlying communities are periodically attracted to easily available food sources. Bears are drawn in by summer bird feeders, and improperly stored garbage. Coyotes commonly

## Canmore's Gone to the Dogs

Canmore has gone to the dogs. It's impossible to walk the paths and trails of Canmore without passing an endless line of Labrador retrievers, huskies, and Jack Russell terriers. With the popularity of dogs in town, locals have had to adapt to the challenges and responsibilities of owning a pet in a small community. Gone are the days of dogs running wild. Owning a dog now involves carrying bags for picking up leftovers and keeping your pet on a leash at all times. The Town of Canmore has installed many handy bag dispensers along the trail system

to encourage dog owners to scoop their poop. Huge numbers of dogs makes the old practice of letting your pup walk beside you on your daily forays impractical. Take your dog to the off-leash area near Quarry Lake for a chance to chase the tennis ball or Frisbee, and don't forget to share the trail with other dogs.

**Local veterinarians include:**
The Canmore Veterinary Hospital, 503 Bow Valley Trail, (403)678-4425
Bow River Veterinary Centre, 1510 Railway Ave., (403)678-9595

*Ha Ling Peak over the Bow River in summer*

attractants, not letting our pets out at night and keeping an eye on our children, we can all enjoy the mountain lifestyle with minimum of risk.

## Canmore Listed as One of 10 Prettiest Towns in Canada

Harrowsmith Country Life is one of Canada's most respected sources on country living and gardening. In its April 2001 issue, it published its list of the 10 prettiest towns in Canada. Not surprising to anyone familiar with Canmore, this small mountain community made the list. As Harrowsmith puts it: "For those who can afford it, Canmore remains a haven for outdoor adventure...In fact, everyone on the streets looks like they've just completed a mountain bike race or a biathlon. Polar fleece and hiking boots are very de rigueur."

Canmore and Kaslo, B.C. are the only communities listed that are west of Ontario. Other communities on the list include Knowlton (Lac Brome), Que.; Elora, Ont.; Kamouraska, Que.; Gagetown, N.B.; Creemore, Ontario; Mahone Bay, N.S.; Bayfield, Ont.; and Dildo, Nfld.

## Festival of Eagles

Each spring and fall, Canmore hosts travellers of a different kind. High above the mountain peaks, for more than 11,000 years, golden eagles have been passing over the

## Bow Valley Wildland Park

**Prior to 1995**, numerous conservation organizations had been working to preserve the Bow Valley. That same year, Harvey Locke, Gareth Thompson, and Wendy Francis of the Canadian Parks and Wilderness Society met to discuss ideas for a wildland park in the Bow Valley. Using a model from the United States called The Wildlands Project (TWP), they put together a proposal for the Bow Valley Wildland Park.

Support was obtained from other conservation organizations, the Town of Canmore, outfitters and local guides. The support of Bert Dyck, then mayor of Canmore, greatly enhanced the process, and finally in December of 1998, the Alberta government announced the creation of the park. While the group was not successful in preserving all of the land that had been proposed, they did manage to have much of the remaining, undeveloped portions of the Bow Valley included.

Recently, with the announcement of the new Spray Lakes Provincial Park, an additional 82 square kilometres was added to the Bow Valley Wildland Park, linking Bow Valley Wildland, Spray Valley and Peter Lougheed Provincial Parks into one contiguous area.

# Canmore

## Restaurant Guide

Canmore's restaurants run the entire spectrum from fine dining to casual lunches. You can enjoy traditional Asian, French, Italian, Swiss, Greek or Cajun dishes in a magnificent mountain setting. Albertans have begun to recognize Canmore as a special place to combine a holiday visit with a reputation for fine food. Be sure to check out some of these restaurants for yourself.

## North American Cuisine

### Canmore Hotel
738-8 Street, (403) 678-5181. Canmore's oldest restaurant, but the second oldest hotel in Alberta. The patio is a popular local summer hangout offering large portions and great burgers, snacks and salads.

### Copper Door Restaurant
726-9 Street, (403) 678-5233. Serving a diverse range of tasty and interesting meals with a funky ambience.

### Crazyweed Kitchen
Main Street, (403) 609-2530. Focused on a global mix of Asian, East Indian, Italian , Mediterranean, and French dishes. You will find this restaurant packed with locals—a sure sign of a great lunch! Not open for dinner.

### The Drake Inn and Restaurant
909 Railway Avenue, (403) 678-5131. Features hearty portions and a separate non-smoking lounge. Specialties include their Famous Drake Burger, Steak Sandwich and Quesadillas.

### Fireside Inn Restaurant
718-8 Street, (403) 678-9570. Offers plentiful portions and family favourites. Their outdoor patio is a favourite location for summer lunches.

### French Quarter Café
#4-102 Boulder Crescent, Elk Run Industrial Park, (403) 678-3612. Your source for spicy Cajun and Creole cooking. Their menu includes traditional gumbos, blackened chicken, and jambalaya. Chef Michael Raso will dazzle you with his cooking—ask about cooking classes. Enjoy jazz most weekends at the French Quarter.

### Grizzly Paw Brewing Company
622 Main Street, (403) 678-9983. This local brew pub mixes fine beer with great food. The beer is brewed on-site and has some very inventive names. Try the Dribbling Moose. Their menu changes seasonally, but always offers selections for the vegetarian, the health-conscious, and the meat-lover. The only outdoor fireplace in Canmore livens up the patio.

### Murietta's Westcoast Grill
737 Main St., 2nd floor Featuring Pacific dishes and a range of wines with fantastic 2nd floor views.

### Quarry Bistro
Main Street, (403) 678-6088. This cosmopolitan bistro boasts a classy yet cozy atmosphere, putting a refined twist on a wide range of elegant dishes.

### Rocky Mountain Bagel Company
830-8 Street, (403) 678-9978 or 6a-1306 Bow Valley Trail, (403) 678-9968. A favourite hangout for locals who savour steaming specialty coffees with one of their 18 varieties of freshly baked bagels. Top your bagel with one of 10 flavours of gourmet cream cheeses.

### Rose & Crown Pub
749 Railway Avenue, (403) 678-5168. Specializing in traditional pub grub with entrees like Bangers and Mash, Steak and Kidney Pie and huge orders of Fish & Chips.

### Sage Bistro
1712 Bow Valley Trail, (403) 678-4878. This rustic log cabin offers pleasant and casual Canadian Cuisine.

### Sherwood House
838-8 Street, (403) 678-5211 Located in a beautiful log cabin, the Sherwood House has a diverse menu featuring buffalo, ostrich, beef, pizza and excellent vegetarian dishes. The large outdoor patio is Canmore's premier summer hangout.

### Sinclairs
637-8 Street, (403) 678-5370. Sitting in the heart of downtown Canmore, Sinclairs has built its reputation on providing innovative beef, lamb and seafood dishes with fine wines and an elegant atmosphere. Their outdoor patio adds mountain views to the menu.

### The Summit Café
200-1001 Cougar Creek Drive, (403) 609-2120. No visit to Canmore is complete without having breakfast at the Summit—an experience to be savoured, whether indoors or on the patio. Lunch is equally wonderful—hearty soups, quiches and sandwiches will tempt you, but save room for delectable desserts and a gourmet coffee to go.

### Tannins Fine Food and Wine
838-10 Street, (403) 609-9200. More than 20 different wines available by the glass, with specialties like cedar planked

*Main Street in Canmore*

salmon, rack of lamb, cheese fondue and an array of tapas.

## European Favourites

### Chez François Restaurant
1604 Bow Valley Trail in the Best Western Green Gables Inn, (403) 678-6111. Canmore's signature French restaurant. Chef-owner Jean-François Gouin prepares traditional French dishes and fresh seafood. An extensive wine list and decadent dessert menu round out the experience.

### Des Alpes Restaurant
702-10 Street, (403) 678-6878. Canmore's most famous Swiss-French restaurant. Specialties include Veal Emincé Zürich Style, Scallops Queen Elizabeth, Steel Head Filet and Lamb Filet "Marianne".

### Evvia's Family Restaurant
837-8 Street, (403) 678-2234. Offers a diverse mix of traditional Greek dishes along with a wide selection of North American favourites.

### Gasthaus Alphorn Restaurant
1716 Bow Valley Trail, (403) 678-9446. Known for its grilled

meats, pasta and fondue dishes. They also have an all you can eat breakfast buffet.

### Patrino's Steak House & Pub
1602 Bow Valley Trail, (403) 678-4060. A favourite of locals for its wide selection of Italian, Greek and North American dishes.

### Renzo's Ristorante
#1 Silvertip Trail in the Four Points Sheraton Hotel, (403) 609-4422. Mixes fresh Californian cuisine with classic Italian dishes. A traditional wood-burning stove and an impressive wine list enhance the experience.

### Santa Lucia Italian Restaurant
714-8 Street, (403) 678-3414. Your source for traditional pizza from a family recipe along with favourites like manicotti, lasagna, and cannelloni.

### Tapas Restaurant
633-10 Street, (403) 609-6583. Specializing in Portugese and Spanish dishes in an elegant atmosphere.

### Zona's Bistro
710-9 Street, (403) 609-2000. A favourite amoung locals that has been discovered by visitors, Zona's offers an eclectic menu unlike anything else in Canmore. A cozy atmosphere indoors is enhanced by jazz bands, while the patio glimmers on summer evenings.

## Asian Specialties

### Famous Chinese Restaurant
629-8 Street, (403) 678-9535 Focuses on providing traditional Szechuan and Peking Dishes in a relaxing family atmosphere.

### Peking Ginger Restaurant
Bay E-1702 Bow Valley Trail, (403) 678-3365. Offering an immense menu with more than 100 items. Specialties include cashew chicken, ginger fried beef, and mu shu pork. The lunch buffet is popular with locals.

### Musashi Japanese Restaurant
7a-1306 Bow Valley Trail, (403) 678-9360. Canmore's source for traditional Japanese sushi, tempura, sukiyaki, and shabu shabu.

*Canmore and the Bow Valley from Mt. Lady Macdonald*

Bow Valley on their north and south annual migrations. For most of that time, they passed without anyone taking notice. Since they fly in small groups at very high elevations, they are very easy to miss, despite the fact that on peak days, upwards of 850 eagles may pass overhead.

The migration was discovered by Calgary naturalist Peter Sherrington and he has been studying the migration ever since (see Eagle Migration page 94). Canmore celebrates this annual event each October with the Festival of Eagles.

## Art Galleries

**The towering peaks**, emerald waters and plentiful wildlife of Canmore and Kananaskis have been inspiring painters, photographers, sculptures, and artists of all kinds for over a century. Canmore's galleries are your best source for original paintings by local artists like Donna Jo Massie, Marilyn Kinsella, Ralph Temple, Alice Saltiel, Linda Evans, and Virginia Hemingson, along with sculptors and potters like Tony Bloom.

**Canmore Public Library.** Changing displays of locally produced art. 950-8 Ave. (403) 678-2468.

**Great Bowls Afire!** Paint your own ceramics, and Great Bowls Afire will glaze and fire it in their kilns. They have over 100 items and a huge selection of idea books and tools. #5-626 Main Street. (403) 678-9507.

**Kinsella Art Studio & Custom Framing**. Original Kinsella watercolours and her trademark hand-painted mattes. #3-1302 Bow Valley Trail. (403) 678-4331.

**Mountainesque**. Paintings, sculptures, glass and native/Inuit carvings. 1-999 Bow Valley Trail. (403) 678-9943.

**Settler's Cabin**. This is your source for folk art, especially by local artists like Linda Evans and Virginia Hemingson. 829-8 Street. (403) 678-5966.

**Stonecrop Studios**. Features the pottery of owner Tony Bloom. 10-102 Elk Run Blvd. (403) 678-4151.

**Sunny Raven Gallery**. Original paintings by local and native artists. 201-630 Main Street (Alley Entrance). (403) 678-6113.

**The Corner Gallery**. Original works by Canadian and local artists, sculptures and pottery. 737 Main Street. (403) 678-6090.

**The Quest Avens Gallery**. Original paintings by local artists like Saltiel, Donna Jo Massie, Ele Hughes, Lory Lemco, Susan Elkins and Nancy Slaught. 709 Main Street. (403) 678-4471.

The two-day event features guided hikes, interpretive presentations and exhibits, displays and guest speakers.

## Local Rituals

### Trout Fishing on the Bow River

On any given day, local anglers can be spotted testing their luck at their favourite eddy along the winding course of the Bow River. Renowned for its excellent trout fishing, the Bow has attracted novice and expert anglers for more than a century. Remarkably, the techniques have not changed dramatically throughout that period. While many of these anglers have computerized cars and high tech jobs, once they wade into the frigid waters of the Bow River, it is them against the fish. Here, technology is limited to hand-tied flies, Kevlar rods and the fisherman's own measure of experience. Today, catch and release is the order of the day, and most serious anglers prefer to let their quarry swim away to challenge them another day.

### Quarry Lake

If you mention to a local that you are heading up to the Quarry, they will know exactly what you mean. This small pond was an open pit coal mine until only a few decades ago, but is now a popular swimming hole. Quarry Lake Municipal Park is located along the road to the Canmore Nordic Centre. It was used as the setting for the movie Mystery, Alaska, and is one of the town's most popular summer hangouts. Its sandy beach and cool waters ensure that it will be busy throughout the summer months. In the evenings, anglers cast a fly, while nesting waterfowl dive in the deep blue waters.

### Recreation Centre

Canmore's Recreation Centre, like similar facilities in other small towns, is one of the community's focal points. The centre includes a large hockey and skating rink, Olympic sized pool, weight room, gymnasium, and community hall. In the winter, it plays host to the Canmore Eagles (Alberta Junior Hockey League), attracting fans from all over the Bow Valley.

### Skateboard Park

Skateboarding has experienced a surge in popularity, and Canmore now offers skateboarders an excellent skateboard park next door to the Recreation Centre. It opened in August of 1997 and features a transition pyramid, pyramid with jibs, rail hip, manual box, high curb, pipe jib and multiple hip curves. There are challenges for users of all abilities. Helmets are mandatory, but there is no charge for admission.

### Cross Zee Ranch

In 1939, Johnny Boychuk registered the Cross Zee Left Shoulder as his brand, and opened a guiding operation in Yoho National Park. In 1950, he moved his operation to Canmore and opened Johnny's Riding Stables. In 1995, at the age of 90, Johnny retired, and the ranch changed hands. Today, the ranch offers trail and sleigh rides, along with special events and group functions.

## Mountain Climbing

Some of the best climbers in the world call Canmore home. Canmore resident Patrick Morrow was the first man on Earth to climb the highest mountain on all seven

## Mountain Bike Races

**Over the past** decade, Canmore has gained an international reputation for its challenging mountain bike races. Not only does the Canmore Nordic Centre host events like the 24 Hours of Adrenalin, it also played host to World Cup Mountain bike races in 1998, 1999, and 2000. Beginning in 2002, the annual Trans Rockies Challenge ("the toughest race in North America") selected Canmore as the finish line for this 7-day, 600 km mountain bike race. The route was designed by the author of this book. The Canmore Nordic Centre has created a network of trails that provide an endless opportunity for events of all kinds.

*Mountain biker*

continents, including Mount Everest. John Amatt and Lloyd "Kiwi" Gallagher, the co-leaders of Canada's first successful Everest expedition (1982), both live in Canmore. Another local, Sharon Wood, was the first woman in the western hemisphere to stand on top of Mount Everest. She summitted during Canada's 1986 expedition. Two of her teammates on that climb, Dave McNabb and Barry Blanchard, still live in Canmore. Barry has become known as Hollywood's mountain climber. He did the climbing for Sylvester Stallone in the movie "Cliffhanger", and did much of the climbing in the movie "Vertical Limit".

Canmore has become internationally renowned as a centre for ice climbing. The annual Canmore International Ice Climbing Festival attracts climbers seeking to learn about the sport, develop their skills or compete against each other. As well, World Champion ice climber, Will Gadd, calls Canmore home.

# Key Local Events

## January

**Canmore Winter Festival**. This 10-day festival celebrates all the great things that a Rocky Mountain Winter provides. Beginning with the **Rocky Mountain Ski Marathon** , the festival also includes concerts, art exhibits, slide shows, ice sculptures, curling, skating and always a few surprises.

## February

**Canmore International Ice Climbing Festival**. This annual event showcases the sport of ice climbing and at-

## Tick Talk

**Ticks are quite** prevalent on Canmore's Benchland area, so check for them before your day's activity is done. Their favourite spots are any warm moist area they can find. These include in the hairline, armpits, and pubic area, and behind tight-fitting clothing (bra and underwear straps).

Similar in appearance to a small spider, ticks have a triangular body and eight legs. To feed, they insert their mouthparts into the skin—only their mouthparts. After anchoring themselves with a secreted glue, they slowly draw blood from you until they've had their fill and drop off. Females swell to several times their body size while males swell less.

Ticks hang on to low-lying vegetation and as you walk by they hitch a ride. Since they usually don't crawl too far, you can discourage them by tucking your pant legs into your socks. If they don't find a suitable site, they simply drop off.

Removal is quite easy. Grab the tick and slowly but steadily pull it out. Make sure that the mouth parts don't break off and remain in the wound. If they do, remove them with a sterilized needle, and then use a little disinfectant on the wound.

While ticks can cause Rocky Mountain Spotted Fever, the incidence is quite low. Lyme Disease has not been recorded in Kananaskis.

Ticks are one of the very few drawbacks of living in the mountains, but with a little attention they cause very little discomfort. Enjoy your hike and remember to check for hitchhikers.

## Dogsled Tours

**Winter in the** Spray Lakes means dogsledding. Over the past decade, numerous companies have been operating dogsled tours along the snow-covered length of the Spray Lakes Reservoir. Companies like Snowy Owl Sled Dog Tours, Howling Dog Tours and Mad Dogs & Englishmen have given thousands of travellers the opportunity to try their hand at mushing. Dogsledding is something unique to the North Country, and is one winter event that everyone should try. Think of it like trying to drive a car with the accelerator stuck. These dogs live to run, and given the opportunity, can't wait to be hitched up and put to work. These truly are "dogs with jobs".

For hundreds of years, dogsleds have been integral to travel in the snowbound North Country. These tour companies have taken the time to create an experience that allows you to experience a piece of that history. For more information, you can contact the following companies:

Snowy Owl Sled Dog Tours, (403) 678-4369

Howling Dog Tours, (403) 678-9588

*Participants at the Canmore International Ice Climbing Festival*

## The Alpine Club of Canada

**The Alpine Club of Canada** is one of the country's oldest outdoor clubs. Founded in 1906, the club has local chapters across the country. In Canmore, the Alpine Club Clubhouse is more than just hostel-style accommodation for climbers and outdoors people. It is their meeting place and headquarters. Head up to the Clubhouse, hang out long enough, and you will find yourself a climbing partner. Along with the main clubhouse, the Bell Cabin offers a private, self-contained accomodation for groups of up to 15.

The mountain section of the Alpine Club is the largest in Canada, with almost 800 members. The members operate a diverse schedule of trips and courses that help local and visitor alike learn more about their mountain landscape.

### Association of Canadian Mountain Guides

Along with the Alpine Club of Canada, the Association of Canadian Mountain Guides (A.C.M.G.) is the central authority for certifying mountain guides in Canada. The ACMG was formed in 1963 and had training programs to certify mountain guides in place by 1966. In 1972, the ACMG became the first non-European member of the International Federation of Mountain Guide Associations, the international body that sets professional standards for mountain guides worldwide

## Mozart on the Mountain

Who says golf courses are for golf only? Canmore's Stewart Creek Golf Course has found a way to turn their pristine mountain location into an outdoor concert venue. In this case, the music is classical, and in September 2003, the Calgary Philharmonic hosted a spectacular outdoor concert at the course. Mozart on the Mountain began in 1990 as an annual event at Nakiska at Mount Allan. In 1995, over 13,000 people showed up, and the Trans Canada Highway, not to mention Highway 40, stopped moving. The tradition ended after the 1996 season and the event seemed like it would slip into the past. In 2003, the event was resurrected to great fanfare. The sold-out event was an instant success and a tradition is reborn. The 2003 event included World Champion Whistler Ray Thoreson and Alphorn player William Hopson to add to the mountain theme. Performances included Mozart's Overture to Marriage of Figaro, Strauss' Radetzky March, and Armitage's Alphorn Ballad. An excerpt of William's music from Harry Potter added a modern touch.

tracts some of the best climbers in the world. As part of the event, organizers erect a huge, man-made ice wall where you can test your skills, even if you've never ice climbed before. Sponsors are on hand with demo gear, letting you try out the latest equipment. In conjunction with the climbing wall, the event includes seminars, demonstrations, slide shows and clinics. The event is held at the beginning of February each year.

For more information, contact Gear Up Sports at (403) 678-1636.

## May

**Canmore Children's Festival.** This two-day event was created to celebrate our children. During this May long weekend event, children of all ages are treated to magic, storytellers, comedy, theatre, puppets, crafts, games and discovery. For more information, contact the Special Events Coordinator for Canmore at (403) 678-1878.

## July

**Canada Day Parade and Celebration.** Canada Day is chock full of events that begin with a pancake breakfast, followed by a parade down Main Street. Celebrations continue throughout the afternoon, finally culminating in a fireworks celebration at dusk. For more information, contact the Special Events Coordinator for Canmore at (403) 678-1878.

**Canmore Miners' Day.** Canmore is a town born of coal, and Miner's Day celebrates the contributions of these pioneers to the growth of Canmore. The mines closed forever on July 13th, 1979, and

Miners' Day is the Saturday closest to the 13th. Events include a parade on Main Street and a special ceremony to honour the town's remaining miners. For more information, contact the Special Events Coordinator for Canmore at (403) 678-1878.

**24 Hours of Adrenaline.** Known as the "Woodstock of mountain biking", this event draws hundreds of racers every year to camp and ride through the night. Stop by on Saturday at noon to witness the start of the race. This annual event takes place at the Canmore Nordic Centre. For information contact Steve Merker. Phone: 905-944-9436

## August

**Annual Canmore Folk Music Festival.** This renowned festival mixes the best musical talent with a weekend festival of music, workshops and fun. (see Canmore Folk Festival – page 87)

## October

**Festival of Eagles.** Each year thousands of eagles fly over Canmore, and during the two days of this event, naturalists interpret the event through presentations, hikes and assisted viewings (see Festival of Eagles – page 82). For more information, contact the Special Events Coordinator for Canmore at (403) 678-1878.

## November

**The Vic Lewis Band Festival.** Vic Lewis was a band leader in the Bow Valley for many years, starting in the 1940s, and this annual festival attracts more than 800 young musicians to compete in this annual competition in his memory. For more information, contact

## Key Contacts

**Canmore Festival of Eagles**, Contact Chris Burr, Phone: (403) 678-1878. Email: specialevents@gov.canmore.ab.ca

**Canmore Golf and Curling Club**, 2000-8th Ave, Canmore, AB, T1W-1Y2. Proshop: (403) 678-5959.

**Canmore Folk Festival**, c/o Ken Rooks, Festival Director, Box 8098, Canmore, Alberta, T1W 2T8. Phone/fax: (403) 678-2524. Email: info@canmorefolkfestival.com. Web site: www.canmorefolkfestival.com.

**Canmore Highland Games**, Box 8102, Canmore, AB, T1W-2TB. Phone: (403) 678-9454, www.discovercanmore.com/highlandgames

**Canmore International Ice Climbing Festival**, Contact Gear Up Sports (403)678-1636.

**Canmore Museum and Geo-Science Centre**, 907 7th Avenue, Canmore, AB, T1W-2A9. Phone: (403) 678 2462. Fax: (403) 678 2216. Email: info@cmags.org, www.cmags.org

**SilverTip Golf Course Limited**, 1000 SilverTip Trail, P.O. Box 8330, Canmore, Alberta, T1W 2V1 Phone: (403) 678-1600, www.silvertipresort.com/aboutsilvertip/

**Stewart Creek Golf Club**, Box 8570, Canmore, AB, T1W 2V3. Proshop: (403) 609-6099. Email: asilberman@threesisters.ab.ca, www.stewartcreekgolf.com

| Pipers at the Highland Games | Heavy events at the Highland Games |

Julie Kehler at (403) 678-2622.

**Canmore Artists & Artisans Guild Christmas Show & Sale.** Canmore has a strong community of artists, photographers and sculptors. Each year, the Canmore Artists and Artisans Guild has their show and sale, and this is your best opportunity to see the work of established and new artists from the area. For more information contact Louise Olinger at (403) 609-2117.

**"Light Up Canmore"** Christmas Season Kick-off. It's not Christmas until the lights go up. This event officially launches the Christmas festivities with the lighting of the Northwest Mounted Police Barracks. Choirs entertain while hot chocolate and prize draws add to the attraction. For more information, call (403) 678-4094.

## December
**Community Party on the Pond.** Every December 31, the town hosts a party for families, with sleigh rides, skating, bonfires, hot chocolate and hot dogs, not to mention fire-

works. For more information, contact the Special Events Coordinator for Canmore at (403) 678-1878.

## Canmore Folk Festival
The Canmore Folk Festival has been running annually since 1978, making it the longest running folk festival in Alberta. The event takes place over the Heritage Day weekend in early August and over time has grown from a one-day event to a three-day extravaganza. The event, which takes place on the Stan Rogers Memorial Stage, attracts the best folk, country, bluegrass, blues and world music performers. Over the years, performers like Valdy, Lennie Gallant, Laura Love, James Keelaghan, Stephen Fearing, Connie Caldar, and Garnet Rogers have wowed local audiences. Attendance averages 2,500-5,500 people each day, and you'll want to come early to stake out your territory.

Along with the events on the main stage, there are nu-

merous afternoon workshops that give performers a chance to meet festival participants and collaborate with other musicians. The themes vary from serious to silly, and the result is always musical magic.

The festival is designed to be a family event. There is a children's concert on Saturday, prior to the main stage show beginning, and there is always a family area with clowns, jugglers, magicians, mascots, and entertainers. Face painting and pony rides are also available, along with craft and food booths.

## Canmore Highland Games
This annual event has been attracting larger crowds each year. Celebrating the Scottish connection in the naming of Canmore with the long tradition of the Highland Games, Canmore's event attracts the strongest competitors from across the country. It is the largest Highland Games in Western Canada.

Since the early days in

Scotland, annual games were designed to test the strength and agility of the country's warriors. It is commonly believed that Malcolm Canmore, after whom the town of Canmore is named, started the first Highland Games in the 11th century. The games were an important training tool to determine the strength of highland warriors, the best of whom would receive the most cherished military positions.

After the defeat of Bonnie Prince Charles at the battle of Culloden in 1746, the Highlanders were forbidden to play bagpipes, wear tartan, or even speak their own brand of Gaelic. This was effective in destroying much of the old clan structure, and it wasn't until the 1820s that the events were revived. They have changed very little since they were reestablished, with events including stone and hammer throwing, tossing the caber, piping and dancing, along with running and jumping events.

# Services

Canmore offers everything the visitor could possibly need. The town is well known for its diverse shops and restaurants, and, while it is well known for its small-town feel, it also offers big-city convenience. Here are some of the essential services for the town.

## Emergency Services

RCMP , call 911, (non-emergency 403-678-5516), 101 Elk Run Blvd, Canmore, AB, T1W 1L1

Ambulance, call 911, 1021 Railway Ave. Canmore, AB, T1W 1P3

Fire Department, call 911,

(non-emergency 403-678-6199) 1021 Railway Ave. Canmore, AB, T1W 1P3

Canmore Hospital, (403) 678-5536, 1100 Hospital Place, T1W 1N2

Conservation Officer, (403) 678- 800 Railway Ave, Canmore, AB, T1W 1P1

## Tourist Information

Travel Alberta Tourist Information, (1-800-661-8888), 2801 Bow Valley Trail, Canmore, AB, T1W 3A2

Tourism Canmore, (403) 678-1295, 2801 Bow Valley Trail, Canmore, AB, T1W 3A2, www.tourismcanmore.com

Canmore/Kananaskis Chamber of Commerce, #12, 801-8 Street, Canmore, AB, T1W 2B3, www.canmorebusiness.com/chambermain.htm

## Groceries

Garden Market IGA, (403) 678-6326, 2-950 Railway Ave., Canmore, AB, T1W 1P4

Marra's Grocery, (403) 678-5075, 638-8 Street, Canmore, AB, T1W 2B5

Rusticana Grocery, (403) 678-4465, 801-8 Street, Canmore, AB, T1W 2B3

Safeway Food and Drug, (403)609-2955, 1200 Railway Ave., Canmore, AB

## Medical Clincs

Canmore Associate Medical Clinic, (403) 678-5585, 703 8 Street, Canmore, AB, T1W 2B2

Canmore Medical Clinic, (403) 678-5511, 901-8 Street, Canmore, AB, T1W 2B4

## Veterinary Clinics

The Canmore Veterinary Hospital, (403)678-4425, 502 Bow Valley Trail, Canmore, AB

Bow River Veterinary Centre, (403)678-9595, 1510 Railway Ave., Canmore, AB

## Pharmacies

Mironuck IDA Pharmacy, (403) 678-4301, 8 Ave & Main St., Canmore, AB, T1W 2B2

## Liquor Stores

Alberta Spirits, (403) 678-2421, #120-1120 Railway Ave., Canmore, AB

Canmore Lodge, (403) 678-5528, 200-17 Street, Canmore, AB, T1W 1L8

Mountain Dew Liquors, (403) 678-8773, 738-8 Street, Canmore, AB, T1W 2B6

## Hardware

RD Building Supplies, (403) 678-2200, 733-8 Street, Canmore, AB, T1W 2B2

Home Hardware, (403) 678-5144, 900 Railway Ave., Canmore, AB, T1W 2T9

## Churches

Rocky Mountain Victory Church, (403) 678-8746, 1-117 Bow Meadows Cr., Canmore, AB, T1W 2W8

Saint Michael's Anglican Church, (403) 678-5191, 709-7 Street, Canmore, AB, T1W 2C3

Ralph Connor United Church, (403) 678-5354, 617-8 Street, Canmore, AB, T1W 2B1

Alpine Christian Ministries, (403) 609-0832, Box 8415, Canmore, AB, T1W 2V2

Canmore Community Church, (403) 678-2399, 1717 Bow Valley Trail, Canmore, AB, T1W 1N8

Sacred Heart Catholic Church, (403) 678-5022, 810-7 Street, Canmore, AB, T1W 2C8

Church of Jesus Christ of Latter Day Saints, (403) 678-3682, Canmore, AB,

Mountain Baptist Church, (403) 678-2861, Box 8227, Canmore, AB

Shepherd of the Valley Lutheran Church,

*Opposite: Policeman's Creek in winter*

# Kananaskis Trail (Hwy. 40)

*Mount Lorette*

The Kananaskis Trail takes you through the most highly travelled corridor of Kananaskis Country. As the most well known and thoroughly developed area, it acts as a funnel, leading most visitors into this picturesque valley. Unfortunately, it also leaves the impression that there is little more to Kananaskis than this one district. I generally recommend visitors use this valley as an introduction to the vast recreational riches that Kananaskis has to offer, and then follow up with visits to some of the other, less travelled areas.

The valley is easy to find. Simply follow the Trans Canada Highway (Highway 1) west from Calgary for approximately 60 km (36 mi.), until you meet the junction with Highway 40. From the south, you can access this area via Longview along Highway 22, southwest of Calgary.

This area was known to the local Stoney Indians for generations. Archaeological sites dating as far back as 6,000 BC have been located within Kananaskis Country. The Stoneys travelled these valleys searching for big game, and later trapped their isolated lakeshores. The valley's European history began with the travels of James Sinclair. He passed through in 1854, bringing settlers to the newly opened Oregon Territory. A few years later he was followed by Captain John Palliser, who did the first detailed surveys. It was also Palliser that dubbed the valley "Kananaskis," after the legend of an Indian named Kananaskis, who had survived a blow to the head by a battle axe.

More recently, it has seen Depression work camps, prisoners-of-war, and endless numbers of sightseers and recreationists. Since the Olympics and the media coverage of the downhill events at Nakiska at Mount Allan, this valley has seen increased pressure from developers. The trick now will be to slow things down, and create a long-term plan to manage growth and maintain the wilderness character that has made this valley so popular.

Make sure you stop in at

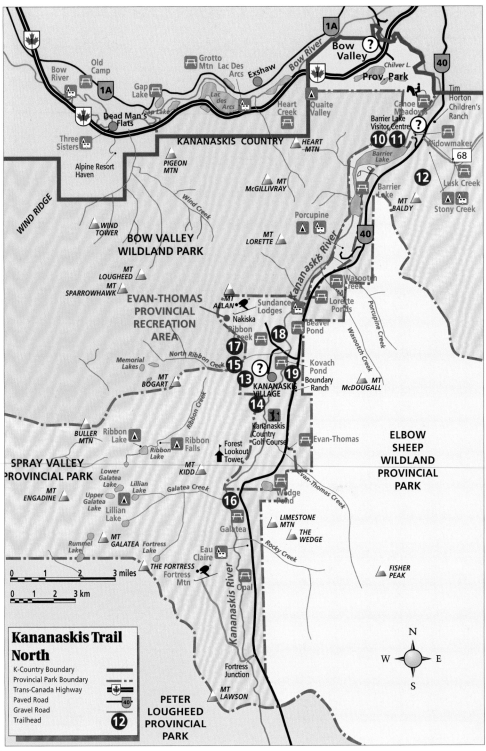

**Kananaskis Trail North**

| | |
|---|---|
| K-Country Boundary | |
| Provincial Park Boundary | |
| Trans-Canada Highway | |
| Paved Road | |
| Gravel Road | |
| Trailhead | |

the Barrier Lake Visitor Information Centre on your way south. It provides updated literature and maps, as well as information on current trail conditions and helpful suggestions on how to maximize your time in the area.

## Canoe Meadows

The Kananaskis River, like so many of our great rivers, has been dammed in several places, which limits the amount of water flowing downstream. As a peak-flow generator, the water is released at sporadic times, depending on power usage and the requirements of TransAlta Utilities. This leads to a potentially dangerous situation as the river can change from an almost empty channel to a competitive-level whitewater course in a matter of minutes. It is very important to stay out of the channel during low water.

This duality led paddlers to custom design a whitewater course. They used earth movers, added some rocks and other obstacles, and created a Class 3 competition course. Over the past few years it has hosted numerous whitewater events, and sees paddlers challenging its waters even during winter. Canoe Meadows forms the take-out point for paddlers, while the put-in is several kilometres further south, at Widowmaker Day Use. For information on dam release times, contact the Barrier Lake Information Centre at (403) 673-3985

## Tim Horton Children's Ranch

Tim Horton, a Canadian hockey great, had a great love for children. He felt very lucky

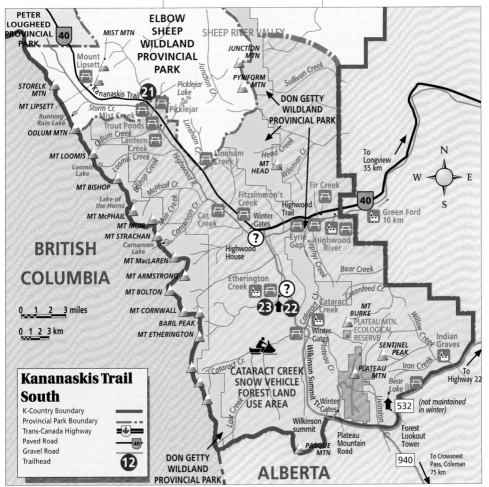

*Mount Baldy and Barrier Lake*

## Eagle Migration

**Eagles abound** in the mountains, especially during spring and fall. Not too long ago it was believed that most of the continent's eagles migrated along routes that kept them out of Kananaskis. Amazingly, several years ago a field biologist from Calgary, Peter Sherrington, discovered a previously unknown migratory route taking large numbers of golden eagles right over the area.

The numbers are quite astounding—approximately 5,500 eagles pass by on each migration, and, according to Sherrington, have likely done so for more than 11,000 years.

During Sherrington's self-financed studies he has noticed that the older eagles seem to appear earliest in the spring, followed by the younger birds. They make use of relatively stable air masses during late February and early March. In the fall, the young birds are the first to vacate the north country and head for warmer climes.

Since eagles mate for life, they usually travel in mated pairs, interacting little with other individuals on the migration. Sherrington describes the migrating birds as being similar to people in rush hour. We may be going to the same place, but our interaction with other commuters is minimal.

When is the best time to watch for eagles? They can be seen beginning at around 9:00 *Bald head eagle* a.m., with the numbers increasing until 4:00 or 6:00 p.m. In autumn, the numbers begin to drop off at around 5:00 p.m. The late-afternoon preference is likely related to the strong thermals created at that time as air rises. This makes travel easier and allows them to fly at speeds of 100–120 km/hr (60–72 mi./hr.).

The area surrounding Barrier Lake and Mount Lorette is one of the prime spots for watching the migration. In fact Peter Sherrington spends around six months a year in this area for his field studies. To celebrate the migrations, Canmore provides an annual event called the Festival of Eagles.

## Prisoners of War

*Barracks at Kananaskis POW camp*

**As the situation** in Europe deteriorated into war, a former work camp beneath the slopes of Mount Baldy was converted and utilized as an internment camp for German nationals. Shortly thereafter, Italians of questionable loyalty were also added to the growing population of internees. The government later released most of the detainees, and those still being held were removed to camps elsewhere. This left the facility vacant, so it was upgraded to hold up to 700 German prisoners of war.

Kananaskis Camp 130—Seebe, as it became known, was inundated with prisoners, primarily commissioned officers with a few enlisted men sent to perform those tasks that were below the dignity of the officers. Over the next several years, the biggest difficulty for the prisoners was finding creative ways to overcome boredom. Some found solace in work—they were paid 50 cents a cord to chop wood and $3.50 a day to work for Calgary Power on hydro projects within the valley. Others retreated into the arts and actually had shows in local communities, including Canmore. Still others managed to talk the commandant into allowing them to leave the camp to climb local mountains, like Baldy Mountain behind the camp, as long as they promised not to escape, which none attempted while free on these passes.

Also, according to the Geneva Convention they had to be fed food of similar quality and quantity as Canadian troops overseas. Many locals, who were experiencing severe rationing, felt the prisoners were being treated better than the people who lived in the valley. The POWs even managed to supplement their monthly pint of beer with a few hidden stills.

As the war ended, many would look back fondly at their years in Kananaskis, and some even attempted to remain in Canada after the war. Although they were all returned to Germany, many subsequently emigrated.

in life and wanted to help those less fortunate than himself. Shortly after his untimely death in 1974, the Tim Horton Children's Foundation was conceived. Operating four wilderness camps across Canada, it provides facilities for children who might not otherwise have an opportunity to go to summer camp. The camps help the dreams of many children come true.

The Kananaskis ranch consists of a spacious three-floor lodge and four rustic cabins. There is also a 669-sq.-m (7,200-sq.-ft.) recreation hall, a full western town, a teepee village, and a stable and corral. The corral holds 40 horses during the summer months.

The Foundation is funded by Tim Horton's Donuts store owners and private donations. The store owners work with local schools, churches, and affiliated helping agencies to select children that would benefit from visiting the camps. Each year over 4,000 children attend 10-day camps at the various facilities, and the memory of Tim Horton lives on in their smiles.

## University of Calgary Environmental Research Centre

This site holds a lot of history. Over the years it has helped usher in many of the changes this valley has seen. Today it is a quiet educational site used for Environmental Research.

Like many developments in Canada and the U.S., this site owes its existence to the Depression of the 1930s. During those difficult times, cities were deluged with unemployed men. There was no work to be had, and provincial and federal governments were forced to take action. The sight of long lines of hungry souls waiting outside soup kitchens and relief stations is forever burned into the memories of many seniors.

In an attempt to deal with the endless numbers of unemployed, the government began a series of relief camps to provide work, along with token amounts of money, for these men. The wage was a whopping 20 cents a day, and the men descended upon the wilderness of western Canada. Some headed toward the mountains of Banff and Jasper to build the Icefields Parkway. Others headed to the Kananaskis, where the government leased 160 sq. km (64 sq. mi.) of the valley for a research centre. The purpose of the facility was to do research on spruce and lodgepole pine in the area.

The first order of business was the building of a series of 12 x 6-m frame huts covered with tar paper. These housed the workers. Shortly afterward, they built a mess hall, a cook house, a wash house, latrines, and a log cabin for an office. Far from finished, they cleared several fire roads, built picnic shelters, thinned some stands of timber, and cleared some old burn sites. In time, this camp served as headquarters for four relief camps built in the area. Their tenure was short lived. By June of 1936, most of the work had been completed, and the relief program was discontinued. The site didn't remain quiet for long, however. As tensions

flared in Europe and war broke out, the camp was taken over for internment of German and Italian nationals whose loyalties were questioned.

While the war in Europe raged, work at the Kananaskis Forest Experimental Station was scaled down significantly. With victory, research began to pick up once again. During the next few years, trees were thinned, soil studies were undertaken, and exotic trees were planted. The period of 1951–60 was unusually busy—Forest and Fish and Wildlife officers trained there as part of the Alberta Forest Service Training School. Forestry research ceased in 1969. How-

ever, in 1966 an area was leased to the University of Calgary for the purpose of environmental research.

## Barrier Lake

The first mountain lake visible along Highway 40, Barrier Lake takes its name from the imposing mountain along its eastern shore. Mount Baldy was originally known as Barrier Mountain, and formed a natural obstacle to travellers following the Kananaskis River prior to its metamorphosis into a man-made lake.

The area in which the lake sits today was first cleared by German prisoners-of-war during the summer of 1945. Al-

## New Parks

**In the summer** of 2001, the Alberta government established two new Provincial Wildland Parks and one Provincial Park within Kananaskis Country. With the addition of Bluerock Wildland Provincial Park (127 km²), Don Getty Wildland Provincial Park (628 km²) and Sheep River Provincial Park (62 km²), the area now contains a total of 10 Provincial and Wildland Parks.

Don Getty Wildland Provincial Park is unique in that it is not a single entity. It is made up of numerous islands of significant habitat that stretch from the Ghost River to the Highwood Region of Kananaskis. In the Highwood Region it protects the entire length of the Continental Divide extending from the south

boundary of the Elbow/Sheep Wildland Provincial Park to the southern boundary of Kananaskis Country.

While these new parks greatly expand the amount of protected lands within Kananaskis, there is growing pressure to protect even more lands within parks. In particular, the Evan-Thomas Provincial Recreation Area is an ecologically sensitive area that is the subject of numerous development proposals. In addition, the Highwood Region has been largely designated for logging by Spray Lakes Sawmills of Cochrane.

Please contact Kananaskis Country for any new Provincial Parks established following the publication of this guide.

*Ribbon Lake*

though they could not be required to perform such manual labour according to the Geneva Convention, they enjoyed the work, and were paid $3.50 a day. The timber, not of saleable quality, was burned. Two years later, on July 18, 1947, the Barrier Plant opened with a capacity of 12,900 kW, and a head of 47 m (155 ft.). The reservoir is 308 ha (770 acres) in size and has a storage capacity of 44,530,000 m³ (1.5 trillion ft.³). Calgary Power, now known as Trans Alta Utilities, uses Barrier as a peak-flow generator. As such, it provides power to the grid during those times of day when the draw is at its maximum.

Although the lake is not natural, few people complain as they drive past its turquoise waters. Its shores are used by picnickers, hikers, mountain bikers, and other curious explorers.

## Mount Lorette Ponds

The five ponds of Mount Lorette were formed by diverting the Kananaskis River. Their linear nature provides an ideal place for families to cast a line for some of the regularly stocked rainbow trout. Completely wheelchair accessible, it is also popular with visitors to William Watson Lodge, and was designed to accommodate physically challenged individuals. The fish are not huge, but they can be more than enough to keep kids of all ages happy during family outings.

During busy summer weekends the site is a buzz of activity, as families and special needs users flock to the site. The fish are visible in the shallow waters, so they disappear rapidly after stocking. In August of 1994, the ponds were stocked with 2,400 rainbow trout, averaging 25 cm (10 in.) in length. Generally the stocking program is fairly consistent

on an annual basis, but you'll want to check with local Fish and Wildlife offices for current information.

## Ribbon Creek

The area around Ribbon Creek is one of the busiest in all of Kananaskis Country. With over 10,000 hikers each year, the Creek is rarely without hikers or skiers exploring its course.

In 1947, the Kananaskis Exploration and Development Company began exploiting coal reserves on Mount Allan. To accommodate the miners and support staff, bunkhouses were built and a village soon sprung up adjacent to the site. Before long, a school, a small store, and a snack bar were added to the growing village. On the opposite side of Ribbon Creek, Calgary Power built its own set of bunkhouses. The growing community was known as "Ribbon Crik" or "the camp," but its official name was "Kovach," named after the district ranger, Joe Kovach.

During its peak, 150 men worked for the company. The coal was removed on site and then trucked to a tipple on the Stoney Reserve. Even with a capacity of 75 tons/h., the mine was short lived. Much of the market for coal was making the change to oil and in February of 1952, the mine shut down for good. With the closing of the mine, the buildings were left to the elements. It wasn't long before the Calgary Power employees also moved on. In 1976, the Alberta Government decreed that there would be no more mining permits within Kananaskis Country.

## Kananaskis Village

Kananaskis Village officially opened on December 20, 1987, shortly before the Olympics. It was located to attract year-round tourism, positioned as it is between the Olympic ski hill (Nakiska at Mount Allan) and the 36-hole Kananaskis Golf Course. It consists of two hotels, the Delta Lodge at Kananaskis, which includes the Delta Signature Club, and the Kananaskis Mountain Lodge.

The largest of the hotels, the Lodge at Kananaskis, is operated by Delta Hotels, and contains 251 rooms, including 58 suites. It also contains a large conference centre with facilities for upwards of 800 people. The dining scene provides a wide selection, from fine cuisine in Seasons Dining Room and Western Classics at the Fireweed Grill, to tastes of the Mediterranean at Brady's

*The Kananaskis Mountain Lodge in Kananaskis Village*

Market. A large fireplace in the lobby, along with pleasant seating adjacent, provides a nice spot to relax.

The Delta Signature Club, in the John Palliser Manor, provides for a more exclusive resort experience. The 70 rooms are large, and all boast a mountain view. The beds are king and queen size and the rooms grand. This is a five star property, and provides all the perks and conveniences that go with such a designation.

Across the small pond from the Delta properties is the Kananaskis Mountain Lodge. This newly-renovated hotel provides reasonable rates, and a less pretentious atmosphere. Its 90 rooms provide comfortable accommodation, and the facility is popular with families. Relax in the evening in Woody's Pub, or grab some diner in the Alpine Garden Cafe. Meeting facilities are also available.

The Village Centre provides numerous services to visitors not staying in the hotels, as well as guests. They have an information desk with current

trail information, brochures, and postal service. A large fireplace, with ample seating, provides a welcome spot to plan the day's activities. You can rent sports equipment right here and hit the trails right away.

For the fun seeker, the village area boasts a children's playground, toboggan hill, outdoor firepit, tennis courts, a sports field, horseshoe pitches, an outdoor volleyball court, and a croquet site. Nearby, a helicopter landing pad offers scenic rides, or quick access to local communities like Canmore.

## Ribbon Creek Hostel

After the town of Kovach was abandoned, the schoolhouse was purchased in 1960, by the Canadian Youth Hostel Association (CYHA). They paid the princely sum of $105 for the old structure. Before long, renovations were required, and in 1963, Jim Lisoway, local president of the hostel association, decided to make the building

*Ski racer at Nakiska*

an A-frame. Unfortunately, the attempt was less than successful. As Ray Marriner, president of the Mountain Region put it:

*"We started out by dismantling the roof, then sawing the side walls off about three feet from the ground. We then used the completely inadequate lumber from the old rafters to make the A rafters. A properly constructed A-frame building is one of the strongest structures, but our new hostel was anything but! By the time the shingles were applied to the roof the whole building was so unstable that the sides of the roof would flap in and out in a strong breeze."*

Draftsman Neil Worley divided the building into two floors and managed to make it more stable. By 1969, a larger hostel was needed for the increasing number of guests. Before long, fundraising was complete, and on July 20, 1970, the doors to the new hostel opened. Designed by Worley, it was again expanded in 1971, with the addition of a large common room, four family rooms, and separate quarters for the house parents. Today the hostel is one of the most popular in the Southern Alberta Hosteling Association's chain of mountain hostels. Busy year round, it seems to change as Kananaskis Country does.

## Boundary Ranch

Originally called Boundary Stables, this ranch has grown substantially since it first opened. Today it houses all manner of groups and individuals, providing a western "cowboy" experience. Trail rides radiate out from the stables, and the ranch's guides will take you on rides to match your ability.

Recreational rides during the peak summer months, followed by extended wilderness hunting trips during the fall, keep them busy. With facilities for large groups, the Ranch attracts conference-goers looking to kick up their heels, and tour groups seeking to take advantage of the guided horseback rides. Evening functions provide plenty of food, dancing, and the relaxing feeling that comes with hangin' out at the ranch.

In 1989, the ranch was featured in the Don Johnson movie "Dead Bang," as the setting of a neo-nazi camp. The barn was renovated, a small stage and fireplace were added, and the walls were redone with tongue-and-groove cedar. When filming concluded, the renovations were left in place. Suddenly Boundary Ranch had a dance hall, that is, once they built a new barn.

Owner Rick Guinn is no stranger to movies himself. As the star of an earlier western film called "Buffalo Rider," he played a cowboy who rode a buffalo instead of a horse—not a simple feat. His father, Alvin Guinn, originally operated another local guest ranch, the Rafter Six Resort. Also, a nearby pass, Guinn's Pass, is named after Rick Guinn's father.

## Kananaskis Country Golf Course

Golf is one of the world's fastest-growing recreational activities, and this course has to be seen to be believed. With 36 challenging holes, the government spent in the neighbourhood of $36 million on its development. Construction began in 1978, and the course officially opened, with 27 of its 36 holes completed, on July 22, 1983. During the development phase, Bob Parkin, the provincial government's project manager, stated : "It will be a public course for Albertans, but it will be a world-class standard." In a good year the course averages over 75,000 rounds of golf during their season, from May to September or October.

Almost 100 m (300 ft.) higher than the Banff Springs golf course, the Kananaskis golf course's elevation allows golfers to hit the ball slightly farther, and use less club, than lower courses. It has numerous par-5 holes, with one topping out at 550 m (600 yd.). An 18-hole round can be as long as 6,000 m (6,560 yd.).

As it's difficult to drop in, you'll need to reserve tee times by calling 261-GOLF in Calgary, 463-GOLF in Edmonton, or (403) 591-7272 from all other locations. Reservations are taken up to 60 days in advance.

## Wedge Pond

Wedge Pond began life as a tiny, shallow body of water. With the building of the Kananaskis Golf Course, approximately 300,000 m³ (10.5 million ft.³) of gravel were removed from it to use as topsoil and contouring material. Today, it has been landscaped and converted into a put-and-take fishing pond. Lying beneath its namesake mountain, it provides a mirror-like reflection of its surrounding peaks, including Mount Kidd to the west and The Fortress to the south.

Occasionally stocked with rainbow trout, the pond is an excellent place for a family outing. It has numerous picnic sites with firepits, and is at the south end of the Evan–Thomas paved bicycle path.

## Fortress Mountain Ski Area

Fortress Mountain is one of the premier family ski hills in the mountains. It doesn't offer the variety of terrain found at Sunshine or Lake Louise, but it does offer excellent ski runs with short lift lines, and great snow. After a heavy snowfall, Fortress is a superb choice for fresh powder.

### Nakiska at Mount Allan

*Olympic ski hill*

**This ski hill** hosted, and was built specifically for, the alpine events of the 1988 Winter Olympics. It consists of 70% intermediate, with 16% novice, and 14% expert runs. The vertical drop totals 760 m (2,494 ft.). Since the hill was designed to move huge numbers of spectators during the games, it has an incredible capacity—8,620 skiers per hour. Lifts include two detachable quad chairs, one triple chair, and one double chair. To ensure an ample snow supply, snow-making facilities reach 85% of the hills surface. Today Nakiska is a popular family ski hill, due largely to the lack of crowds and the hill's proximity to Calgary. It is also much less expensive than its more famous counterparts in Banff.

Despite this popularity, the site was almost never built. There was a long debate over potential locations for the Olympic downhill events, and this site was not always the front runner. Mount Sparrowhawk, along the Smith–Dorrien/Spray Trail, was also in the running. In November of 1982, the final word came down—Mount Allan was in, Sparrowhawk was out. The Calgary Olympic Development Association had made its final decision, and a new facility would be constructed to the exacting specifications of the International Olympic Committee. Right up until the games ended, the area was under heavy pressure to perform. Skeptics predicted that there would be no snow and the events would flop. In the end, the mountain performed flawlessly. A few wind delays postponed some events, but to the 20,000 fans spread all over the hill, the events were perfect.

*Skiers at Fortress Mountain*

Development of "Snowridge Ski Area," as the site was first named, began in 1966. The development proceeded at the 1,950-m (6,435-ft.) elevation of Fortress Mountain, at the end of a winding 8-km (4.8-mi.) road. When it opened in 1969, the basic facilities included a single chairlift, two T-bars, and a 140-bed hotel.

Within a year, Brewster Transportation acquired the hill, but was no more successful, and after a year and a half the operation went bust. Following a test during the 1974/75 season, while still in receivership, the hill began operation. During the summer of 1975 a triple chairlift was constructed. Although the hill has changed hands numerous times, it remains an enduring part of the Kananaskis landscape. Today it is operated by Skiing Louise, as is Nakiska farther north on Highway 40. Be forewarned, however—after a large dump of snow, the access road can be a slippery, snowy challenge.

## O'Shaughnessy Falls

Waterfalls are always a welcome site along roadsides, even if they are not completely natural. This falls was built by John O'Shaughnessy in 1973, during upgrading of Highway 40. When he tried to divert the water from this small stream through a culvert, it stubbornly refused to cooperate and continued to spill over the highway. By building this small falls, the problem was solved. He followed up with a wishing well and some general landscaping.

Unfortunately vandals damaged the falls in 1981, and for several years it looked like it would continue to deteriorate. Thankfully, Exshaw resident Warren Harbeck circulated a petition asking that the government

*O'Shaughnessy Falls*

repair the site. After 400 people signed their names, the government announced that it would fund restoration. The announcement was made in September of 1983, and the repairs done shortly after. It is now a pleasant place to stop and watch the water tumble over numerous steps on its way towards the Kananaskis River. The name O'Shaughnessy Falls was officially approved on December 5, 1984.

Occasionally people bring water jugs to fill. However, this is not recommended since this water, like most local streams, must be suspected of containing *Giardia lamblia*. This small organism can cause a variety of unpleasant symptoms collectively known as "beaver fever." Better to let the water flow, and drink from a proper tap.

## Kananaskis Lakes Trail

This section of Kananaskis Country is one of the most popular—and most developed—recreation areas. The facilities along the Kananaskis Trail are treated at length in the next chapter, *Peter Lougheed Provincial Park*.

Just south of the junction with the Kananaskis Lakes Trail, a winter gate limits access south on Highway 40. The highway passes through critical winter wildlife habitat, and is closed between December 1 and June 15 to reduce impact during this sensitive season. In winter, cross-country skiers traverse this road, and in spring, before it opens to vehicle traffic, it is an excellent road to cycle. The road closure extends all the way to the Highwood Junction, where Highways 940 and 541 meet.

## Valley View Trail

This short side trip, which is located 5 km (3 mi.) south of the Kananaskis Lakes Trail turn-off, provides a winding alternative to the main highway. Although it meanders only a few kilometres, there are two main viewpoints—Elpoca and Lakeview. From

**Mount Kidd**

*Mount Kidd reflected in the Kananaskis River*

**One of the** most impressive mountains in the Kananaskis Valley, Mount Kidd dominates the scenery as you travel south beyond Kananaskis Village, or north past Galatea Creek. As a classic example of a Main Range mountain, its thick limestone layers tower above the surrounding valley. On its north shoulder, a tiny fire lookout perches high above Kananaskis Village.

This peak is named after Stuart Kidd (1883–1956), an early Alberta rancher who also managed Scott and Leeson's Trading Post at Morley. Following his stint at Morley, he operated the Brazeau Trading Company in Nordegg. The mountain was named in 1907 by D.B. Dowling, the surveyor responsible for assessing the value of the Ribbon Creek coal seams in 1903.

Kidd was fluent in the Stoney language and eventually became an honorary chief in 1927. He was given the Stoney name "Tah-Osa" which translates to "Moose Killer."

*Kananaskis Lakes from Opal Range*

Within this rocky slope, many animals have taken up residence. The Columbian ground squirrel may utter its peeping call, the tiny pika may call its name, or the golden-mantled ground squirrel may scurry past your feet. Always alert for intrusions of weasels—the only predator able to follow these animals into their rocky home—they keep a constant vigil. Other dangers include hawks, which silently swoop down and carry off unsuspecting residents of the rock pile.

these partially treed pull-outs, you get a panoramic view of the valley and the Upper and Lower Kananaskis lakes. This perspective is only obtained from this route; the main highway doesn't provide this lofty lookout. If you feel energetic, you can scramble higher up the Opal Range and get an unobstructed view of the lakes. This is, however, not a trail, and caution is advised whenever heading off the beaten path.

## Rock Glacier

At the base of Mount Rae and the Misty Range, there is a huge debris slope. Although it may seem like a lifeless rock pile, it's a place where nature has left behind a world of opportunity amidst rocky rubble. Not a true glacier, it is a large accumulation of rock that, due to the extreme angle at which it lies, slowly moves downhill, mimicking the movement of its icy namesake.

## Highwood Pass

From the junction with the Kananaskis Lakes Trail, the road climbs steadily from 1,700 m (5,610 ft.) until it crests Highwood Pass at an elevation of 2,206 m (7,280 ft.). With the gentle appearance of the pass, it surprises most people to learn that this is the highest engineered road in Canada.

## The Battle of Jutland and the Canadian Rockies

**One of the** most pivotal battles of World War I occurred off the Danish coast of Jutland. The only major naval engagement of the war, it dragged out over two days—May 31 and June 1, 1916. The battle began between the battle cruiser squadrons of Germany's Franz von Hipper and British Admiral David Beatty. The H.M.S. Galatea, flagship of Britain's 1st Light Cruiser Squadron, fired the opening volley. Eventually, the battle escalated to include both main fleets—the British, commanded by Admiral Sir John Jellicoe, and the German, under Admiral Rienhard Scheer.

British losses were immense, but the Germans were prevented from breaking the Allied blockade. For the remainder of the war, the German high fleet never left port again. The Allies lost many more sailors, but the battle is seen as a draw. In terms of the war, it was a turning point.

Throughout the Rockies, a seemingly endless number of peaks commemorate this battle. Mounts Inflexible and Nestor honour battleships of the same name. While Mount Nestor remains, its namesake was sunk during the battle. Mounts Chester, Cornwall, Engadine, Galatea, and Glasgow were

named for many of the battle cruisers in the engagement. The battle cruiser Indefatigable (Mount Indefatigable) exploded after being hit by five shells fired from the German battleship Von-der Tann. Only two of its 957-member crew survived. The Invincible (Mount Invincible), part of the 3rd Battle Cruiser Squadron, was sunk, and only six of its 1,034-member crew survived. The cruiser H.M.S. Warspite (Mount Warspite), on the other hand, was nicknamed "The Old Lady," and survived both world wars.

*Wedge Pond reflects the square summit of The Fortress*

Lying beneath the summits of Mounts Rae and Arathusa of the Misty Range to the east, and the folded slopes of Mount Tyrwhitt of the Elk Range to the west, the location is one of alpine splendour. In all directions the action of glaciers can be seen etched into the rock faces.

From the parking lot, a short, self-guided interpretive trail takes you on a stroll through an exceptional alpine meadow. This is one of the most accessible alpine meadows in the Rockies, and every July the field explodes with flowers such as western anemone.

In the spring of 1994, an interesting encounter took place high up on the pass. A small plane was tracking a local grizzly bear as part of a research study. Suddenly the plane began to experience mechanical problems. An emergency landing was necessary, and the plane managed a rough touchdown on the closed highway along Highwood Pass. As it was the first week of June, the pass had not yet opened for vehicle traffic. Once on the ground, the bear must have

## Highwood Meadows

**During the short** alpine summer Highwood Pass comes alive with all manner of wildflowers. Situated at the margin of the treeline, it supports a diversity of alpine plants. In the deep forest cover across the road, many of these plants could not survive. Alpine meadows provide a self-contained ecosystem where these sun-loving plants can endure. Life isn't easy in the alpine. The growing season may only be a few months long and the climate is similar to that of the arctic tundra.

With the melting of winter's heavy snow blanket comes the explosion of flowers into flaming reds and yellows. The paintbrush's deep purple looks as if it has been freshly dipped into a paint can. The western anemone quickly trades in its white flowers for its shaggy seed head, earning the pet name "Hippie Flower." The alpine forget-me-not, with its delicate blue flower, forms groups just large enough to make sure not only that you don't miss them, but that you pull out your camera to record them.

*Western anemone*

figured that turn-about was fair play, and it began to track the wardens, until they found themselves treed by the very bear they had been tracking.

# Highwood Junction

As you descend from Highwood Pass and continue the final 35 km (21 mi.) to High-wood Junction, you drop more than 600 m (1,980 ft.) . The narrow valley of the Pass widens dramatically as you approach the Junction. Gradually the prominent faces of the Elk Range give way to the towering cliffs of the High Rock Range. North of the junction the narrow Highwood Range terminates with Mount Head, at 2,782 m (9,181 ft.). Named by Captain John Palliser when he travelled through the valley in 1858, it commemorates Sir Edmund Walker Head (1805–1868), who was Governor-in-Chief of Canada from 1854 to 1861. He was a major contributor to the early work on the concept of confederation, and returned to England

## Lost Lemon Mine

**The story of** the Lost Lemon Mine is one of the enduring legends of the Canadian Rockies. Like most stories, this tale has grown and changed over the years. The basic tale tells of a group of prospectors who, in 1870, left Tobacco Plains, Montana in search of gold. They planned to prospect along the North Saskatchewan River, a river which still bears some gold today. Along the way, two prospectors, Blackjack and Lemon, headed out on their own.

Senator Dan Riley wrote the classic account of the legend for the Alberta Folklore Quarterly in 1946:

*"Blackjack and Lemon found likely showings of gold in the river. Following the mountain stream upwards toward the headwaters they discovered rich diggings from grass roots to bedrock. They sank two pits and, while bringing their cayuses in from the picket line, they accidentally discovered the ledge from which the gold came…*

*In camp that night the two prospectors got into an argument as to whether they should return in the spring or camp right there. After they had bedded down for the* night, Lemon stealthily crawled out of his blankets, seized an axe and split the head of his sleeping partner. Overwhelmed with panic when he realized the enormity of his crime, Lemon built a huge fire and, with his gun beneath his arm, strode to and fro like a caged beast till dawn.*"

The story doesn't end here. Apparently two Stoney Indians had followed the group and witnessed the entire episode. Later, their chief, Moses Bearspaw, made the braves promise to remain ever silent about the incident. He was afraid the white man would invade their hunting grounds and forever alter their traditional way of life.

Since that time, numerous expeditions have searched for the gold. According to the legend, most of these, at least all that came close to finding the gold, met with tragedy. On several occasions, Lemon tried to lead expeditions to the mine, but whenever he approached the area, he got progressively more agitated. In the end, he was never able to rediscover the location of the gold.

Shortly after Blackjack's death, a mountain man named John McDougall was dispatched to bury the unfortunate prospector. This he did, and was later re-engaged to lead a party back to the site. He never arrived. On his way to meet them he had stopped at Fort Kipp, Montana and drank himself to death.

Lafayette French, the man who had funded Blackjack and Lemon, was also determined to find the mine. For many years French searched for the gold, and it appears that he may have finally succeeded. He wrote to a friend, stating that he had found the mine, but was fatally burned when the cabin in which he was staying burned to the ground. He did not live long enough to share the secret of the mine's location. The gold had thwarted its seekers once again.

Since then, the story has not died. Throughout the past 125 years, many people have been looking for the mine. Numerous small gold rushes have begun through quiet rumour, but none have located the mother lode. Will it ever be discovered? Who knows? But one thing is evident—stories like this add much to the folklore of the Canadian wilderness.

in 1861 to became Governor of the Hudson's Bay Company.

This intersection forms an important juncture. It marks the southern extent of the winter highway closure, and provides the option of continuing east to the town of Longview, or heading south on the good gravel of the Forestry Trunk Road. The southern boundary of Kananaskis Country is 24 km (14.4 mi.) south along this road. Once there, you can exit along steep, secondary Highway 532, or continue to the Crowsnest Pass.

East of Highwood Junction the paved highway becomes Highway 541, and meanders through pleasant foothills until it meets the town of Longview, 35 km (21 mi.) distant. As you travel this stretch, the mountains quickly lose their imposing nature and the foothills become the dominant landform. Passing the eastern boundary, you enter ranching country with its high, grassy, south-facing slopes. Keep your eyes open for golden eagles soaring overhead, on the lookout for ground squirrels.

## Forestry Trunk Road

Following the Forestry Trunk Road provides quiet, dusty diversion. Away from the hustle and bustle of Highway 40, you can explore areas of Kananaskis that see very little traffic. The road has a good gravel surface, but during the winter it closes between Cataract Creek Campground and Wilkinson Summit. From the Cataract and Etherington campgrounds a diverse system of summer trails and winter

*Highwood Pass summit*

snowmobile trails radiate. Heading west towards the Continental Divide, they provide excellent views of the surrounding peaks of the High Rock Range. For more information on the trails in this area, see the descriptions at the end of this section.

At the south boundary of

## Chickadees and Nuthatches

**It's funny how** we always tend to focus on superlatives—the biggest, the strongest, and the most dramatic. Two of the most common, but rarely noticed, birds in Kananaskis are the black-capped chickadee, and the red-breasted nuthatch.

The chickadee is about 11 cm (4.4 in.) long and has a tiny beak. It has a distinct black cap and throat patch separated by whitish cheeks. Its back is a drab greyish-brown and the underside is lightly coloured. It quickly gives away its presence as it opens its beak and calls out its name: "chick-a-dee-dee-dee." This, along with its distinctive markings quickly identifies this common resident. There are three different types of chickadees living in this area, but the black-capped is by far the most common.

Chickadees eat small insects, larvae, and seeds. Very agile flyers, they can be seen perched upside down as they peck away with their little beaks in search of food. When they take a large seed, they hold it between their feet, and peck away at it until they get at the fleshy meat beneath the shell.

Their neighbour, the red-breasted nuthatch, is equally easy to identify. It has a bluish-gray back, a rusty breast, and a dark head patch and eye streak. Usually you'll see it working its way down a tree, checking behind the tops of the bark scales for anything worth eating. Like the chickadee, it likes insects and seeds, and quickly finds any new bird feeder within its turf.

Like the chickadee, the call of the red-breasted nuthatch is quite distinctive. It's a nasal-sounding "eenk" which can't be confused with any other local bird. You may need someone to point the call out to you for the first time.

Kananaskis Country, Highway 532 steeply winds its way eastward towards Highway 22. Climbing over 200 m (660 ft.) in the first few kilometres, it drops off the summit just to the east of flat-topped Hailstone Butte. Over the next two kilometres, it plummets 300 m (990 ft.) along a gear-grinding gradient. Following the route of a gas pipeline, it winds its way to a junction with Highway 22, through pleasant rolling country. Following its drop off the summit, the gradient becomes more bearable and the driving smooth. This route would not be safe in anything but good conditions, as the steep drop could become dangerous when wet or icy.

## Logging

**With the coming** of the railway, the forests of the Kananaskis and Spray valleys soon came under the axe. Following surveys from 1883–84 by L.B. Stewart, the area was divided into timber limits. First to the draw was James Walker. A former mounted police constable, his mill operated in the Kananaskis Valley between 1883 and 1886. During this period he employed 15–70 men, depending on the season. In 1884, his sawmill processed two million feet of logs. He later managed the famous Cochrane Ranche, and was a long time civic leader and founding father of Calgary. In 1975, during Calgary's centennial celebrations, Walker was voted the citizen of the century for his long affiliation with that city.

Almost simultaneously, Ottawa lawyer Kutusoff MacFee began planning his own logging operation. On a trip to Eau Claire, Wisconsin, a major timber-producing area in the midwestern U.S., he managed to pique the interest of several key people in that area.

Following an exploratory trip down the Kananaskis and Spray valleys, MacFee acquired the rights to 250 sq. km (100 sq. mi.) of timber along the Spray, Bow, and Kananaskis Rivers. With this, the Eau Claire and Bow River Lumber Company was officially

*Logs ready for the spring drive*

registered.

MacFee got underway in 1886 with a sawmill in Calgary and opened a logging camp along the Kananaskis River, with another near Silver City in Banff National Park. Much of the cutting took place during the winter months, when as much as five million feet of timber was cut. With spring runoff, the logs were floated downstream to the mill in Calgary. The drives were an annual affair, from their inception in 1887 until 1944. Not an overly efficient delivery system, the drives took two months and 30–40 men.

The main camp was located on the site of the present Eau Claire campsite, whereas a secondary camp was located along the south fork of Ribbon Creek. As it was difficult to keep good workers in these isolated camps, the company brought in a wagon-load of prostitutes twice a month to keep the men happy.

By the 1930s and 1940s, the companies were using more and more trucks to move logs to the sawmills. The quality of the wood in the valley dropped following a large fire in 1936. This limited the company to salvage cutting and signaled the beginning of the end of logging in the Kananaskis Valley. The company's mill in Calgary closed in 1945, and the main Eau Claire camp was taken down in 1948 by Joe Kovach, the district ranger at the time. He built a kitchen shelter using some of the scrap lumber. In Calgary, Prince's Island Park was named after Peter Prince, a manager of the Eau Claire Lumber Company between 1886 and 1916.

# Peter Lougheed Provincial Park

*Upper Kananaskis Lake*

**K**ananaskis Provincial Park, as Peter Lougheed Provincial Park was originally known, was dedicated on September 22, 1977. One of the largest Provincial Parks in Alberta, it encompasses 304 sq. km (122 sq. mi.) around the Kananaskis Lakes. The park was created as part of the much larger Kananaskis Country. More than 20,000 people travelled to the park in its inaugural year, and things have been on an uphill swing since then.

The Kananaskis Lakes Trail takes you to the Upper and Lower lakes and past most of the facilities of Peter Lougheed Provincial Park. As one of the busiest corridors in Kananaskis, its 16 km (9.6 mi.) often seems like an urban jungle. Cyclists breeze along the paved bicycle path, hikers head into the backcountry, and mountain bikers grunt their way towards the top of one more hill—the valley pro-vides something for everyone. With some of the most picturesque landscape in all of Kananaskis, it begs to be explored.

## Kananaskis Visitor Centre

During the early days of Kananaskis Country, money was plentiful and no expense was spared. Things have changed today, with cutbacks and deficits, but the legacy of this early period of prosperity can be seen in the quality of facilities located in Kananaskis. This attention to detail can be clearly seen in the Kananaskis Visitor Centre.

An abundance of slide shows and displays keep visitors busy for quite some time. The focus here is on interaction. Many of the displays require some form of input from the viewer, and several laser-disk pro-grams provide high-tech access to trail information.

The staff at the Kananaskis Visitor Centre are experts on the area, and are an excellent source of information on current trail conditions and campground availability.

Beyond the desk a large sitting room with immense windows provides views of the surrounding Opal Ranges. With a roaring fire in the fire-

*Opposite: The Opal Range*

place and extensive seating, it's the perfect place to warm up after a cold winter ski, or just relax after a summer hike. The centre can be contacted by calling (403) 591-6322.

# William Watson Lodge

Every once in a while someone designs a facility that is so unique that it deserves accolades. William Watson Lodge is such a facility. Kananaskis Country has built a lodge specifically for guests with physical and mental challenges. This provides opportunities to experience the splendour of Kananaskis in a barrier-free environment. The development includes eight specially-designed cabins and a main lodge. Guests don't need to restrict themselves to the cabins; there is also a barrier-free campground adjacent to the lodge. It accommodates six units and provides equally-accessible walk-in tent sites.

The lodge commemorates William Watson, a man who spent his life trying to improve the lives of disabled persons. He was born in 1904 in Scotland, and due to an injury at birth, spent his life without the use of his arms. Not one to give up, he still managed to earn a Bachelor of Arts degree and, later, a Bachelor of Laws, both from the University of Alberta. His handicap prevented him from practicing law, so he devoted his life to empowering

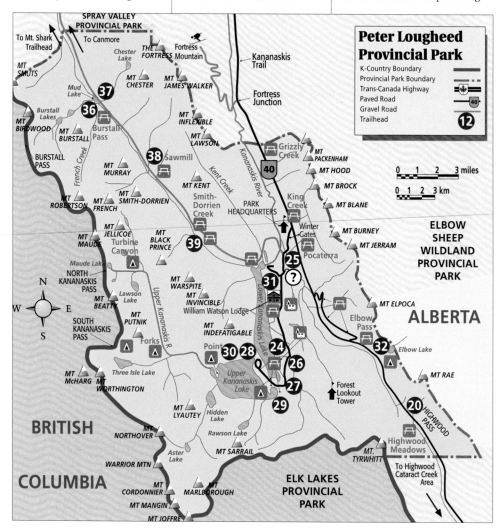

*Lower Kananaskis Lake and the Opal Range*

the disabled. He helped lay much of the groundwork for today's greater acceptance of persons with disabilities.

This facility is designed to be used by anybody with a physical or mental challenge. It doesn't provide attendants, but an eligible person may book a lodge for up to six people, and stay with them to provide assistance.

Surrounding the lodge there are numerous trails that are accessible to wheelchairs. These include Spruce Road Audio Trail, Marl Lake Trail, Rockwall Trail, and the Highwood Meadows Interpretive trails. The paved bicycle path, which snakes its way along the Kananaskis Lakes Trail, also provides a pleasant stroll or roll. The Evan–Thomas paved bicycle path, farther north on Highway 40, is yet another option. Finally, don't forget Mount Lorette Ponds, designed to provide barrier-free put-and-take fishing.

When you consider all of these opportunities for enjoying Kananaskis, the value of this facility begins to really shine. Few wilderness preserves in North America provide a similar service, and the prices are very reasonable. As you can imagine, these facilities are exceedingly popular, so reservations need to be made well in advance by calling (403) 591-7227.

## Cottages

Hidden along the shores of the Lower Kananaskis Lake are a series of cottages. The only private residences in Kananaskis Country, the cottagers have worked hard to protect their secret. Even the access road is camouflaged. It joins with the Kananaskis Lakes Trail as a loose gravel road, but follow it a short distance and it quickly becomes paved. As the road passes the cottages, it becomes evident that this is prime real estate. In

1961, 70 cottage lots were leased for the princely sum of $5 plus a $30 annual fee. The new leasees had two years to build a cottage, and before long there were 75 stretched out along the shoreline. The cottages vary from deluxe to rustic, as each resident finds his own way to appreciate the beauty of the location.

## Kananaskis Lakes

How does one describe the Kananaskis Lakes? They are a perfect combination of mountain, magic, and man. When explorer John Palliser first laid eyes on them in 1858 he remarked:

> *"We came upon a magnificent lake, hemmed in by mountains, and studded by numerous islets, very thickly wooded. This lake, about 4 miles long and 1-1/2 miles wide, receives waters from the glacier above, and is a*

Upper Kananaskis Lake in winter

*Upper Kananaskis Lake in summer*

*Three Isle Lake*

## Pocaterra

**George Pocaterra** was one of this area's most colourful, yet lesser-known pioneers. Born in Rocchette, Italy in 1883, he spent many years trapping and exploring the area now known as Kananaskis.

When he arrived on Canadian shores in 1903, he had $3.75, and began working on a small farm in Southern Manitoba. In the fall of 1904, the banks of the Highwood River became home, as he began work on what would eventually become one of the area's first "Dude Ranches"—the Buffalo Head Ranch. Soon he encountered his first "real" Indians, and this chance encounter led to a lifelong friendship with the Stoney Indians. One of those he met that day, Three Buffalo Bulls, later took him as a son. His other

*George Pocaterra in 1911*

son, Spotted Wolf, became Pocaterra's blood brother.

George, Spotted Wolf, and another Stoney named Dog Nose ran a trapline up the Kananaskis Valley. After dividing up the territory, Pocaterra trapped the area around both lakes and along a small stream that now bears his name. The winter of 1906-07 became known as the "year of the blue snows"—the year that the Chinook did not come. Pocaterra and his Stoney companions had a harrowing winter, almost not escaping the frozen grasp of the Kananaskis valley. Despite this ordeal, Pocaterra continued to hunt and trap in the area for another 20 years. He also filed several mineral deposits, but was unable to stimulate development of the sites. Although he opposed the hydro developments in the Kananaskis, one of the dams, a creek, and a group camp still bear his name. He died in 1972 at the age of 89, but his name lives on in the Kananaskis.

*favourite place of resort to the Kootenie Indians."*

The two lakes are joined artificially through a penstock, a long pipe-like canal built between 1947 and 1955. Prior to this diversion, the lakes were linked by a small stream and waterfall.

George Pocaterra later described the changes brought about by hydro development. *"The most beautiful scenery in the world, as far as I am concerned, was at these lakes but now is completely spoiled by the power*

*dams, the drowning of the marvelously beautiful islands and exquisitely carved beaches, the cutting down of the centuries old trees, and the drying up of the twin falls between the two lakes, and the falls below the lower lake."*

The lakes provide numerous opportunities to hike, mountain bike, or fish. In 1994 the Lower Kananaskis Lake was stocked in August with 84,300 cutthroat trout, and the Upper in both August and September with 43,800 rainbow trout. Boat launches are

provided at the Upper Lakes day use for access to the Upper Lake, and at Canyon day use for access to the Lower Lake.

## Power Generation

**In 1912** Calgary Power sent a survey party to assess the Kananaskis Lakes for their potential for hydroelectric development. They had already built the Horseshoe Dam on the Bow River and would soon complete the Kananaskis Falls Power Plant at the confluence of the Kananaskis and Bow rivers. The Kananaskis Lakes were almost spared in 1914, when a representative of the federal Water Power branch, M.C. Hendry, released a report suggesting that the development would be far too expensive to warrant consideration.

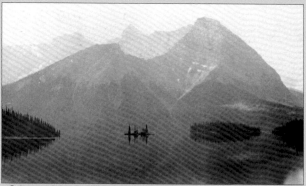

*Schooner Island on Upper Kananaskis Lake in 1911—now inundated*

Unfortunately for the Lakes, as technology improved, so did the ability to make marginal dams pay off, and in 1932 a hand-hewn spillway on the Upper Kananaskis Lake was begun. This first dam was a primitive affair, with water flow being controlled by manually pulling out logs at two-week intervals in the spring and fall. Although this raised the water level, and pro-

vided a storage capacity of approximately 44 billion litres (11 billion gallons), a second dam was built 10 years later to almost triple the capacity to 126 billion litres (33 billion gallons), an area of 868 ha (2,170 acres). In 1955, Interlakes Plant was completed, and the storage capacity of the Upper Lakes was finally used to generate electricity. The capacity was small—just 5,000 kW, with a head of 39 m (127 ft.).

Even the Lower Kananaskis Lake was not spared to the

hunger for increased power generation, and clearing for its reservoir began in 1954. The following year, the Pocaterra Plant came on line with a usable storage of 63 billion litres (16 billion gallons), and an area of 641 ha (1,603 acres). Its power-generating capacity was 14,900 kW and its head 63 m (207 ft.). This, the Interlakes Plant, and the Barrier Plant are operated by remote control from the town of Seebe.

# The Smith-Dorrien/Spray Trail

*Mud Lake*

This 60-km road links the town of Canmore with the Kananaskis Lakes. While it is unpaved and exceedingly dusty in dry weather, its virtues far outweigh these relatively minor inconveniences. Travelling beneath the glacier-scoured peaks of the Spray Mountains and the Goat Range,

along with the picturesque shoreline of the Spray Lakes Reservoir, it is a splendid driving route. As of January 1, 2001, the expansion of Bow Valley Wildlands Park, and the establishment of Spray Valley Provincial Park have protected this magical landscape. These two parks were created to protect the wild character of this valley by ensuring that there would never be any large-scale developments within this sensitive corridor. Their designation reflects Albertans' overwhelming belief that this area of Kananaskis needed a much higher level of protection than was previously available.

Also located along its length are numerous hiking, and mountain bike trails, along with a remote, but pleasant campground. The south end of the road was little more than a forestry road hacked out of the wilderness around 1936, ending at the Mud Lakes area. The north end wasn't developed until hunger for power in 1951 prompted construction of a steep road from Canmore to the newly created Spray Lakes Reservoir. Spray Lake Sawmills logged the valley in the 1950's. The highway has been dramatically upgraded since Kananaskis Country's incep-

tion, and now boasts a wide gravel surface along the southern 49 km, while the north end remains narrow and winding. The drop down to Canmore also requires some confidence, as you drive along a steep mountain traverse—but the views during the descent are well worth it.

## Spray Valley Provincial Park

On September 20, 2000, Alberta's Minister of Environment, Gary Mar, announced the creation of a new provincial park. Spray Valley Provincial Park protects 266 square kilometres (103 sq. mi.) of the Spray Lakes

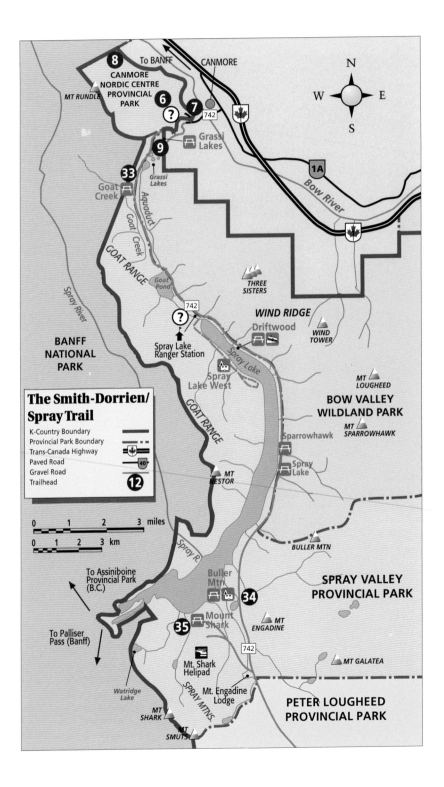

*Mount Shark*

Valley. This newly created park ended talks of large-scale developments within this sensitive valley and has been highly lauded by the Alberta public and conservationists alike.

The new park, along with the adjacent Bow Valley Wildland Park and Peter Lougheed Provincial Park, now creates an uninterrupted stretch of protected wilderness that stretches 550 km (330 mi.) from Kakwa Wildland Park in the north to Peter Lougheed Provincial Park in the south. This new park fills a large hole in the protected network of parks running along the Continental Divide. It also adds a valuable component to the Yellowstone to Yukon Conservation Initiative.

## Gypsum Mine

On the steep slopes of Mount Indefatigable you may notice a faint diagonal line trending up the side and cutting through the trees near the summit. This cutline is all that remains of a gypsum mine attempted atop this remote mountain.

In 1964, a report published by the Geological Survey indicated deposits of gypsum along the north slope of Mount Indefatigable. Almost as soon as the report hit the presses, the Canadian Pacific Oil and Gas company applied for a permit. In 1965, it received a 21-year lease for the site. The lease was subsequently assigned to Alberta Gypsum.

The difficulties of building a road to the site proved nearly insurmountable. The first road came close, before reaching an impassable point. A second road was built along the northern side of Mount Indefatigable, the road still visible traversing this steep face.

Despite all this effort the deposit was of poor commercial quality, and only one carload of gypsum was ever taken out. In 1970, when Alberta Gypsum failed to pay for land restoration on the site, their lease was cancelled. With the advent of Kananaskis Country, mining was forbidden within its boundaries. Today the deposit remains where it lies, high on the slopes of Mount Indefatigable.

**119**

*The Goat Range over Spray Lakes*

## Mount Engadine Lodge

This splendid wilderness lodge was built in 1986 by Rudi and Elizabeth Kranabitter and Eric and Dorle Lomas. It provides the only lodge-style accommodation along this wilderness corridor, and is located at the junction of the Smith–Dorrien and Mount Shark roads. To the south, the three-peaked summit of Mount Birdwood dominates the skyline, and Mount Shark looms to the west. The lodge takes its name from Mount Engadine to the east, which in turn commemorates a light battle cruiser engaged in the Battle of Jutland during World War I.

Pleasantly rustic, it boasts a common sitting room with a large stone fireplace, a large dining area with plentiful European cuisine, and quiet rooms exuding simple luxury. From the lodge, a variety of exploring options are possible. Track-set cross-country ski trails lead out from the lodge, hiking trails are located close by, and certified mountain guides are able to take you up the surrounding mountains. Options include simple accommodation packages and week-long adventure tours.

## Glacial Nurseries

**Along the** southern end of the Smith–Dorrien/Spray Trail, the western skyline is dominated by the glacially-carved faces of Mounts Invincible, Warspite, and Black Prince. Large bowl-like depressions have been carved into the mountain faces, and these bowls were once the birthplace of a glacier.

Mountain glaciers are formed by the slow accumulation of snow within a small depression. Later, as the depth of snow increases, the lower layers become compressed into ice. As the ice layers get thicker with each passing year, pressure on the lower layers causes them to flow, slowly, like a thick liquid. As ice moves within these alpine depressions, the glacier carves out a large bowl, or cirque, before flowing into the surrounding valley.

Later, the ice disappears from most of these glacial bowls. Some were trapped in the bottom and later melted to become one of the many glacial lakes found in the Rockies. These cirque lakes are called tarns and are quite common within Kananaskis Country. Black Prince Trail takes you to one such tarn. In some instances, the water carved a channel through the bowl's lip, and formed a waterfall to the valley bottom. Ptarmigan Cirque on Highwood Pass shows this post-glacial carving—the water flows down Mounts Rae and Arathusa.

*Mt. Assiniboine*

## Mount Shark

The Canmore Nordic Centre lies in the Bow Valley and may not receive significant amounts of snow during the early part of the cross-country ski season. To ensure early- and late-season racing options, the Mount Shark ski trail system was designed. A former logging road provides easy access, and the trails provide a series of loops throughout this former clear-cut. The views down the valley towards the Spray Lakes Reservoir are attractive, and the network of trails challenging.

The trail system includes 2-km, 5-km, 10-km and 15-km racing trails (1.2, 3, 6, and 9 mi. respectively) as well as the Ruedi Setz biathlon range. Ruedi was a former racer and a pivotal figure in the growth of biathlon in Alberta. He provided much of the impetus for the building of this facility.

Mount Shark also forms the main access point to Mount Assiniboine Provincial Park. The road to the trailhead passes a helipad, allowing for more leisurely access, whereas the main trail is used by hikers, horseback riders, and skiers.

## Mount Assiniboine

Shortly after passing the Mount Shark Road, you'll pass a small pond on the western side of the highway. Looking across Buller Pond, as it is known, you can see the towering wall of Mount Assiniboine. This mountain has captured the dreams of many travellers to the mountains. Walter Wilcox, who unsuccessfully attempted climbing the mountain in 1899, described it reflected in Lake Magog at its base:

> *The majestic mountain, which is a noble pyramid of rock towering above snow fields, was clearly reflected in the water surface. Such a picture so suddenly revealed aroused the utmost enthusiasm of all our party, and unconsciously everyone paused in admiration.*

It was named in 1884 by surveyor George Dawson after the Stoney Indians of the Assiniboine nation. Assiniboine loosely translates to "stone boiler." Prior to the introduction of metal cook pots, the Stoneys would heat rocks and place them into cooking receptacles, thus heating water to cook their food.

The mountain is often referred to as the "Matterhorn of the Rockies." Its craggy summit has been carved by glacial ice on four sides, giving it a striking similarity to its European namesake. It rises 3,618 m (11,870 ft.) and is visible from very few areas in the Kananaskis. This sight is a special treat on clear days.

*Ice fishing on Spray Lakes*

## Ski Hills on Mount Sparrowhawk

High above Sparrowhawk Day Use Area are the towering slopes of its namesake mountain. This site has seen numerous failed proposals to develop a world class ski resort. As early as 1970, developers were trying to coax approval from a reluctant Alberta government. The attempts were politely rejected, but the proposals continued to come. In 1978, a group called the Spray Lakes Ski Corporation submitted a $300 million development proposal. It was tentatively approved, but following an election, subsequently turned down as being too grandiose.

The proposal was scaled down to a more manageable $50 million, again rejected and again scaled down. Even the modest $25 million dollar development finally proposed would have supported 5,000 to 8,000 skiers per day.

During this same period, there was speculation that this site could double as the host site for the downhill events of the 1988 Winter Olympics. The Calgary Olympic proposals for the Games used Sparrowhawk as the mountain of choice. It could easily support the 300 metre (1,000 foot) vertical drop necessary for an Olympic event. In the end, the mountain was rejected on both hands. Mount Allan was chosen for the 1988 games, and the proposal for a ski resort was turned down.

This was hardly the end of the story, and in 1999 Genesis Land Corporation in Calgary came forward with a proposal for a massive development. The plans included a four-season ski resort on Tent Ridge with a daily capacity of 6000 skiers, a 27-hole golf course and a 400-room hotel. They also planned a boat tour operation on Spray Lakes Reservoir and a heli-ski operation on Mount Sparrowhawk.

The proposal was well funded and Genesis had worked very hard during the approval process. While it looked to many that the proposal might get the green light, on September 20, 2000 Environment Minister Gary Mar announced the creation of a new provincial park, Spray Valley Provincial Park, along with an expansion of the adjacent Bow Valley Wildland Park. Together with Peter Lougheed Provincial Park, these three parks protect the entire Spray Valley and finally end any possibility of future ski hill development in this valley.

The Spray Valley will stay as it is. It will have limited trail access and winter cross-country ski facilities, but will not see any large-scale developments.

## Mountain Goats and the Goat Range

**Along the shores** of Spray Lakes Reservoir, the western sky is filled with the impressive faces of the Goat Range. Named after the mountain goat, an animal that eschews the valleys for the inhospitable alpine summits, it implies ruggedness, and it delivers. The south end of the range begins with Mount Nestor, named for a destroyer sunk at the Battle of Jutland.

Mountain goats are one of the most highly adapted of our mountain wildlife. No other animal has the ability to survive on the summits like goats. Even bighorn sheep, another well-known climber, defers to the mountain goat. Easily recognized by its white, shaggy coat and black goat-like horns, it is rarely seen along the roadways. Despite its name, it is actually related to the mountain antelope of Asia—it's not a goat at all!

Animals that stay white year-round are rare in nature, but the goat has found this to be an advantage. For most animals, a white coat in summer is too visible, making them vulnerable to predators. For the goat, though its white colour is clearly visible, it is often discounted as a patch of summer snow—that is, until it begins to move. Often you will see numerous goats in an area, and you may find collections of their pellets beneath rocky overhangs, which serve as shelters.

Even mountain goats sometimes fall, but more fall victim to the unpredictable nature of avalanches. In winter they prefer the wind-blown summits, which keep sufficient grasses exposed for feeding. Ironically, when the hunt for food results in the release of an avalanche, they provide food for grizzlies. As these large eaters wake from their winter sleep, they head to the avalanche slopes to feed on the carcasses of winter-killed sheep and goats. The main predator of the mountain goat is the cougar, but the rocky crags provide protection from most non-human hunters.

Each spring, mountain goats shed their winter coats. This brings on a desire for salt, which may bring them down to the valley bottoms. Occasionally they appear along roadsides, where they lick glacial gravels that provide some of these minerals. Unfortunately, they are rarely seen at road level in Kananaskis. In some areas in Kananaskis, mountain goats are being reintroduced: the Picklejar Lakes area south of Highwood Pass and near the summit of Nihahi Ridge in the Elbow River Valley. If successful, this program will allow their shaggy coats to be seen more widely within the boundaries of Kananaskis Country.

## Spray Lakes

The Spray Lakes began as a small series of mountain lakes enhanced to provide hydro-electric power. To this end, it puts the capabilities of the Kananaskis Lakes to shame. As early as the 1920s, negotiations with the federal government over the status of the lakes were being undertaken. At that time, they were within the boundaries of Rocky Mountains Park, now Banff. The park was much larger then, and included Canmore, the Spray Lakes, and Lac Des Arcs within its boundaries. In 1928, the Department of the Interior agreed to remove Spray Lakes from the Park if the province would guarantee a flow of 350 second-feet down the Spray River to Banff. The Crag and Canyon Newspaper, on December 10, 1928, described the Spray Lakes as:

*"A valley full of muskeg…and old burnt stumps, the largest slope of the Canadian Rockies, that breeds uncountable numbers of mosquitoes, and flies. Surely a place to clean up, and what more fitting way than to submerge it in a big lake, where the natural sloping of the ground and feeding place, will increase the fast vanishing fishing of the Spray Lake…*

*Spray Lakes sports a fish rarely caught anywhere else in the mountains. All these trout weigh close to four pounds each and time and again it has been said, by fishermen who know the streams of Europe, that they never had better sport than what they got from Spray Lakes, so that with the raising of Spray Lakes, these fish would be preserved indefinitely and mean an income to all the Dominion."*

The Spray System finally came on line in 1951, and is composed of three power plants and several dams. Spray Lakes is formed by Canyon and Three Sisters dams. Together, they create a reservoir 1,987 ha (4,968 acres) in size, with a storage capacity of 421,850,000 $m^3$ (18 trillion $ft.^3$). This makes it larger than the combined capacity of the Upper and Lower Kananaskis lakes, and Barrier Lake. Canyon Dam is located at the southwestern end of Spray Lakes, where the Spray River enters the lake. Three Sisters Dam keeps the water contained at the northern end. After leaving Three Sisters Dam, the water drops 20 m (66 ft.) to Three Sisters Power Plant. This drop is enough to generate only 3,000 kW, making it the smallest power plant operated by Trans Alta Utilities. Continuing through a series of canals, the water passes through Goat Pond on its way to Whiteman Dam and the Spray Power Plant. As it drops 274 m (904 ft.) from this dam, through a dual penstock, it generates an additional 102,800 kW. The final power plant in the Spray System is just west of Canmore, where the water drops a final 98 m (323 ft.) to join the Bow River at the Rundle Power Plant, and produces an additional 49,900 kW. The total energy production of the Spray System is 155,700 kW—enough to provide power to a city of 100,000 people. This generating system far surpasses the Kananaskis System's combined capacity of only 33,800 kW.

## Penstock

As you drive past the Whiteman Dam Reservoir, you'll notice a large metal pipe dropping from the dam down into the valley. Built in 1960, this penstock, as it is called, carries water from the reservoir down a drop, or head, of 274 m (904 ft.). This is the largest drop in the Trans Alta system. At the base of this steep cliff, the water enters the Spray Power Plant, and the energy generated during the drop is used to turn the blades of several large turbines. This in turn generates hydroelectric power. This one penstock produces 52,900 kW of energy. Hidden within the mountain face is a second penstock, the original. It opened in 1951 with a capacity of 49,900 kW. The combination of the two generating units allows for the generation of 102,800 kW .

The metal penstock is the result of wartime technology. Prior to World War II, there were few metals strong enough to be used for external penstocks, so they were routinely built into the hillsides. As more durable armaments were developed for battle, these technologies were used for more peaceful pursuits.

# Bow Valley Provincial Park

*Mount Yamnuska*

Along the Trans-Canada Highway, Bow Valley Provincial Park provides a unique combination of aspen parkland and plains, beginning at the base of Mount Yamnuska and extending south along the northern section of Highway 40. It explodes into a yellow green colour each May, as the aspen leaves burst out of their winter buds. The valley seems to breathe a sigh of relief as the colours change from the drab brown of winter to the wonderful greens of summer. Even before the leaves appear, wildflowers like the prairie crocus add their pink flowers to the landscape.

During the final advance of glacial ice, known as the Canmore Advance, the Bow Valley Glacier reached only to present day Bow Valley Provincial Park. To the east, the huge continental ice sheet had also petered out before reaching this ideal location. Numerous landforms in the park area tes-

tify to the terminal position of the ice. As ice retreated, it left behind depositional landforms, and numerous kettle lakes. Kettles form when huge blocks of ice are buried under glacial debris. When the ice later melts, it creates a meltwater pond. This was how some of the park lakes originated.

Today, the facilities in the park include numerous campsites, along with several pleasant interpretive trails. The easy access to the highway makes it a perfect staging area for day trips into the surrounding valleys. After all, the park sits in an ancient travel corridor that

has hosted visitors for more than 10,000 years. A recent expansion to the park now protects the northern section of Highway 40 (along the west side of the highway) as far south as Sundance Lodges Campground.

## World Scout Jamboree

In 1983 Kananaskis Country was "invaded" by a force of 15,000 uniformed troops from 74 countries. Luckily, however, the troops were scouts, participants in the XV World Jamboree held in Bow Valley Provincial Park from July 6–16, 1983. The logistics for this

*Opposite: Trembling aspens*

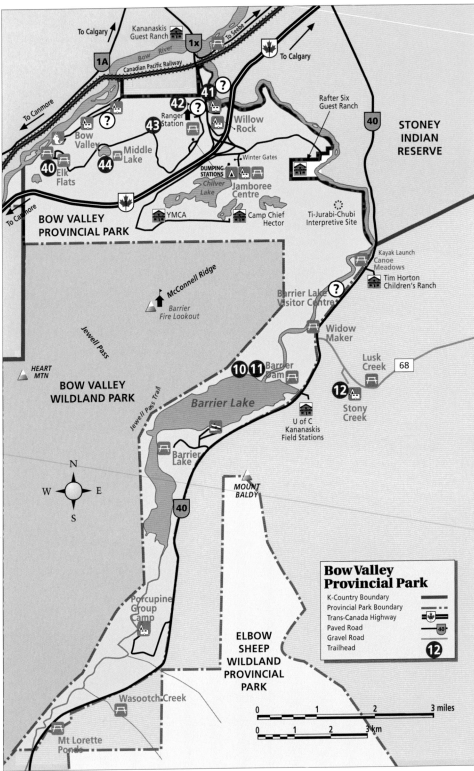

Bow Valley Provincial Park

To Calgary
Kananaskis
Guest Ranch
1x
To Seebe
To Calgary
Bow River
1A
Canadian Pacific Railway
To Canmore
41
42
Ranger
Station
43
Willow
Rock
Bow
Valley
Middle
Lake
44
40
Elk
Flats
DUMPING
STATIONS
Chilver
Lake
Jamboree
Centre
Winter Gates
To Canmore
BOW VALLEY
PROVINCIAL PARK
YMCA
Camp Chief
Hector
Rafter Six
Guest Ranch
40
STONEY
INDIAN
RESERVE
Ti-Jurabi-Chubi
Interpretive Site
Kayak Launch
Canoe
Meadows
Tim Horton
Children's Ranch
McConnell Ridge
Barrier
Fire Lookout
Barrier Lake
Visitor Centre
Widow
Maker
Jewell Pass
HEART
MTN
Lusk
Creek
68
BOW VALLEY
WILDLAND PARK
Jewell Pass Trail
10 11
Barrier
Dam
12
Stony
Creek
Barrier Lake
U of C
Kananaskis
Field Stations
Barrier
Lake
N
W        E
S
MOUNT
BALDY
40
Porcupine
Group
Camp
ELBOW
SHEEP
WILDLAND
PROVINCIAL
PARK
Bow Valley
Provincial Park

K-Country Boundary
Provincial Park Boundary
Trans-Canada Highway
Paved Road
40
Gravel Road
Trailhead
12

Wasootch Creek

Mt Lorette
Ponds

0        1        2        3 miles
0    1    2    3 km

*Mount Lougheed*

## Orchids

**Orchids are very** primitive flowers, yet they are one of the most diverse, both in appearance and in the relationships they have with their pollinators. The yellow lady slipper is one of a large number of orchids found in Kananaskis Country. Other lady's slipper types include the white sparrows-egg orchid and the calypso orchid. These both have a large lip-like lower petal, which makes bees force their way in to collect nectar. This results in their collecting a rather large amount of pollen, which is transferred to the next orchid they land on, fertilizing it.

Another orchid, the northern green bog orchid, has selected an unlikely pollinator—mosquitoes. Male mosquitoes spend their lives collecting nectar. This plant has evolved to take advantage of this so when they come for their nectar, they also pick up some pollen as well. Without mosquitoes, we may not have this orchid. Maybe there is a reason for everything.

Other orchids found in Kananaskis include the blunt-leafed orchid, round-leafed orchid, striped coral root, and spotted coral root.

*Yellow lady slipper*

**129**

event were mind-numbing. Ray Andrews of Kananaskis Country was the manager in charge of the event. He spent more than a year organizing staff and training leaders. The event was deemed a success by none other than Lord Baden Powell, the grandson of the movement's founder. The purpose of the event was to celebrate the diversity of world cultures. A miniature international village featured displays, exhibits, and foods from the countries represented.

The scouts didn't remain on site the whole time, but were provided with trips to the many nearby attractions. Some visited the Columbia Icefields and others headed to the Calgary Stampede. How do you say "yahoo" in Bangladesh? Other scouts went whitewater rafting, hiking, and mountain climbing, not to mention western mainstays like roping, riding, and gold panning.

## Elk

*Stag elk*

**Bow Valley Provincial Park** supports an elk herd of approximately 75 animals. Their tan coats and large antlers are easily identified. Each antler can weigh more than 12 kg (26 lbs.). Elk are grazers, and spend most of the summer munching on the grasses and flowers of the local meadows. Within the park the snow is often shallow due to the powerful Chinook winds. The elk paw through the snow to get at the grasses only a few inches below. In years where the snows are deep, they may resort to chewing the bark of aspen trees. This contributes to the dark bark on the lower part of many such trees.

In the fall, the rut brings a little romance to the park. The stags are in peak condition, and the competition between them can be intense. Their strategies are based on a single male mating with as many cows as he can collect, and keep. The strongest male mates, and when the game is done, often so is he. He limps away, wilted and weak, just before the harsh winter. Needless to say, the reigning male changes regularly.

The calves appear in the spring, and the cows become very protective at this time. Don't approach a cow with a calf, as you may end up with a serious injury—elk are incredibly fast, and very strong.

## Guest Ranches

**Ever since ranching arrived** in the foothills, guest ranches were destined to become a popular vacation option. The concept is simple—invite guests in to see life on a ranch. Offer them the opportunity to ride the range, and provide good food and rustic accommodation. Bow Valley Provincial Park is host to two separate ranches—the Kananaskis Guest Ranch and Rafter Six Ranch Resort.

### Kananaskis Guest Ranch

When John and Isabella Brewster arrived in the Banff area in 1886, the whole nature of the valley changed. The Brewsters opened a dairy, and this humble start led to the building of an empire. During the winter, when business was slow, the family homesteaded beneath the face of Mount Yamnuska, at the site of the present ranch. Two of the sons, Bill and Jim, loved the wilderness and became insatiable explorers. When the Banff Springs Hotel asked them to guide a party of fishermen when they were at the tender ages of 12 and 10, they set in motion the beginnings of the Brewster Mountain Pack Trains Company. The two brothers also started the successful motor coach company that still bears the family name, but it was purchased by Greyhound Canada in 1965, leaving the family to concentrate on their guiding operations.

Over the years the ranch expanded. The main lodge was built in 1922. The1930s were difficult, but Bill's wife Sylvia (better known as "Missy") and her eldest son Claude kept things going. Claude's sons Jack and Bud in turn took over the ranch. Bud added the famous Do-nut tent and the Lyster paddle wheeler seminar room in the 1960s. In 1987, more renovations were needed to keep pace with the times. Today, it is managed by a fifth generation of the Brewster family. With over 100 years of tradition behind them, the Brewster family welcomes you to the Kananaskis Guest Ranch. For more information call (403) 673-3737.

### Rafter Six Ranch Resort

Rafter Six Ranch Resort sits south of the Trans Canada Highway, hidden from sight. As you pull up, past the chipmunk-crossing signs, the ranch suddenly looms into view, and you wonder how you could have missed it. In 1873 Colonel James Walker, a member of the Northwest Mounted Police, opened a sawmill on the site to supply the outpost at Fort Calgary. It was later acquired by a crusty curmudgeon known as Soapy Smith. After Smith died, his young wife Eva married Alvin Guinn, the son of a local rancher. In the 1930s they turned the site into a guest ranch. It grew slowly, but eventually tents were replaced by log cabins. A main lodge was built, which includes the present dining room.

Hollywood discovered the location in the 1950s, and Marilyn Monroe was filmed at the site in "River of No Return." Later movies such as "Grizzly Adams," and "Across the Great Divide," also used the site. In 1994, the comedy "How the West Was Fun," was filmed here.

In 1978 the ranch was taken over by Stan and Gloria Cowley. The lodge was expanded and the tradition continues. For more information, call (403) 673-3622.

# Sibbald Creek Trail

*Mount Baldy from Sibbald Creek Trail*

Just 8 km (4.8 mi.) south of the Trans Canada Highway, the 36-km (21.6-mi.) Sibbald Creek Trail (Highway 68) provides access to a quiet foothills valley with numerous exploration opportunities. Andrew Sibbald settled near Morley in 1875. His son Frank settled along Sibbald Creek 15 years later, and introduced cattle to the area.

The rolling country along this road owes much of its character to the huge glacier that flowed up the Bow Valley to the north. Although this valley seems separate from the Bow Valley, things were quite different at the peak of the ice age. As the Bow Valley Glacier left the mountains and suddenly found itself unrestricted by the valley walls, it began to spread out. This piedmont glacier, as this squat river of ice is known, literally spread right over the surrounding hills and spilled into this valley. Since the ice came from the northwest, features in the valley caused by the moving ice are oriented in that direction. As the ice melted, huge lakes formed in front of the shrinking glaciers. This major advance ended approximately 40,000 years ago. Subsequent advances were more limited in extent, and did not supply enough ice to spill over to the Sibbald area, leaving the valley ice-free. This freedom from ice led to its use as a travel corridor, and the earliest example of Fluted Point projectiles in western Canada were found there. Fastened to the tips of lances, they were a primitive, yet effective, hunting tool.

## Highway 68

Highway 68 follows the route of Sibbald Creek and the Jumpingpound River. From its western entrance to the north of Mount Baldy, it climbs over the small divide between the Stoney Creek and Sibbald Creek drainages. From here it follows Sibbald Creek as it becomes a tributary of the Jumpingpound Creek. Eventually, it abandons the river to head north to its junction with the Trans Canada Highway (Highway 1). It meets Highway 1 just east of the Scott Lake Hill, the second-highest point on the Trans Canada Highway.

As the highway parallels

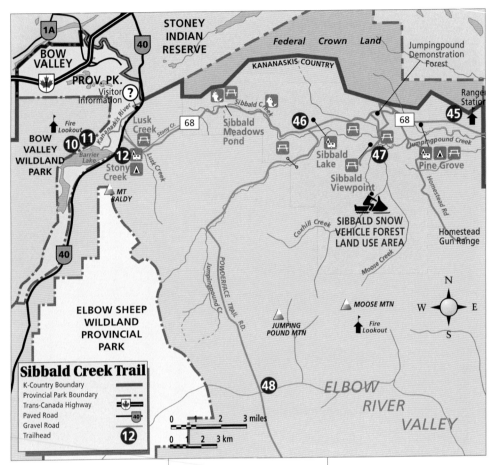

## Sibbald Creek Trail

| Legend | |
|---|---|
| K-Country Boundary | |
| Provincial Park Boundary | |
| Trans-Canada Highway | |
| Paved Road | |
| Gravel Road | |
| Trailhead | |

Map labels: 1A · BOW VALLEY PROV. PK. · Visitor Information · 40 · STONEY INDIAN RESERVE · Federal Crown Land · KANANASKIS COUNTRY · Jumpingpound Demonstration Forest · Kananaskis River · Fire Lookout · BOW VALLEY WILDLAND PARK · 10 · 11 · Barrier Lake · 12 · Stony Creek · Lusk Creek · Stony Cr. · 68 · Sibbald Cr. · Sibbald Meadows Pond · 46 · Sibbald Lake · 47 · 68 · 45 · Ranger Station · Jumpingpound Creek · Pine Grove · Sibbald Viewpoint · Homestead Rd · MT BALDY · Coxhill Creek · SIBBALD SNOW VEHICLE FOREST LAND USE AREA · Homestead Gun Range · Moose Creek · 40 · Jumpingpound Cr. · POWDERFACE TRAIL RD. · JUMPING POUND MTN · MOOSE MTN · Fire Lookout · ELBOW SHEEP WILDLAND PROVINCIAL PARK · 48 · ELBOW RIVER VALLEY · N W E S · 0 1 2 3 miles · 0 1 2 3 km

Sibbald Creek, it passes numerous sloughs and beaver ponds. These sloughs can be quite productive. Having shallow water, they warm up dramatically, and soft, muddy bottoms promote plant growth. Winter kill can be a problem for fish, as winter decomposition of plant material depletes the ponds of oxygen.

The channel of Jumpingpound Creek is considered a "misfit" stream. When it was originally carved, it was fed by incredible amounts of water as the mountain glaciers melted. Once the supply of ice was gone, a small river was left behind in a channel seemingly far too large for it.

## Sibbald Lake

This tiny, shallow lake was formed when a large block of glacial ice was buried beneath a series of outwash deposits as the Bow Valley Glacier melted 40,000 years ago. When a block of ice is buried, it may remain as ice for a lengthy period before melting. As it melts, the material lying on top of it collapses into the hole left behind. This hole fills with the now-released water, and a lake results. Many of the small lakes at mountain fronts were formed in this way. Sibbald Lake is not very deep, only 2.1 m (7 ft.) at its deepest point. Some of its water supply today comes from underground springs, which helps keep the level consistent. Large glacial deposits adjacent to Bateman Creek nearby, reflect the deposit of glacial debris that originally held the pond-forming ice chunk.

The lake is popular with campers, but also with fishermen that like to test their luck in its placid waters. It's regularly stocked with rainbow trout. The day use area also serves as a trailhead for numerous hiking trails in the area, including Deer Ridge,

Eagle Hill, Ole Buck Loop, Sibbald Flat, and Reforestation Trail.

## Sibbald Meadows Pond

This pleasant little pond is rarely without a fishermen or two, with fly rods a-flicking. It looks like it has always been part of the landscape, but it was artificially created in 1982. At that time, the Sibbald Creek floodplain was dredged, and the fill removed. This depression was supplemented with a partial dam to raise the water level even more. It covers 4.8 ha (12 acres) and has a maximum depth of 4.5 m (15 ft.). With the consistent water level created by the dam, the lake sees many families spending time along its shores. Small inflatable boats or family canoes find their way into its calm waters.

## Jumpingpounds

*Bison once ruled the plains*

**For generations,** bison were crucial to the survival of the Plains Indians. Little of the animal was wasted: its meat provided nourishment and its hide kept them warm. The immense herds seemed like they would last forever. Before the introduction of the horse and the gun, a very creative method had to be devised to hunt these potentially dangerous beasts. For most of the prehistory of the plains, the method of choice was the jumpingpound. Since bison are a herd animal, the hunters needed to enlist the assistance of neighbouring family groups, and before long the annual bison hunt became an important social and religious event.

The bison were slowly gathered in areas known as collection basins. Rock cairns and man-made changes to the landscape help trace the route through which the bison were moved. To these early hunters it was critical that every bison die. They believed bison could talk, and if any survived, they would warn the others. That would end the chance of any future hunts on that cliff.

On the final day, dozens of hunters would line the route to the cliff. Some would cover themselves in animal hides and try to look inconspicuous. At the last minute, they would all jump up and whip the herd into a frenzy. The bison stampeded toward the cliff and their poor eyesight never warned them of their impending doom. By the time they saw the chasm, it was too late to stop, and they tumbled over the edge to their death. Jumpingpound Creek has numerous pound sites, though they are further downstream, where the banks are high and steep.

Another site south of Calgary is known as Head-Smashed-In Buffalo Jump. It is the most heavily studied of these hunting sites, and was used consistently for more than 5,000 years.

*The mountains of western Kananaskis rise from the plains*

# Powderface Trail

Winding south from the Sibbald Creek trail, this narrow, 36-km (21.6-mi.) gravel road provides excellent fair-weather access to the Elbow Valley. It climbs gradually to crest a small divide between the Jumpingpound and Canyon Creek drainages. It follows the dividing point between foothill and mountain. The jagged faces of the Fisher Range to the west contrast with the rolling foothills to the east. Along its length the road provides access to numerous trail systems, and is the only vehicle link between the Kananaskis and Elbow Valleys. It is recommended in fair weather only.

The road was built around 1952 to link the valleys of the Elbow and Jumpingpound rivers. During this period, the Eastern Rockies Forest Conservation Board was expanding facilities and improving roads, to ensure access in the case of forest fire. The Forestry Trunk Road was part of this same program of expansion.

## Tom Lusk

**Lusk Creek** and Lusk Pass take their names from one of the most colourful guides in the area. Tom Lusk was a hard-working, hard-drinking man. He was Martin Nordegg's guide when he prospected the coal seams on Mount Allan. Lusk was a tough Texan who arrived in the area around 1895 and quickly established a reputation as a man who could get the job done. He wore a big stetson and a red bandanna. Any who saw Tom in town may have assumed, as did Nordegg, that he was a drunk. However, on the trail he never touched a drop. It was too difficult to justify the weight of all the liquor, and the bottles were too easily broken. But when the season was done, he'd retire to his cabin with several cases of whiskey. He would divide them up for the six winter months and never drink more than his ration. When the Stoneys saw the smoke stop billowing, they would stop in and either re-light his fire, or arrange a funeral.

*Opposite: View from Jumpingpound Ridge*

# Elbow Falls Trail (Hwy. 66)

*Rainy Summit in the Elbow district*

The hamlet of Bragg Creek provides services for the Elbow Valley, as well as the surrounding ranching country. The area has seen many visitors over the years. Long before the white man entered the wilderness, the ancestors of today's native Indians were hunting the shores of the Elbow River. Later, men like David Thompson ushered in the fur trade by living and learning from the Blackfoot nations, as well as their neighbours, the Sarcee, both residing in this area in the early 1800s.

Before long the missionaries made their way westward, setting up the first catholic mission in southern Alberta just north of Bragg Creek. Not far from today's Clem Gardner Bridge, it was called "Our Lady of Peace Mission." A lonely stone cairn marks the spot today. Not far from the mission was a trading post operated by Sam Livingston.

Whiskey traders moved in around 1869 and then the Northwest Mounted Police, the forerunners of today's Royal Canadian Mounted Police. With the stability of police presence, settlers were not far behind.

Bragg Creek takes its name from Albert Warren Bragg. He arrived in 1886 with his younger brother John and attempted to set up a cattle ranch in the area. He was less than successful, and left prior to the turn of the century to look for greener pastures. To his surprise, a survey crew attached his name to the creek, and later a town sprung up around it.

Today, Bragg Creek boasts bustling shopping malls, with visitors flocking in during the weekend and almost as quickly disappearing. It forms a jumping-off point for explorations of the nearby Elbow Valley, and is quickly growing into a popular artisans community with its numerous galleries.

## West Bragg Creek

Few visitors explore the ranching country in the foothills west of Bragg Creek. It supports a growing number of housing developments, as Calgarians continually look to

*Opposite: View west from Nihahi Ridge*

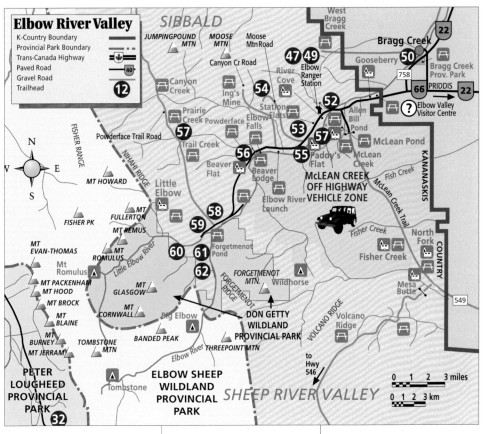

move out of the city. It provides a wonderful opportunity for country living within easy distance of Calgary. Slowly, the old ranches seem to be vanishing as more of these housing developments come on stream.

Not far from the town of Bragg Creek, Wintergreen ski hill provides a nice mix of moderate level skiing close to Calgary. Night skiing also makes this hill quite popular, as there is little in the way of night skiing opportunities farther into the mountains.

Farther west, where the west Bragg Creek road ends just within Kananaskis Country, a network of winter cross-country ski trails double as

summer horseback and mountain-bike trails.

## Ranching

It was not long after the arrival of the first cattle in southern Alberta in 1873 that ranching became a vital industry in the west.

By 1881 the local Indians had settled on reserves, the Mounties had brought stability to the area, and the railroads were moving westward, providing easy access to distant markets. Soon a flood of cattle moved into the area. The government allowed leases of up to 100,000 acres per man, spawning the large ranching operations of the early days. Most, like the

Quorn Ranch, were farther south, along the Sheep River. The Elbow was left to the independents, men like Sam Livingston and Albert Bragg.

During the summer, cattle would range far and wide. Each fall, representatives from area ranches got together for a roundup to bring the cattle in. The days were long, and the work hard, but as one pioneer rancher, Fred Ings, put it: "In looking back how I can see it! Hear it! Live it again! A roundup day! From the first call to roll out in the dawn till we stamped out the last coal of our fire and turned in, a little stiff and no-end weary, to sleep the dreamless sleep of youth."

*Powderface Creek trail summit*

## Highway 66—The Elbow Falls Trail

Travelling Highway 66 today, it's hard to believe the difficulties experienced by early travellers to this remote valley. Meandering west from Bragg Creek towards the Little Elbow Campground, its 100-km/hr (60-mi./hr.) speeds whisk visitors into the valley.

In the past, access was this valley's biggest challenge. With oil and gas wells appearing in the late 1920s, road quality was one of the major limitations to success.

The road was little more than a wagon trail beyond

## Wild Horses

*Wild horses still roam the foothills*

**Between the valleys** of the Elbow and Sheep rivers, numerous bands of wild, or feral, horses roam. Descendants of formerly-domestic stock, their wild spirit can be seen in the fire in their eyes. It's hard to imagine horses as "wild," but the first time you set eyes on a feral band, their proud and wary nature quickly removes any doubts.

These stocky animals resemble a draft horse, with thick joints and heavy build. Their manes blow untamed in the breeze, and the mares are often accompanied by young colts. Although they add a touch of romance to the valley, they can be a real hazard to equestrian users. Wild studs are very aggressive in their attempt to increase their herd, and steal mares in season.

Bert Ostroski, a former Kananaskis employee and range rider, had one of his prize mares stolen by a "wildie." It took him two months to track her down, and after he finally recaptured

her, he was rewarded with the birth of a half-wild filly. Make sure you avoid bringing mares in season into the area.

At certain times in the past, permits were available to capture wild horses. These animals were generally sold to meat-packing plants, but the lucky ones were trained and used as pack animals. The main areas for wild horses include the McLean Creek, Quirk Creek, Mesa Butte, Death Valley, and Muskeg Creek areas.

The numbers are small, but the lucky traveller may get to see them wandering their range.

They are very territorial, with the stud marking his territory with "stud piles." These manure heaps warn other studs to stay clear, unless they wish to challenge the resident stud. Today, the wild horses of Kananaskis have protected status, and are free to roam unmolested.

Bragg Creek. Heavy loads would sink in the mud. Trucks would unload at Bragg Creek and the gear was transferred to wagons for the bumpy ride down the valley. The early wells disappeared, but the road lived on. In the 1950s, a gate was placed across the road near the present ranger station, and visitors were checked in by the local ranger. The rangers used pick and wheelbarrow to keep the road passable.

Upgrading during the 1980s brought a smooth surface to this formerly bumpy highway. As gravel was needed to resurface the road, it was taken from several large gravel pits adjacent to the highway. When the work was completed, the pits were flooded, and Allan Bill, McLean, and Forget-me-not ponds were formed. With the increased speed of traffic came the danger of hitting animals, particularly cattle, on the road. Drive slowly, and enjoy the view.

## Moose Mountain

Over the years Moose Mountain has seen a lot of use. A.W. Bragg first settled along its lower slopes in 1886. Then it was mined for coal at the turn of the century. More recently it has been a fire lookout and a gas well site.

Dr. George Ings, also known for the Ings' Mine along Canyon Creek, was a Calgarian with a keen interest in coal. Beginning in the 1890s, he prospected the Bragg Creek area and discovered a seam of coal at the base of Moose Mountain. Unfortunately, despite a thousand tons of coal being taken out of this deposit, it never made it to market. Lack of proper transportation was the bane of many would-be mines.

Later, as forest fires became a concern, a lookout was built on the rocky summit of Moose Mountain. Completed

## Rangers

**The forest ranger** is an enduring part of the history of the Rocky Mountains. As early as 1889 the Dominion Government began to worry about the impact of random logging on the health of forests. The Forestry Branch was organized, and rangers began to patrol what would later become southern Alberta. There were only two rangers for all of the southern part of this province, but they regulated cutting and kept an eye out for forest fires.

Dick Mackey was the district ranger in the Elbow Valley from 1952–60. As he put it:

"In those days when they wanted to hire a ranger, they wanted either some cowboy or logger or trapper; somebody who could live by himself, go back in the jungle by himself, look after himself, and, if you could read and write, so much the better."

Over the years the duties changed. As cattle moved into the valley, the ranger was placed

*Park Rangers at a formal function*

in charge of the rangeland. As coal mining and oil expansion increased, the forest rangers were kept busy regulating them. For many years the rangers controlled recreational access to the valley.

Until 1942 the rangers were laid off every fall. A seasoned ranger would arrange to be on the edge of his district by first snowfall. It would then take several weeks before he would receive his layoff notice.

The role of the ranger is still evolving. Today, the original duties of the forest ranger has been divided among several agencies. The Alberta Forestry Service still takes care of forest and resource concerns, but the Fish and Wildlife Department protects the area's wildlife, and Recreation and Parks facilitates recreation in the area.

*Entrance to the Canyon Creek Ice Caves*

the pipeline to help satisfy the growing demand for natural gas.

## Canyon Creek

Canyon Creek has played an important part in the valley's history. One of the first wells, drilled by Moose Dome Oils, was drilled along the creek in 1927. Without transportation or pipelines, however, the gas stayed in the ground. What it did accomplish for the area was a road, allowing access to this pleasant valley and opening it up for future development.

Natural gas started the ball rolling and it still plays a vital role along this roadway. Today, Shell operates a compressor station adjacent to the road. Since 1985 the compressor station has piped their gas 28 km (16.8 mi.) to a processing plant at Quirk Creek. Here it is processed to separate the sweet gas from the liquids and to remove the sulphur content. Following processing, the gas follows pipelines to Edmonton, and on to various other markets. From the end of the main road, a gated access road provides Shell with the ability to service some of its well sites.

Adjacent to the Canyon Creek Roads junction with Hwy. 66 is the Elbow River launch, which provides paddlers easy access to the river.

## Ice Caves

Caves are not uncommon in the Rockies. Limestone, one of the predominant rocks of the mountains, is easily dissolved. The Canyon Creek ice caves were discovered in 1905 by Stan Fullerton. They are dark,

around 1929, it worked in conjunction with other lookouts to the south and north. Fires could quickly spread and threaten ranches downstream. Packhorses had to wind their way up a treacherous trail, where a single slip could mean tragedy, to the lookout site. Unlike most lookouts, the Moose Mountain site had its own spring for water.

After a truck road was built up to the summit in 1950, a new lookout was constructed beside the original. From its completion in 1952, until 1958, the old tower served as a source of firewood. Other towers, perched in locations too difficult to access by roads, were abandoned. In 1974, the lookout was again replaced, this time on its original 1929 foundation.

While the Alberta Forest Service struggles to ensure the Moose Mountain lookout station has sufficient propane each season, the tower sits on a "gold mine" of fuel—natural gas. The mountain's twin summits form a perfect geological storage system for gas. The first well, Moose Dome 1, was drilled in 1927, and a second, Moose Dome 2, in 1935. Model Oil drilled a well in 1936, and McCall–Frontenac in 1941. Although these wells are no longer active, the mountain is still providing gas. Shell drilled their first well in 1960, right next to the McCall–Frontenac well. Unfortunately, with no compressor station or pipeline, the gas remained in the ground. Four other wells were drilled over the years, and finally, after a long public consultation process, Shell received approval to further develop the gas wells. In 1985 they opened the Moose Mountain Compressor Station, to which the five wells were attached. The gas from the wells travels by pipeline to Esso's Quirk Creek gas plant, 28 km (17 mi.) south. It is processed there, and then it continues along

*Elbow Falls*

## Whiskey Traders

**In 1869 the** Hudson's Bay Company relinquished its claim on Canada's vast western lands. With their departure the west was left devoid of Government representation. Whiskey traders from the United States flooded north into Canadian territory, to sell "rot-gut" to the Indians in exchange for furs. Lacking the long-term perspective of the Hudson's Bay Company, they had no interest in the well-being of the natives with whom they traded, and in short order, whiskey destroyed many villages.

Jean L'Heureux, a self-appointed missionary, wrote the Dominion Government begging for assistance. In his letter describing a two-year period at one post, he stated:

*"Twelve thousand gallons of liquor were sold to Indi-*

*ans…Without counting the more than six hundred ounces of strychnine distributed to the Indians, more than one hundred and twelve persons have perished in these orgies and horrors."*

Several posts were opened in the Elbow Valley area. The most notorious was operated by Fred Kanouse. He arrived on the banks of the Elbow in 1871 and built a three-room log post. The Indians traded by way of a long tunnel with a trap door. If a customer got out of hand and tried to break in, the trap could be released.

After an argument with one customer, Kanouse was wounded. In retaliation he killed the battle chief, White Eagle. The resulting battle lasted three days. Rein-

forcements arrived on day four, and the fort was saved for the time being.

Kanouse returned for one more season of trading, and described it as "quite successful." That same year, trader Dick Berry set up a post 20 km (12 mi.) upstream from Kanouse, but he was ambushed and killed by one of his customers.

In the fall of 1874, the Northwest Mounted Police arrived on the prairies, and brought an end to the whiskey trade. Crowfoot, the famous Blackfoot Chief, stated: "If the police had not come to this country, where would we all be now? Bad men and whiskey were killing us so fast that very few of us indeed would have been left today. The police have protected us as the feathers of a bird protect it in winter."

damp, and full of ice. In the 1970s, more careful studies were undertaken, revealing 494 m (1,630 ft.) of tunnels. In 1983 four different caverns, located well inside the mountain face, were accessible. In subsequent years, variations in weather caused the entrances to seal with ice, making all but the main cave entrance impassable. Due to the potential dangers of caving, it is not recommended that novices attempt to penetrate beyond the main cavern.

## Elbow Falls

The waters of the Elbow River plunge over a hard outcrop to form one of the highlights along Highway 66. It is the largest waterfall in Kananaskis Country, and one of the most popular stopping points along the valley.

Even at the turn of the century, people travelled long distances to see the falls. One such visitor was Monica Hopkins, who travelled for 2.5 days and reached the falls in 1910. She wrote in a letter: "The Falls are beautiful, not very large or high, but above them the river comes down in rapids, and the background of snow tipped mountains with dark tinges on the sides, and nearer the river the poplars in all the beauty of their autumnal colouring was a perfect picture."

Today, the falls still conjure up the same feelings. In keeping with Kananaskis' mandate to provide access for all users, the falls site was renovated around 1984 to make the trail wheelchair accessible. It also added railings to discourage climbing near the cliff edge. Some silly souls have jumped from the rocks into the deep pool beneath the falls—a very dangerous game. Park rangers have had to install a permanent rescue cable beneath the rock face to facilitate the rescue of some of these swimmers. There are dangerous undercurrents beneath the foam. Please don't go beyond the railings.

## North America's First Hostel

*Raising the tent wall at the first Bragg Creek Hostel*

**Also in** west Bragg Creek was the first Youth Hostel in North America. It was spearheaded by Mary and Catherine Barclay, who tried to sell the idea to just about anyone who crossed their paths. Converts included Ida and Harry White, who rented them the land for their first venture. On July 1, 1933, they set up a 12 ft. x 14 ft. tent, with cupboards made of apple boxes, a grass floor, and a primitive toilet.

In 1936, the hostel was moved to a site donated by Tom Fullerton. The hostel building was later replaced, only to burn down in 1984. That fire marked the end of hostelling in Bragg Creek, but hostels still remain popular elsewhere. The Ribbon Creek Hostel is now Kananaskis Country's sole hostel. To Mary Barclay, hostelling was "A right idea that once seen could never be destroyed!"

## Rainy Summit

The forests within the Bow corridor would burn, if left alone, about every 80 years. In 1981, this site had a 110-ha (275-acre) fire, which was followed by a salvage cut, meaning commercially salvageable timber was removed. To these forests, fire is an essential force, a process of renewal, and is required for life by many fire-adapted species. Some, like the lodgepole pine, rarely reproduce in the absence of fire. Its cones are tightly sealed with a hard wax and generally will not open until the wax is melted by the heat of a fire.

Poplars and aspens send out horizontal roots just below the surface that will, in turn, periodically send up a new shoot. When a fire moves through the stand, the trees are killed, but the root system will often survive. Before you know it, suckers start appearing and a new stand begins.

*Mount Romulus*

For local animals, when the fire burns itself out there's an abundance of exposed seeds. Grouse and squirrels take advantage of these easy pickins', and those they miss quickly sprout in the carbon-rich soils. Soon new trees and shrubs are replacing the blackened stumps, and a whole new generation has begun.

Deer and elk wander the margins and take advantage of a healthy food supply as new growth takes over the burn. Studies show that many shrubs important to grizzlies are more prevalent on burn sites when compared to old growth. The same study found that increasing fire suppression since the 1920s has led to the encroachment of conifers into shrub fields, leaving less food for the bears and, in the long run, fewer bears.

## Cobble Flats

This pleasant day use area, located along the shores of the Elbow River, is a quiet, remote site for a picnic. It lies beneath the slopes of Forget-me-not

## Ings' Mine

*Dr. Ings at one of his claims*

**Dr. George Ings** was a Calgarian who had a keen interest in geology, particularly coal and oil geology. Beginning in the 1890s, he often rode through the foothills looking for potential deposits. His first venture near Bragg Creek was a failure due to a lack of transportation. In 1914 he discovered another coal seam, just as Bragg Creek's first oil well began drilling. He hired Bob Parker to operate the mine, and the coal supplied the Mowbray–Berkley oil well with fuel. The mine site was only accessible during the summer, due to the rugged nature of the road, but despite this, several thousand tons of coal were transported to the Bragg Creek well site.

Mountain, and links up with the Mount Quirk Exploration Road on the other side of the river. In the early 1990s, Shell drilled a well on Mount Quirk. During this time, a bridge provided easy access to this area, but as the well turned out to be a dry hole, the bridge was removed and the access closed.

## Powderface Trail

In the shadow of Nihahi Ridge, Powderface Trail trends northward towards the Sibbald Creek Trail. Captain John Palliser passed this way in 1858 while doing the first surveys of the area. The name of the road and the surrounding ridge honours Tom Powderface, a Stoney Indian who lived in the Bragg Creek area.

Signs indicate that it is not recommended for travel, but in good weather it is a wonderful alternate route, providing access to Sibbald Creek Trail and Highway 40. It is the only alternate to backtracking along Highway 66, and is worth the adventure.

As it winds its way north, Powderface Trail passes beneath the convoluted slopes of Compression Ridge, and Mount Bryant to the west. To the east, the slopes of Powderface and Jumpingpound Ridges, as well as Cox Hill, have a rolling appearance. The route is important, as the road follows the juncture of foothill and mountain. To the west, Nihahi Ridge, named for the Stoney Indian word for "rock," forms the official start of the Front Ranges of the Rocky Mountains.

Because of Kananaskis Country's multiple-use mandate, numerous logging projects have been undertaken along this road. The logging traffic means that it will require some extra caution to traverse this narrow road.

## End of the Line

At the western end of the valley, Highway 66 is blocked by a solid wall of mountains. Suddenly the rolling foothills give way to the jagged peaks of the Rockies. Highway 66 meets Powderface Trail and the road crosses Ford Creek and ends in a campground. Henry Ford (1866–1933) was a rancher in the Priddis area near the turn of the century. For many years this site used his name. The name "Little Elbow" recognizes the water source flowing to the south of the campground.

Although the mountain faces stop traffic today, they did not always do so. In past years 4x4 routes followed the rocky shores of the Little Elbow River, providing easy access to the backcountry. The route continued south to the Sheep Valley and made it possible to drive from one valley to the other. Today, the route is only used as a backcountry trail.

## Sam Livingston

Sam Livingston

Sam Livingston was one of the pivotal settlers of this area. He had a knack for being at the right place at the right time. He arrived in the west during the 1860s, and settled near Fort Edmonton at a small post known as Fort Victoria. He and his wife Jane operated a trading business between Fort Garry (Winnipeg) and Edmonton. As the buffalo herds began to vanish in the early 1870s, the family began to look elsewhere. After all, Sam needed 700 buffalo pelts a year just to cover his costs.

They eventually settled near Our Lady of Peace Mission, along the Elbow River. Here the buffalo were still plentiful. They even used the Livingston's cabin as a scratching post on occasion. During the summer of 1875 the Livingstons witnessed the end of an era. One morning, Sam watched a rider approach from a distance. He knew it was not an Indian by the way he sat in his saddle. It turned out to be one of the first mounted policemen to arrive on the plains. Soon thereafter the Livingstons packed up and moved to Fort Calgary, to become one of that community's first settlers.

# Sheep River Valley

*The Sheep Valley explodes into golden fall colours*

Turner Valley is the primary access point for the Sheep River Valley, and it is known for its pivotal role in the development of the oil industry in Alberta. But long before the rigs arrived, the ranchers took over the plains. Southern Alberta was settled much later than areas farther

north. Among the first large ranches were the O.H. (later the Rio Alta), established in 1879, and the Quorn Ranch, in 1884.

Not far behind the ranchers were prospectors, who moved into the foothills. Harry Denning Sr. opened a coal mine along the shores of the Sheep River in 1888. Today Denning is recognized as Turner Valley's first settler.

In 1887 Sam Howe and John Ware, took an empty whiskey bottle and filled it with oil they discovered in a slough. The site was right where Turner Valley is located today.

By 1891, with the influx of settlers on the rise, the need for timber brought the loggers. Donald Morrison began to run logs down the Sheep River for use in the railway under construction between Calgary and Fort MacLeod.

When Dingman No. 1 well came into production in May of 1914, an oil boom was set off. Over the years hundreds of oil companies have come and gone, but Turner Valley is still producing oil and gas today.

To access the Sheep River Valley, head west on Highway 546.

## Highway 546

Winding through some of the province's premier ranching country, Highway 546 provides a pleasant introduction to the prosperity of the Sheep River valley .

The first road down this valley serviced the Lineham Logging Camp, and passed Harry Denning's coal mine. Cutting trees in the valley as early as 1891, they built the first rough road. Numerous other mines were attempted in the lower part of the valley, and in 1903 Pat Burns opened a coal mine farther up the valley, beyond the limits of the present road. The Burns com-

*Opposite: Gibraltar Mountain*

**149**

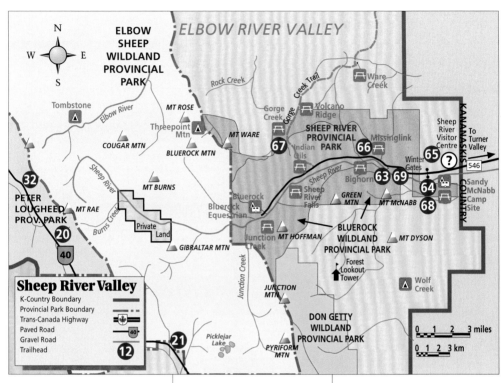

pany had to build and maintain much of the road beyond Gorge Creek themselves. A planned railroad never materialized.

In 1948 surveying for a Forestry Trunk Road south to Coleman began. Four years later, in 1952, it was completed, along with numerous secondary roads designed to provide access to adjacent valleys. One route led from the upper Sheep past the Burns mine site and on to the Elbow Valley. With the naming of Kananaskis Country in 1977, this route was restricted to non-motorized traffic only.

## Sheep River

The Sheep River was a vital waterway long before the first humans moved through its valley. From the early bands of nomadic hunters, to today's bands of nomadic hikers, it has formed the nucleus of this picturesque valley.

Although the river is responsible for carving this valley, glaciers had a dramatic impact on the landscape we see today. Numerous glaciers flowed down the valley of the Sheep, all converging near present-day Bluerock campground. At the height of glaciation the ice would have been approximately 275 m (908 ft.) thick at this point. As the glacier became less constricted by the narrow valleys of the upper Sheep, it spread out into several piedmont glaciers. As these glaciers melted, a 15-km-long (9-mi.-long) lake formed between Turner Valley and the eastern boundary of Kananaskis Country. It was short-lived, and quickly drained away as more ice melted to the east.

By 40,000 years ago the main Sheep River valley was free of ice. Later advances were limited to small cirque glaciers, which flowed only as far as Gorge Creek.

Sharing its Mount Rae headwaters with the Elbow River, the Sheep was the victim of stream "piracy." As the Elbow River extended its headwaters, runoff was diverted from the Sheep. Its many tributaries join the Sheep, and they combine to include more than 1,000 km (600 mi.) of channel.

The upper Sheep River follows the landscape, the mountain ramparts determining the route of its channel. East of Bluerock Campground the river cuts across the landscape to take on an eastern course.

Now its waters are diverted

*Denning's cabins, Sheep Trail*

for irrigation. Its waves see the occasional whitewater paddler, and free-ranging cattle still drink from it. It is as important today as it was when the first natives wandered this remote wilderness.

## Sandy McNabb

Sandy McNabb recreation area is one of the focal points of the trip along the Sheep River. Its day use area provides wonderful picnic sites along the Sheep River. There is also an interpretive trail with panoramic views of the surrounding valley and some slopes covered with wildflowers.

The site has a terraced landscape, with numerous steps gradually dropping towards the river. These were formed as the river cut away at glacial deposits. The campground takes advantage of these levels and allows for a variety of views and camping options.

Sandy McNabb, after whom the site is named, was employed in the oilpatch during the 1920s and 1930s. He worked for companies like Dalhousie Oil and Imperial Oil. Royalite Oil developed an association with Imperial during the depression. McNabb, lucky to have a job during trying times, worked on behalf of Royalite to provide food assistance to the oilfield workers. He would buy cows and, with the help of some of the men, butcher them and deliver the meat to the families he felt needed it most.

An avid camper, McNabb's favourite site was at the mouth of Coal Creek; it became known as "Sandy McNabbs Camp" as early as 1916. As the site became increasingly popular, the Alberta Forest Service began to provide simple facilities. It was upgraded again during the 1950s for camping, and improved road access brought more people into the valley.

McNabb was also an avid sportsman, and helped organize a hunt club in Turner Valley. Early every Thursday, two members would head out and lay a trail, and the hunt would commence in the evening. As more and more fences were put up, it became increasingly difficult to find a good site for hunting.

## Sheep Ranger Station

The Sheep Ranger Station forms the headquarters for information on the Sheep River valley. Located just before you reach the Sandy McNabb recreation area, it can provide you with any information you require to make your time in the valley more enjoyable.

Alberta Recreation and Parks is responsible for, as its name implies, recreation. Over the years, they have taken over some of the early duties of the Alberta Forest Service, allow-

## Oil and Gas

*Turner Valley, 1935*

**Alberta's Oil Boom** began in the Turner Valley area. When Dingman No. 1 blew in during May of 1914, the whole character of this sleepy area changed. During one 24-hour period, more than 500 oil and gas companies were formed in Calgary.

The early drills were cable tool rigs, which worked by lifting and dropping heavy cutting tools repeatedly. This setup was so successful that they became known as "Canadian Rigs."

At the helm of Calgary Petroleum Products Company was A. W. Dingman and W. S. Herron. Their Dingman No. 1 well was the deepest well drilled at that time. The oil was a light naphtha, which was quite pure and could be burned in car engines without refining.

In 1924 another major strike, Royalite No. 4, brought renewed interest to the Turner Valley fields. Subsequent studies showed that most of the wells had been abandoned before being drilled deep enough. Most had struck gas, and further evaluation of drilling data showed that

the gas was merely a cap over the larger oil reserves. Armed with this new knowledge, Royalite No. 4 drilled to a record depth of 1,949 m (6,395 ft.) in 1936, and became the area's first big producer of crude oil. Almost overnight, towns like Turner Valley and Black Diamond doubled in size. Other tiny communities grew from the plains with names like "Little Chicago," and "Little New York." The latter survives today under the more fitting moniker of Longview.

In 1949 oil was discovered in Leduc, near Edmonton, and the importance of Turner Valley quickly declined. Many of the wells are still producing, among them the Quirk Creek gas field developed in the 1960s. Owned by Imperial Oil, the gas is processed at the Quirk Creek Gas Plant and then moved to market through a series of pipelines.

In 1929 the Indian Oils Company started drilling in the Sheep Valley, but abandoned the effort the same year.

**Hell's Half Acre**

The early wells wasted much of

the natural gas produced, as there was little market for it at that time. Pipelines to Calgary had yet to be built, so there was little means to move the gas to market. Some was used to heat the bunkhouses and local homes, and most of the remainder was burned in countless flare stacks around Royalite No. 4. The gas production during the peak, in excess of 5.7 million m$^3$ (200 million ft.$^3$) daily, was enough to have heated New York City. The combination of strong skunk-like odour and flames led to the area's nickname— "Hell's Half Acre."

Goddy McRae of Turner Valley, in the book "In The Light of the Flares", recalled: "The view was breathtaking! A great fairyland was before us…The brightness of the light and the intensity of the heat were frightening at first. Only those, who have stood as we did, understand. We turned northward to see Hell's Half Acre, where a gigantic flame played in the embankment. We stood and marveled at the strange light and the deafening roar."

*A quiet moment at Sheep Falls*

ing that agency to focus on their area of expertise. Over the years, recreational use has increased, and now is the principle use of this valley. The oil wells and coal mines have disappeared, and logging is much more limited in extent. With the increasing demands of hikers, mountain bikers, horseback riders, hunters, and fishermen, the park's staff are kept busy.

This building is relatively new, and provides a new home for the park's staff. Previously, they based their operations within the Bighorn Sheep Sanctuary, as the Alberta Forest Service had done before them. This modern centre places them at the entrance to the valley, creating a higher profile and allowing them to keep better tabs on valley use.

## R.B. Miller Station

With the natural potential for research in the sanctuary, the R.B. Miller Biological Station of the University of Alberta is well situated.

R. B. Miller was a biologist engaged in fish studies in the area during the 1950s. He founded the Alberta Biological Station in 1950. Over the next seven years it expanded in size and scope. When Miller died in 1959 it was renamed the R. B. Miller Biological Station. During the summer months, students do research on everything from ground squirrels to grouse. The findings are regularly published in scientific publications and theses.

At various points in the valley, tall poles topped with chairs are visible. These are used as part of ground squirrel studies. The birds-eye view allows researchers to better study a colony of animals. They are one of the visible signs of ongoing research in the area.

## Gorge Creek Trail Junction

This winding secondary road provides fair-weather adventure as it climbs from the Sheep Trail to access McLean Creek Trail and, in turn, the Elbow Valley.

The road crosses over three divides, creating a roller coaster of steep driving. The first separates Gorge Creek from Ware Creek. It is followed by a second divide to join Link Creek, and concludes with a serious climb towards Threepoint Creek. This final stretch ascends more than 200 m (660 ft.) in just over 4 km (2.4 mi.) before dropping almost as rapidly to join the McLean Creek Trail.

The road was built along an old pack trail to link up with the Elbow Valley during the Eastern Rockies Forest Conservation Board tenure. They undertook extensive improvements to road access to facilitate watershed and forest fire protection. Good roads meant that fire crews could rapidly attack fires in remote areas.

During upgrading of this route during the late 1970s and early 1980s, archaeological studies uncovered a long-lived and diverse culture. Finds showed a steady occupation from approximately 3,500 BC to 1,000 AD. Some of the artifacts included tools, made of both local and distant materials. This indicates that these early residents had extensive trading networks extending to the east and south.

## Coal Mining

This valley contains a lot of coal, but its rugged landscape and limited road access, has repeatedly thwarted attempts to commercially mine the resource.

Early settlers occasionally dug some coal for their own use, but the amount was small. The first commercial coal mine was undertaken by Harry Denning Sr. in 1888. His mine was located west of the town of Turner Valley, and the excellent quality of the coal led to further interest in the reserves. Names like Coal Creek and Indian Oils reflect this early period of exploration.

George Austin, a Dominion Land surveyor, surveyed many of the early coal leases. In 1906, Government reports list two mines in operation–Denning's and another along Coal Creek. Many claims were filed along the creek due to its rich deposits, but few were developed. Coal Creek mine, near present-day Sandy McNabb Campground, was opened in 1915 by Dave Blacklock. To get the coal out, Blacklock waited until winter when a sled could be dragged over the frozen river.

Frank Swanson opened the Windy Point Coal Mine about 1918. Slightly west of the present day Ranger Station, the coal was of poor quality, almost as soft as peat, and provided little heat. Despite this, the site was worked again between 1920 and 1931.

## Ranching's Golden Era

**Cattle arrived in** southern Alberta in 1872, and it wasn't long before the Sheep River valley became important to the fledgling cattle industry.

There were several factors that slowed settlement in southern Alberta. The Blackfoot Indians discouraged incursions into their territory, and few settlers took the risk. With the signing of Treaty Number 7 in 1877, the Blackfoot, along with the Stoney and Sarcee Indians, were assigned to reserves. The coming of the Northwest Mounted Police added stability to the west, and finally, the arrival of the railroad in the early 1880s provided a feasible transportation link with lucrative eastern markets.

The first ranches were huge, some as large as 40,000 ha (100,000 acres). In 1881 the government introduced a land lease policy that allowed 21-year leases and a maximum of 40,000 ha. The cost was a tiny one cent per acre. Before long,

*Rolling ranchland along Highway 546*

wealthy investors opened ranches like the Quorn and the O. H. (later the Rio Alta). The growth was rapid. In 1880 there were only five ranchers with herds outside the Fort MacLeod market. By 1882 there were as many as 75 such operations.

Most of these ranches were British owned; though the image is of the American-style cowboy, the true picture also included polo, horse racing, cricket, and tennis.

The large ranches tried to limit the influx of smaller operations. The Quorn in particular often used force. When Harry Denning opened his coal mine along the Sheep River, the

The Indian Oils Company operated a mine from 1929–31. It was situated near the present Indian Oils day use area. The site was reopened in 1940, and the tunnel mined until 1945. Then a strip mine opened on the site, which was worked until 1951.

The only mine with any staying power was the Burns Mine. Registered in 1903, the company acquired mining rights to 85 quarter-sections along the upper Sheep River Valley. The mine site remained in private hands, even after the Forest Reserves Act of 1906 and 1911 restricted private ownership within the reserves. It still remains as the only private land in the valley.

Prospector Julius Rickert discovered coal along the upper Sheep River at the turn of the century. He managed to interest Pat Burns in the site, and was assigned a one-twentieth interest in the holdings. The mine was doomed from the start. Although three mines were opened, one strip mine and two tunnel mines, transportation remained the major difficulty. The coal had to be taken out along a rough road. The Burns Company built and maintained the road beyond Gorge Creek, while the Forestry Department kept the rough cart track passable to the east of the creek. For years, Burns pushed to have a railway built to the minesite, and in 1918, the Calgary and Southern Railway was incorporated to do just that. Although much of the right-of-way was cleared over the years, not a single track was ever laid. The fortunes of coal were falling and the oil industry was beginning to boom. The mine ceased operation in 1923, but in 1944, Allied Industrial Ltd. tried to reopen the site. In 1948 another attempt

Quorn sent John Ware to warn him to either move on or risk being burned out. Denning informed Ware that he could also play with fire, and was subsequently left alone. Another family, led by Agrippa and Walter Vine, was burned out.

By the mid-1880s, the government had developed new policies designed to quickly settle the west. This created difficulties for the large operations. The west was parceled into numbered sections of land, all open to purchase. Fences began to appear all over the area, restricting the cattle of the large operations. The golden age of ranching lasted less than 20 years, and was followed by the age of settlement.

In the Sheep River Valley, although there were few settlers living in the reserve area, the cattle roamed freely. One settler, Harry Holness, homesteaded in the location of the Old Sheep Ranger Station, located within the present Sheep Sanctuary. In 1911, when the Bow/Crow Forest Reserve was established, he was evicted, and moved his holdings to Calgary.

## Death Valley

The first ranchers descending upon the west were amazed at the wonderful Chinook winds that blew from the mountains. The winds always kept enough forage exposed for the wintering herds. The thought of putting up hay in preparation for winter was considered a waste of time and money. They could always depend on the Chinooks.

After the hard winter of 1886-87, some ranchers began to question this decision, but it was the winter of 1906-07, "the year of the blue snows," that really changed their minds. That winter, several hundred horses and cows were trapped in a small box canyon in the Sheep Valley. In the spring, the winds carried the smell of rotting flesh, and to this day that valley is known as "Death Valley." That very spring the ranches started putting up hay, and they've been doing it ever since.

## John Ware

John Ware was one of Alberta's most famous black cowboys. Born into slavery in South Carolina, he headed to Texas after the Civil War to become a cattle hand. He made his way to Alberta in 1882, helping Tom Lynch drive cattle north. He later worked for the Quorn Ranch before filing his own homestead claim in 1885, at the junction of present day Threepoint and Ware creeks. His "9999" brand became famous. He left in 1902 and moved to the Red Deer River where, only two years later, he died when his horse fell on him. Canada lost its most celebrated early black rancher the same year Alberta became a province. In 1970 a memorial was erected on the site of his original homestead.

*Dysan Falls*

was made by eastern promoters. Neither was able to create a viable enterprise. Finally, in the early 1960s the mine was sealed for the last time.

When Kananaskis Country was named, mining was prohibited within its boundaries.

## Sheep Falls

From the Indian Oils day use area, a short walk takes the visitor to Sheep Falls. The river and falls were known to the early native travellers of this valley as the "itou-kai-you." This name was used on David Thompson's first map of the area, and was later translated to "Sheep."

The falls have also been known as Shepherd Falls. Several documents relating to the Indian Oils coal mine refer to it by this name. The origin is unknown.

The falls are not large, but the water tumbles over the rock outcrop with a low rumble. It is created by a resistant layer of rock overlying softer shales. The shales are easily eroded, whereas the harder rock (sandstone or limestone) remains. As the soft rocks beneath the falls are removed, an overhang of hard rocks is created. In time, the weight of the water snaps off the overhang, and the falls move slightly upstream.

## Logging

Like most of the Kananaskis, the Sheep River valley has been extensively logged. Settlers arrived on the scene and the valley quickly fell under the axe. In the late 1880s, the Lineham Lumber Company began cutting along the Sheep and Highwood rivers. Crews cut during the winter months and the logs were floated down the river during the spring flood.

By 1912 most of the valley's marketable timber had been cut. Large fires over the years took care of much of the remaining timber. Salvage cutting was the name of the game for much of the 20th century. The Bluerock Creek area was logged in 1947 by Napp Lefavre, but he was allowed to remove green timber as well as burned wood. Anything less than 25 cm (10 in.) in diameter had to be left untouched.

About the same time, the Price Logging Camp operated along March Creek. Near the camp, a falls on Dyson Creek found a unique use. The foreman apparently used the falls as a walk-in "cooler" by storing fresh meat in a small cave hidden behind the waterfall.

## Bluerock

The western extent of Highway 546 is marked by Bluerock Campground. However, prior to Kananaskis Country's official designation, four-wheel-drive vehicles regularly continued all the way to the Elbow Valley. The campground takes its name from Bluerock Mountain, and has facilities for equestrian as well as traditional users.

## Sheep Sanctuary

**The Sheep River Wildlife Sanctuary** was first established in 1973 to protect critical bighorn sheep winter range. This is increasingly essential, especially with improved access to the valley over the past few years. This, coupled with hunting pressures adjacent to the sanctuary and numerous grazing allotments overlapping its boundaries, is putting the squeeze on the area's sheep population. In 2001, the Alberta Government upgraded the status of the sanctuary by establishing Sheep River Provincial Park. The area surrounding the sanctuary was also upgraded to park status with the establishment of Bluerock Provincial Park and Don Getty Provinical Park.

Bighorn sheep are an animal unique to high places. Female sheep are often mistaken for mountain goats, due to their short goat-like horns. However, goats are snow-white in colour and have black horns. The females, or ewes, spend the summer at low elevations with the lambs, while the rams prefer to stay in bachelor herds higher up the mountains. In late fall they congregate for the rut on the wide flats near the research centre. The sound of two rams butting heads echoes like a gunshot, and carries for miles on the wind. The successful male wins the right to mate with the harem. The rut leaves him in a weakened condition just before the long winter. This can have fatal consequences if sufficient reserves to survive this difficult season are lacking.

The diet of bighorn sheep includes grasses, flowers, and other foliage. During winter, they climb towards high ridges, where ever-present winds keep the grasses exposed. Occasionally they become part of the diet of predators, primarily cougars and wolves.

With the large resident sheep population, the sanctuary is an ideal place for research. Studies focus on diseases (lungworm), die-offs, grazing conflicts, and overpopulation. As part of the study, the sheep are ear-tagged, and some are radio-collared.

The sanctuary has also been the site of a number of reintroduction programs. Although the Sheep District of Kananaskis includes parts of four different registered traplines, fishers were trapped in northern Alberta and transplanted to the Sanctuary. During the same period, peregrine falcons were also reintroduced. Neither program was successful, and both animals are rare within the valley.

The Sheep River valley was also the home of a cougar study. The study took place in the early 1980s and dogs were used to track cougars, which were in turn tranquilized and radio-collared. Over a four-year period 28 different cougars were collared. As of 1985, estimates suggested that approximately six to eight females and two to three males were in the area.

*Bighorn Sheep*

The junction of Bluerock Creek and the Sheep River marks the official start of the Front Ranges of the Rocky Mountains. To the west, the sheer face of Gibraltar Mountain is a tribute to the extensive glaciers that scoured it.

## Forest Fires

Fires are a natural part of the mountain ecosystem. During this century numerous fires made their way down the Sheep Valley. In 1910 most of the valley was charred by a huge fire. The summer had been hot and dry, with less than 1 cm (0.4 in.) of rain. A crew working for the Lineham Logging Company lost control of their campfire while working on the other side of the Misty Range, and the flames quickly jumped over the divide and spilled down the Sheep Valley.

In 1919 a fire was started by workers clearing the right-of-way for the Burns Coal Mine. It burned out the Indian Oils mine, luckily defunct at the time, and continued down the length of the valley. Because of the large number of fires that year, cattle had been moved out of the reserve as a precautionary measure.

The years 1929, 1936, and 1940 saw more fires. Fred Nash was District Ranger during that period, and he worked relentlessly to preserve his forests. One reporter described Nash's dedication: "He came dashing up on horseback, his face black with smoke and grime and his horse played out. He dashed into the corral, unsaddled, threw his saddle on a fresh Mount and galloped off—back

*Sheep River*

to the fire line."

Despite the dangers, wages were kept low during the depression to discourage arson. Fire fighters were paid 15 cents per hour for long days and dangerous work.

The last fire of note burned 26 ha (65 acres) around Bluerock Creek in 1964. It was contained quickly by fire crews flown in by helicopter. The modern age had arrived, and fire roads built only 20 years earlier were suddenly obsolete. The Alberta Forest Service had made the final transition from horses to helicopters.

*Opposite: Three Point Gorge*

# Hikes of Canmore & Kananaskis

*Hikers on bridge over Galatea Creek*

T he trails surrounding Canmore and the adjacent Kananaskis Country offer some of the premier viewpoints in the Canadian Rockies. Take short walk to Grassi Lakes and view fossilized coral reefs and prehistoric rock paintings. Climb the Centennial Ridge Trail and stand

atop the highest hiking trail in the Canadian Rockies. Wander through golden stands of alpine larch on Burstall Pass, or climb the official start of the Front Ranges on Nihahi Ridge. It doesn't matter if you are an athlete or a novice hiker; there are trails for every fitness level.

Kananaskis Country's trails cover thousands of kilometres of landscape stretching from the rolling foothills to the rugged Front Ranges of the Rocky Mountains. Kananaskis is also less famous than neighbouring Banff National Park, leaving many of the trails quiet and serene. Absent are the

lines of hikers that are so common on many of Banff's trails. Keep this quiet character in mind as you head out, you may not meet other hikers along the trail. You need to be fully prepared for variable weather and the possibility that other hikers may not be available to assist you should something go wrong. Be sure to register at one of the park information centres, or at the very least tell a family member where you are hiking and when you expect to return.

Each of the trails in this section begins with clear information on finding the trail-

head and a breakdown of the route information. There are also descriptive icons used to indicate the highlights of the trail. Use these as a quick guide to find trails that are especially scenic, great for flowers or fall colours, perfect for the family, or that allow bikes or horses.

## Trail Closures

As more and more visitors begin to head into the wilderness of Kananaskis Country, it has become more important for Kananaskis to work toward reducing the potential for negative interactions between hu-

*Ribbon Lake reflection*

## Ten Tips for Safe and Ethical Hiking

**As you hike the trails of Kananaskis Country, please show respect by following these recommendations:**

1. Before you head out, register at a park information centre or make sure your family knows your route and estimated return time.
2. Keep dogs on leashes.
3. Avoid picking plants or flowers.
4. Keep a safe distance from wildlife to avoid danger to you AND the animal.
5. Be sure to pack out all your garbage.
6. Keep a close eye on the weather and be ready to retreat if a storm approaches.
7. Always carry a day pack with first-aid kit and extra clothing.
8. Pack a lunch and carry plenty of water. Don't forget that trailside water sources will need to be boiled for at least 30 minutes, or treated with a water filter or purification tablets. Be sure these items are capable of filtering out Giardia lamblia cysts.
9. Always carry a good map and a compass (and make sure you know how to use them). A GPS sensor is another great addition.
10. Follow proper backcountry hygiene. Move at least 50 metres from any water source before defecating, washing or cleaning dishes. Bury the solids and carry out the paper.

*Buffalo berries*

## Legend for Trail Maps

| | | | |
|---|---|---|---|
| A | Campground | — | River |
| 🎿 | Cross Country Skiing | ◯ | Lake |
| 🏕 | Day Use Area | ◯ | Glacier |
| ⛷ | Downhill Skiing | ●➊ | Featured Trail |
| 🏌 | Golf Course | ------ | Adjoining Trail |
| Ⓗ | Historical Sight | ▨ | Town |
| ⑦ | Information Centre | | **Elevation** |
| △ | Mountain Peak | ▨ | Up to 1500 m |
| Ⓟ | Parking | ▨ | 1500-1750 m |
| ⒧Ⓐ | Road Sign | ▨ | 1750-2000 m |
| — | Minor Road | ▨ | 2000-2250 m |
| — | Highway | ▨ | 2250-2500 m |
| ⬥ | Trans-Canada Highway | | 2500 m + |
| +++ | Railway | | |

## Kananaskis Country Backcountry Campgrounds

| Area | Campground | # of sites | Horses |
|---|---|---|---|
| **Bow Valley** | Quaite Valley | 20 | |
| **Kananaskis Valley** | Jewell Bay Equestrian | 9 | 🐎 |
| | Ribbon Falls | 11 | |
| | Ribbon Lake | 20 | |
| | Lillian Lake | 18 | |
| **Peter Lougheed** | Elbow Lake | 15 | |
| | Point | 20 | |
| | Forks | 15 | |
| | Three Isle Lake | 16 | |
| | Turbine Canyon | 12 | |
| | Aster Lake | 5 | |
| **Sibbald** | Lusk Pass Equestrian | 20 | 🐎 |
| **Elbow Valley** | Big Elbow | 6 | 🐎 |
| | Mount Romulus | 14 | 🐎 |
| | Tombstone | 11 | 🐎 |
| **Sheep Valley** | Three Point | 6 | 🐎 |
| | Wildhorse | 5 | 🐎 |
| | Wolf Creek | 5 | 🐎 |

mans and wildlife. August in particular is a critical month for black and grizzly bears along the eastern slopes. This is the time of year that the buffalo berries ripen. These berries represent one of the most critical food sources for our local bear population. During this limited berry season, an adult grizzly can eat upwards of 200,000 buffalo berries per day. In fact, many grizzly bears actually continue to lose weight throughout the summer until this single food ripens.

Buffalo berries grow best along valley bottoms, along the margin of open area and forest. This also describes many of our trail systems, and park managers need to monitor the berries and the bears to reduce the chances of hikers and mountain bikers running into bears. Trail closures are a critical management tool designed to allow the bears to feed safely during this short window, while at the same time reducing negative animal human interactions. Please respect trail closures and if you do see a bear, cougar or wolf, please take the time to report your sighting to park officials. We can all play a role in protecting trail users as well as our wildlife.

# 1. Benchlands Trail System

Map pg 165  👥 📷 🌿 🍃 🐎 🚲

## Trailhead

In Canmore, follow Benchlands Trail to the junction with Elk Run Boulevard. Turn right at this junction and the Cougar Creek Trailhead Parking lot is immediately on your left. Park here.

## Route

| Route | Elevation | | Distance | |
|---|---|---|---|---|
| | metres | feet | km | mi. |
| Trailhead | 1370 | 4,494 | 0.0 | 0.0 |
| Junction with Lady Macdonald Trail | 1420 | 4,658 | 1.0 | 0.6 |
| Benchlands Trail Junction | 1440 | 4,723 | 1.2 | 0.8 |
| High Point of Route | 1610 | 5,281 | 3.0 | 1.9 |
| Join Lower Bench | 1365 | 4,477 | 6.2 | 3.9 |
| Four Points Sheraton Hotel | 1355 | 4,444 | 7.5 | 4.7 |
| Back to Trailhead | 1370 | 4,494 | 9.0 | 5.6 |

This fabulous labyrinth of trails has become one of Canmore's most popular hiking and mountain biking destinations. The trails are located on several parallel benches along the lower slopes of Mount Lady Macdonald. The views are spectacular, as the exposed benches reveal the entire Bow Valley at your feet. To the south, Mount Rundle, Ha Ling Peak and the Three Sisters dominate the skyline, while the views to the west stretch all the way to Cascade Mountain in Banff National Park. To the east, you have unobstructed views all the way to Pigeon Mountain and Mount Allan.

The Benchlands trail system is a network rather than a single trail, and most trail users explore the network a section or two at a time. This description follows the upper bench for several kilometres before dropping down onto the lower bench to make a 9 km (5.6 mi.) loop.

From the Cougar Creek Trailhead, follow the wide path as it leaves the parking lot. Stay along the creek bed for almost 1 km (0.6 km) where a rough rock cairn marks a fork in the trail. Head left, and almost immediately begin a sharp ascent straight up the side of the hillside. Mountain bikers will push, and hikers will puff their

way up this steep slope which provides access to both the Benchlands Trail network as well as Mount Lady Macdonald. As you climb this steep slope, turn left at the third rough junction after 0.2 km (0.12 mi.) of steep climbing. Take this narrow single-track and begin winding towards the open benchland, leaving the Lady Macdonald Trail behind.

Once you leave the creek behind, the trail moderates and cyclists will be able to ride again. Stay right at an informal junction at kilometre 1.4 (0.9 mi.). Soon, the trail begins to traverse the base of Mount Lady Macdonald with a high slope up to your right. By kilometre 2 (1.3 mi.), the views begin to open up, and the valley is spread out below you. The trail eventually makes a hard right to circumnavigate a runoff channel that drops towards the Silvertip Golf Course below you. As you reach the far side of this channel, you can make a nice loop by following a narrow trail forking left and dropping straight down the fall-line. If you want some more elevation, stay on the high line and you can follow this trail all the way to the community of Harvie Heights. For a shorter roller coaster route, turn left here and drop down towards the golf course.

The sharp drop is short-lived, and bottoms out at a T-junction at kilometre 3.8 (2.4 mi.). Turn right and wind through an open Douglas fir, spruce and lodgepole pine forest atop a carpet of pine needles. Cyclists will enjoy the technical rolling terrain that drops quite steadily towards the lower bench. Stay straight at a junction at kilometre 5.7 (3.6 mi.) and climb a short hill and emerge onto the lower bench. As you wander along this lower bench, the Trans-Canada Highway is visible below you to your right, while one of the holes of the Silvertip Golf Course is partially hidden through the trees to your left. Enjoy these final views, as they end all too quickly at the top of a steep drop down to the Four Points Sheraton Hotel. Descend this steep embankment and meet the Silvertip Drive at 7.5 km (4.7 mi.). You can follow Benchlands Trail (road) if you wish to make a loop back to the Cougar Creek Trailhead. This will add an additional 1.5 km (0.9 mi.) to the trail.

*Mountain biking is popular on Benchlands trail*

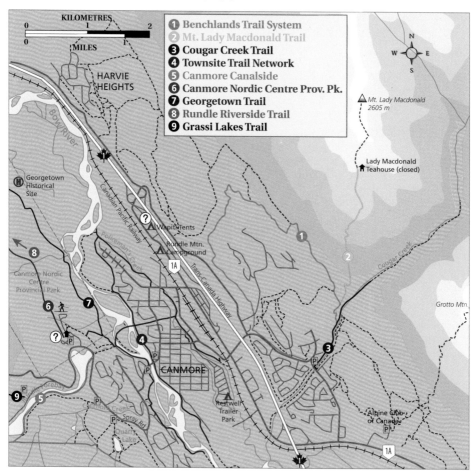

KILOMETRES

MILES

HARVIE HEIGHTS

❶ Benchlands Trail System
❷ Mt. Lady Macdonald Trail
❸ Cougar Creek Trail
❹ Townsite Trail Network
❺ Canmore Canalside
❻ Canmore Nordic Centre Prov. Pk.
❼ Georgetown Trail
❽ Rundle Riverside Trail
❾ Grassi Lakes Trail

N
W    E
S

△ Mt. Lady Macdonald
2605 m

Lady Macdonald
Teahouse (closed)

Bow River

Georgetown
Historical
Site

Canadian Pacific Railway

Policeman's Creek

Wapiti Tents

Rundle Mtn.
Campground

1A

Trans-Canada Highway

Cougar Creek

Canmore Nordic
Centre
Provincial Park

Grotto Mtn

❻

❼

P

❹

P

CANMORE

❽

❸

P

Forbes

❾

❺

Restwell
Trailer
Park

Alpine Club
of Canada
P

Cougar Creek

Spray Rd

Quarry
Lake

1A

# 2. Mount Lady Macdonald Trail

Map pg 165 📷 🌱 🍃

## Trailhead

In Canmore, follow Benchlands Trail to the junction with Elk Run Boulevard. Turn right at this junction and the Cougar Creek Trailhead Parking lot is immediately on your left. Park here.

## Route

| Route | Elevation | | Distance | |
|---|---|---|---|---|
| | metres | feet | km | mi. |
| Trailhead | 1370 | 4,494 | 0.0 | 0.0 |
| Junction with Lady Macdonald Trail | 1420 | 4,658 | 1.0 | 0.6 |
| Benchlands Trail Junction | 1440 | 4,723 | 1.2 | 0.8 |
| End of Formal Trail | 2260 | 7,413 | 3.5 | 2.2 |

The Lady Mac Trail (as this route is often referred by locals) represents one of the first mountain ascents for many Canmore residents. It is a steep, sharp ascent towards the site of a helicopter landing pad on the upper slopes of the mountain. The higher you climb, the more the views open up. To the south, all the peaks of the Bow Valley lie at your feet. The trail is not signed, but is easily followed for its entire route. This is not to say that the trail is easy. This is a mountain summit you are attempting, and the climb gains approximately 890 m (2,919 ft) over just 3.5 km (2.1 mi).

Beginning at the Cougar Creek Trailhead, Lady Macdonald Trail forks to the left at the 1.0 km (0.6 mi) point. The steep climbing begins immediately and after climbing 0.2 km (0.12 mi), the Benchlands Trail Network forks off to the left. The main trail is now reserved for those intrepid souls bent on climbing towards this wind swept summit.

Take a break at a rustic bench at 1.3 km (0.8 mi) before continuing the sharp climb. After winding to the left to leave the valley of Cougar Creek behind, the trail makes a sharp right switchback at 1.6 km (1.0 mi) to begin heading back towards the Cougar Creek valley. This is also the point at which novices will begin to feel the exposure. As the trail re-approaches the Cougar Creek canyon, it winds to the left and continues climbing. Soon, the trail leaves Cougar Creek behind. The exposure gradually increases, but even those that turn around will be well rewarded by the views up to this point. The higher you climb, the more the valley opens up below you.

By the half way point, the climbing gets very steep and increasingly intimidating. It climbs exposed scree slopes with steep downhill drops. The trail winds to the right at approximately 3.0 km (1.8 mi), and soon makes a left to head towards the summit ridge. After a tricky rocky section (bypassable on the right), you ascend the final ridge towards the helipad. For most hikers, this will be sufficient. Beyond the helipad, it becomes a serious scramble and should only be attempted by experienced mountaineers.

# 3. Cougar Creek Trail

Map pg 165 📷 🍃

## Trailhead

In Canmore, follow Benchlands Trail to the junction with Elk Run Boulevard. Turn right at this junction and the Cougar Creek Trailhead Parking lot is immediately on your left. Park here.

## Route

| Route | Elevation | | Distance | |
|---|---|---|---|---|
| | metres | feet | km | mi. |
| Trailhead | 1530 | 5,018 | 0.0 | 0.0 |
| Lady Macdonald Junction | 1420 | 4,658 | 1.0 | 0.6 |
| Trail deteriorates | 1560 | 5,117 | 3.0 | 1.9 |

Cougar Creek Trail is one of Canmore's most popular wandering trails. The trail follows the gravelly bed of Cougar Creek ascends the valley between Mount Lady Macdonald and Grotto Mountain. This trail begins as a wide paved path, but quickly deteriorates into a winding meander that includes innumerable creek crossings. The trail is rocky, and may require you to get wet feet as you pick your way upstream. While the parking lot may be busy, the

*Views from Mt. Lady Macdonald*

*Ha Ling Peak above the Bow River*

vast majority of trailhead users are either heading up to the Benchlands trail network or making the steep ascent towards the site of the helicopter pad on Mount Lady Macdonald. Cougar Creek takes its name from a time when large carnivores were not welcome. During the early days of Banff National Park, Canmore and Cougar Creek were included within the parks boundaries. The official policy was to kill all predators, and Predator Control Officer Ike Mills killed 18 cougars in this valley. Thankfully, such policies have long since been abandoned.

From the trailhead, the wide trail quickly narrows to become a single-track hugging the left bank of the creek. Across Cougar Creek, numerous large luxury homes are visible. After 1 km (0.6 mi.), the trail leading to the Benchlands and Lady Macdonald leaves on the left, and the main Cougar Creek trail continues to follow the streambed. As you cross the creek time and again, you may pass climbers heading towards the popular climbing faces located up this valley. As you follow the stream, the sheer face of Grotto Mountain rises to the east and the more gradual ridge of Mount Lady Macdonald is visible to the west.

By the 2 km (1.9 mi.) point, the trail has deteriorated into a full-on bushwhack with numerous options for exploration available to more adventurous hikers.

# 4. Townsite Trail Network

Map pg 165

## Trailhead

The town network has many access points. The best way to use this trail system is to use the town map on the preceding pages. This trail system is clearly marked on the Canmore map.

## The Trails

Within the townsite itself, there is a great network of wide trails that make for a pleasant day's outing. They join many of the local roads and housing subdivisions and are marked on the map on the following page. The gradients are minimal and they are always busy with walkers, cyclists and joggers. While they do not need full descriptions like other hiking trails, no visit to Canmore would be complete without spending some time exploring this pleasant network.

*Mt. Rundle rises above Canmore Nordic Centre Provincial Park*

# 5. Canmore Canalside

Map pg 165 🚻 📷 🌿 🍃 🚲

## Trailhead

There are two alternate trailheads. The first, and most popular, is along the road to the Canmore Nordic Centre. As you approach the Nordic Centre, you will notice a gated access on the left side of the canal. An alternate access is in the Peaks of Grassi subdivision. To reach this trailhead, follow the Old Haulage Road to its junction with Peaks Drive. Turn right onto Peaks Drive and park near the powerlines. The trail follows the powerlines west.

## Route

| Route | Elevation | | Distance | |
|---|---|---|---|---|
| | metres | feet | km | mi. |
| Trailhead at Spillway Dam at South end of Spillway | 1400 | 4,592 | 0.0 | 0.0 |
| | 1400 | 4,592 | 2.0 | 1.2 |
| Peaks Drive | 1380 | 4,526 | 4.6 | 2.9 |

This picturesque walk is very popular with locals out for a summer stroll. The trail is level and wide, offering panoramic views in all directions. To the south, the sheer face of Ha Ling Peak dominates, while to the north, the many peaks of the Fairholme Range are reflected in the calm waters of the canal (also known as the Rundle Forebay). The canal is part of the Spray Lakes hydroelectric system, and the sheer drop from the Spray Lakes Reservoir provides enough electricity for 100,000 people. Rolling along the spillway, the mountain vistas dominate, but once you leave the spillway behind, the powerline trail rolls east, and in late June is lined with yellow lady's-slipper orchids.

The powerline section of the trail is more rolling than the canal, and winds past Canmore's local swimming hole. The Quarry, as it is known, is the perfect place to relax after a long walk or ride. The trail ends at the intersection with the powerline trail and Peaks Drive.

# 6. Canmore Nordic Centre Provincial Park

Map pg 169 🚻 🚲

## Trailhead

To access Canmore Nordic Centre Provincial Park, proceed up the Smith-Dorien/Spray Road, following the road signs from the Town of Canmore.

## The Trail Network

Built for the 1988 Winter Olympics, Canmore Nordic Centre Provincial Park has evolved into

*Mountain bikers at the Nordic Centre*

a four-season outdoor recreational resort. The vast network of cross-country ski trails has been expanded to become a world-class Nordic skiing, mountain biking, and hiking facility. Since hosting the Olympics, the network has also hosted World Cup cross-country skiing and mountain bike races. Other events include the annual Canada Cup Mountain Bike Race, the Alberta International Sled Dog Classic and numerous other events.

Of the many trails that comprise the network, park managers have developed a system of colour-coded signs to help trail users navigate the labyrinthine network. Hikers and mountain bikers can also use all of the more popular winter routes. In particular, the Georgetown Trail, Banff Trail and the Recreational 5 km, 10 km and 15 km loops are popular winter and summer routes. The major routes are signed using coloured arrows. As an example, the yellow arrows mark the Recreational 10 km Loop.

Summer users have dozens of other trail options in addition to the signed winter network. Hidden amidst the wide winter trails are many unsigned narrow single-track routes. These trails require some exploring and a good map to learn their secrets. The upper single-track network climbs from the stadium and leaves the formal network behind near junctions 78 and 79. These single-tracks follow the World Cup route through the Killer B's, Ziggy's, The Oven, Nectar Noodle and the Albertan. These unmarked trails can be difficult to find, so be sure to bring along a copy of the Canmore Alberta

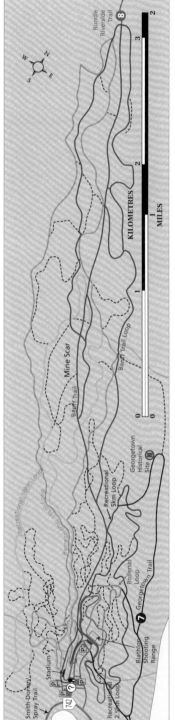

*Trail map for Canmore Nordic Centre Provincial Park*

Recreation Map, which is available at most local stores.

One of the best things about the Nordic Centre is that the trails allow for endless variation. You never need to follow the same route twice, but rather you can vary your experience based upon your interests.

# 7. Georgetown Trail

Map pg 169  🚻 📷 🚲

## Trailhead

To access Canmore Nordic Centre Provincial Park, proceed up the Smith-Dorien/Spray Road, following the road signs from the Town of Canmore.

## Route

| Route | Elevation | | Distance | |
|---|---|---|---|---|
| | metres | feet | km | mi. |
| Trailhead | 1420 | 4,658 | 0.0 | 0.0 |
| View of Fairholme Range | 1350 | 4,428 | 1.4 | 0.9 |
| End of Loop | 1420 | 4,658 | 5.8 | 3.6 |

The Georgetown Trail is a local favourite, as it winds past the remains of an old coal-mining town and offers a great glimpse into the history of coal mining in the area. Along the route, interpretive signs detail the Georgetown story, and some of the old housing foundations are still visible through the trees. The Georgetown mine opened in 1913, but, like most coal mines in the Bow Valley, the operation was short-lived and closed 1916.

The ride begins beside the day lodge and starts by following the paved access for the Bill Warren Training Centre. Continue beyond the centre, and turn right at the Biathlon Team Room. As you leave the parking lot, join the trail immediately. As the trail crosses under the first bridge, turn right following the brown signs for the Georgetown Trail. At most junctions, these signs will indicate the correct route. After two signed junctions, the trail drops down to another bridge at kilometre 0.7 (0.4 mi.). Do not cross the bridge, but rather go left just before the bridge, and then immediately right (basically to the left of the bridge). At this point the trail is signed "Canmore Trail". This trail soon begins to drop off the bench with good views to-

wards Skogan Pass and Pigeon Mountain to the east. Go left at a signed junction at kilometre 1.1 (0.7 mi.), and left again at a subsequent junction. The trail begins to wind left at kilometre 1.4 (0.9 mi.) as it emerges onto a steep embankment with excellent views across the valley towards the Fairholme Range.

After a short uphill, the trail passes several chin-up bars, forks to the right and begins a long descent. Along this stretch, there are several interpretive signs, and the trail bottoms out at kilometre 2.9 (1.8 mi.). The trail emerges in a clearing at 3.7 km (2.3 mi.). At this point, the trail makes a sharp left and begins the infamous Georgetown climb. Mountain bikers will find themselves challenged as the hill begins with a short, sharp pitch, followed by a long uphill grind for 0.7 km (0.4 mi.). Along the climb, you'll pass several more interpretive signs and numerous old foundations.

The top of the climb is reached when you meet Junction 29. Stay straight at this point and continue to climb on a much more gradual gradient. Go left at Junction 30, following the red arrow of the Lower 5km Loop, and soon begin to parallel the wide course of the Banff Trail. At 5.4 km (3.4 mi.), a Georgetown trail sign takes you left, towards Junction 18. Most riders will go left at this junction and join the paved biathlon loop. Turn right onto the pavement and complete the loop at kilometre 5.8 (3.6 mi.).

# 8. Rundle Riverside

Map pg 171  🍃 🚲

## Trailhead

The east access for this trail is at the day-lodge in Canmore Nordic Centre Provincial Park. To get there, simply follow the road signs within the Town of Canmore. The west trailhead is along the access road for the Banff Springs Golf Course. The trail leaves the pavement 2 km (1.9 mi.) along this wide road.

## Route

| Route | Elevation | | Distance | |
|---|---|---|---|---|
| | metres | feet | km | mi. |
| Trailhead | 1390 | 4,559 | 0.0 | 0.0 |
| Banff Park Boundary | 1400 | 4,592 | 8.2 | 5.1 |
| Canmore Nordic Centre | 1420 | 4,658 | 14.1 | 8.8 |

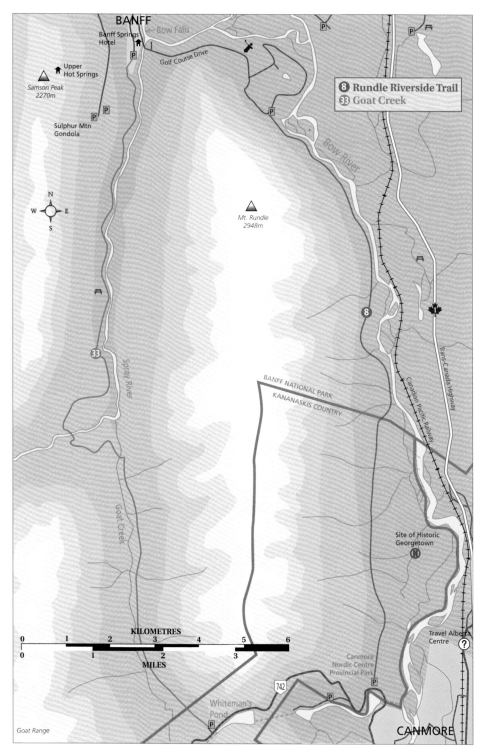

BANFF

Bow Falls

Banff Springs
Hotel

Upper
Hot Springs

Samson Peak
2270m

Golf Course Drive

**8** Rundle Riverside Trail
**33** Goat Creek

Sulphur Mtn
Gondola

Bow River

N
W - E
S

Mt. Rundle
2948m

Spray River

**33**

**8**

BANFF NATIONAL PARK
KANANASKIS COUNTRY

Trans-Canada Highway

Canadian Pacific Railway

Goat Creek

Site of Historic
Georgetown
**H**

Travel Alberta
Centre
**?**

KILOMETRES
0   1   2   3   4   5   6
0       1       2       3
MILES

Canmore
Nordic Centre
Provincial Park

742

Whiteman's
Pond

Goat Range

CANMORE

The Rundle Riverside Trail is most often used for mountain biking, and occasionally hiking. Most mountain bikers ride this trail from Banff to Canmore, often linking it with Goat Creek Trail to make a loop of approximately 48.5 km (30.1 mi.). As the trail leaves the golf course behind, it quickly narrows to become a winding, rough, single-track. Hikers will enjoy the serene nature of the trail as it periodically skirts the fast flowing Bow River. Mountain bikers will find it a challenging, bumpy ride. The trail bounces its way over tree roots, rock falls, and avalanche slopes for 8.2 km (5.1 mi.) until it leaves Banff National Park at a boundary sign. After a short uphill climb, the character changes as it joins Banff Trail, which acts as a vehicle access road for the Canmore Nordic Centre.

The wide gravel of Banff Trail ends at the Day Lodge at 14.1 km (8.8 mi.), however the Nordic Centre offers an endless variety of options for cyclists or hikers looking to extend their route.

*Grassi Lakes*

# 9. Grassi Lakes

Map pg 173 👫 📷 🍃

## Trailhead

The trailhead is at the start of the Smith-Dorrien/Spray hill, along a signed access road veering to the east.

## Route

| Route | Elevation | | Distance | |
|---|---|---|---|---|
| | metres | feet | km | mi. |
| Trailhead | 1530 | 5,018 | 0.0 | 0.0 |
| Second Grassi Lake | 1625 | 5,330 | 1.7 | 1.1 |
| Back to Trailhead | 1530 | 5,018 | 3.1 | 1.9 |

This short loop is only 3.1 km (1.9 mi.), but is a trail that everyone should walk at least once. There are many trails within Kananaskis Country, but this one holds a special fascination with its combination of colour, water and history.

The trail begins along a closed access road, but quickly leaves the road along a narrow trail that forks to the left near the metal gate. Winding through this lodgepole pine forest, keep your eyes open for large piles of cones, scales

and needles. These large piles, called middens, reveal favourite feeding spots and nests of the red squirrel, the self-appointed guardian of this forest. Soon, you'll begin to hear water flowing and after passing the remains of an old bench alongside the trail, you'll meet the weeping wall coming down from the right. In high runoff, you may get wet feet, but you can usually make your way across without too much difficulty. The views across the valley to Grotto Mountain and Mount Lady Macdonald open up here. Below you, the emerald green of the canal reflects the surrounding summits, while a beautiful waterfall (popular with winter ice climbers) is visible ahead of you.

The character changes at kilometre 1.2 (0.8 mi.), as the trail begins to climb sharply. As you ascend, there are stone steps climbing beside the weeping wall, built to aid the climb—but you'll find yourself puffing anyway. This section of trail holds snow and ice well into May, so don't attempt this trail too early in the season. As you climb, try to imagine Canmore Pioneer

*Old cabin off the Grassi Lakes trail*

*Pictographs at Grassi Lakes*

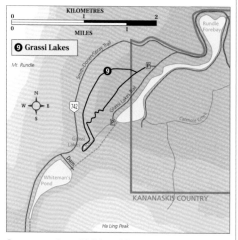

Lawrence Grassi hiking this route in the 1920's. He, along with several other Canmore miners, built this trail to facilitate access to the "Twin Lakes", as the lakes at the end of the trail were originally known. Grassi loved these mountains, and in 1938, the lakes were renamed in his honour. Over the years, the trail has been upgraded and repaired, but remains true to his original route. While the trail has stayed the same, the views have changed dramatically with the rapid development in this valley.

After a short, sharp climb, the trail winds left, and crosses a bridge over Grassi Creek. You reach the top of the climb at kilometre 1.4 (0.9 mi.). You can see the metal penstock above you

as the trail widens. Turn right at this junction and follow the trail as it brings you to the first Grassi Lake. Beyond this, the second lake lies at kilometre 1.7 (1.1 mi.). The deep blue ponds are bound on one side by a steep cliff face. This ancient coral reef is full of evidence of its marine origins. Climbers love these cliffs due to their easy access and good hand and footholds.

To the left of the upper lake, a loose scree slope takes the intrepid explorer further up the valley to view Indian pictographs that are likely more than a thousand years old. If you are comfortable with a little scrambling, make your way up the scree slope to the left of the second lake. A hundred metres beyond the top of the scree, the valley is partially blocked by a large boulder. If you look carefully, you'll see the ancient rock paintings. Remember though, just touching the pictographs can damage them, so please look, but do not touch.

When you return to the lake, walk around to the left and rejoin the access road. This road provides a quick exit to the trail, returning you to the trailhead in just 1.4 km (0.9 mi.). As you plod down the road, you'll pass the remains of an old cabin. Return to the trailhead at approximately 3.1 km (1.9 mi.).

# 10. Prairie View Trail

Map pg 175 👫🏼 📷 🌿 🍂 🚲

*Mt. Lorette*

## Trailhead

The trailhead is at Barrier Dam day use area, 8.4 km (5.2 mi.) south of the Trans-Canada Highway on the Kananaskis Trail (Highway 40). From the parking lot, the trail begins on the far side of the dam.

## Route

| Route | Elevation | | Distance | |
|---|---|---|---|---|
| | metres | feet | km | mi. |
| Trailhead | 1384 | 4,540 | 0.0 | 0.0 |
| Main Viewpoint | 1871 | 6,140 | 5.5 | 3.4 |
| Old Fire Lookout | 1960 | 6,429 | 7.9 | 4.9 |
| Jewell Pass Junction | 1620 | 5,314 | 8.4 | 5.2 |
| Stoney Trail Junction | 1400 | 4,592 | 11.5 | 7.2 |
| Return to Barrier Dam | 1384 | 4,540 | 16.1 | 10.0 |

This 5-km (3.1-mi.) out-and-back trail crosses Barrier Dam before climbing 420 m (1,377 ft.) along an old fire lookout access road. From the summit of McConnell Ridge, the views south to Barrier Lake and Mount Baldy are dramatic and unobscured. The emerald-green water of Barrier Lake reveals its glacial origin. If you feel energetic, scramble up to the site of the old fire lookout for a panoramic view of the Bow Valley. The old lookout tower had been relocated from a prisoner of war camp once located on the opposite side of Barrier Lake. When its duties as a tower were fulfilled, it was returned to the site of the camp,and still stands there today.

## Trailhead to Barrier Lake Viewpoint

The walk across the dam is windy and exposed. On the opposite shore, stay right at the first junction, and climb gently until a second junction at the 1.3-km (0.8-mi.) mark. Go right for a few steps, and the Prairie View Trail will branch to the left. Steady climbing along a high-quality fire road rapidly takes you to the open, exposed viewpoint along the shoulder of this high rocky knoll.

## Barrier Lake Viewpoint to Old Fire Lookout

From the viewpoint, you have three options. You can either return along the same route, scramble up to the site of the old lookout, or descend the far side towards Jewell Pass Trail. From the viewpoint, follow the trail along the ridge for a short distance. At 5.9 km (3.7 mi.), you'll meet a large white panel. At this point, the hiker-defined route heading to the former lookout location atop the summit of McConnell Ridge forks off to the right. This trail is not signed, but is well-defined through heavy use. The summit is crested after an additional 2 km (1.2 mi.) and a climb of 125 m (410 ft.). To the north, the imposing slopes of Mount Laurie (Îyâmnathka), locally known as Mount Yamnuska, mark the beginning of the Front Ranges. To the northwest, the cement plant at Lac Des Arcs billows smoke into to the sky.

## Barrier Lake Viewpoint to Jewell Pass Junction

From the large white panel marking the junction with the lookout trail, stay to the left and you'll soon find the trail dropping towards the south side of the ridge. Cyclists will find the scrambling between the main viewpoint and this junction difficult to negotiate, but a little perseverance is rewarded with a great downhill slalom course on the opposite side as you descend to Jewell Pass.

For cyclists or hikers doing the loop, the Prairie View Trail drops down a scree slope before heading into an airy aspen grove. The trail meets with the Jewell Pass Trail at kilometre 8.4 (mile 5.2).

## Jewell Pass Junction to Barrier Dam

To return to Barrier Lake, turn left at this junc-

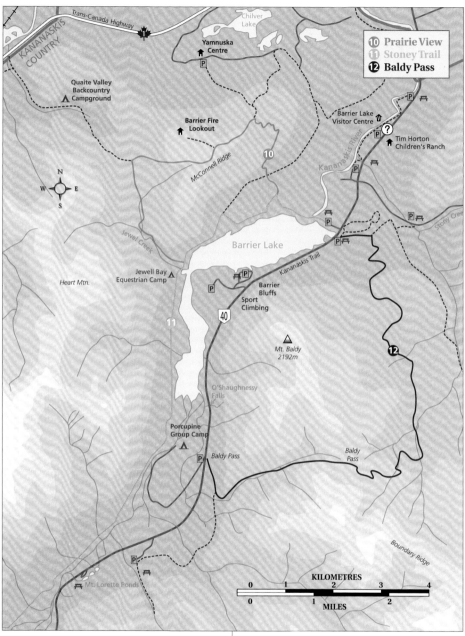

tion. This stretch provides a technical mountain bike route and a pleasant hike through the aspens. Meet the junction with Stoney Trail at kilometre 11.5 (mile 7.2). Turn left and follow this wide trail as it wanders north towards Barrier Dam. Keep your eyes open for another junction at kilometre 13.1 (mile 8.1). Go right at this junction. If you miss it and go straight, the trail continues for an additional 7 km (4.4 mi.) away from the trailhead.

When you meet the junction to Barrier Dam at kilometre 14.6 (mile 9.1), turn right and return to the trailhead at the 16.1-km (10.0-mi.) point.

# 11. Stoney Trail

Map pg 175 🌱 🍃 🏇 🚲

Trailhead: The north trailhead is at Barrier Dam day use area, 8.4 km (5.2 mi.) south of the Trans-Canada Highway on the Kananaskis Trail (Highway 40).

### Route

| Route | Elevation | | Distance | |
|---|---|---|---|---|
| | metres | feet | km | mi. |
| Trailhead | 1384 | 4,540 | 0.0 | 0.0 |
| Jewell Pass Junction | 1400 | 4,592 | 4.2 | 2.6 |
| South Trailhead | 1460 | 4,789 | 16.6 | 10.3 |

Following a power line right-of-way, this trail follows the west shore of Barrier Lake and the Kananaskis River all the way to the Ribbon Creek trail system. Totaling 16.6 km (10.3 mi.) one way, it provides an excellent mountain bike trail, but a rather mediocre hiking route. The trail is wide and rolling, with a good grade all the way.

Cross Barrier Dam and climb a small hill to a junction at kilometre 1.1 (mile 0.7). Turn left onto Stoney Trail and right at an unsigned junction at kilometre 2.2 (mile 1.4). Half a kilometre beyond this junction, go left at a signed junction. This is a critical junction if you return along the same route. Should you miss it on the return trip, you will find yourself heading away from the trailhead.

Beyond the previous trail sign, the wide trail winds towards Barrier Lake, meeting the junction with Jewell Pass Trail at 4.2 km (2.6 mi.). By 6.7 km (4.2 mi.), the trail begins to leave Barrier Lake behind as it climbs above the south end of the lake. As you pass the midway point, the views to the southwest open up and you get your first glimpse of the Olympic downhill site, Nakiska at Mount Allan, along with the Wasootch valley to the east. The trail continues to roll along the cut line until it meets the road to Nakiska and the Kananaskis Village at kilometre 16.6 (10.3 mi.).

# 12. Baldy Pass

Map pg 175 📷 🍃 🚲

From the Trans-Canada Highway, follow Highway 40 south for 7.9 km (4.9 mi.) and turn left onto Highway 68 (Sibbald Creek Trail). After less than 1 km, turn right into the Stoney Creek Group Camp parking lot. From here, the trail leaves the gravel road.

### Route

| Route | Elevation | | Distance | |
|---|---|---|---|---|
| | metres | feet | km | mi. |
| Trailhead | 1390 | 4,559 | 0.0 | 0.0 |
| Baldy Pass | 1850 | 6,068 | 10.4 | 6.5 |
| Wasootch day use | 1450 | 4,756 | 17.0 | 10.6 |

Follow the wide path as it leaves the dusty gravel of Sibbald Creek Trail (road) behind. Stay left at each of several junctions in the first kilometre (0.6 mi.). The trail winds past a junction to Stoney Creek at kilometre 2.6 (mile 1.6) and another junction with Lusk Pass Link Trail at 4.4 km (2.7 mi.). The wide trail climbs gradually through a mixed forest of aspen and lodgepole pine, heading through some old fire scars at kilometre 5.6 (mile 3.5). The trail continues to climb, passing an unsigned junction at 8.1 km (5 mi.). Narrowing beyond this point, the trail begins its final ascent towards the pass at kilometre 10.4 (mile 6.5).

At the summit, the steep face of Mount Baldy dominates the northwest, and Wasootch Tower stands to the southwest. While the views are not as dramatic as those of Prairie View across the valley, they offer a more rugged rustic appeal.

From the pass, drop down the scree on the west side for a little over a kilometre (0.6 mi.) before heading back into the trees. Eventually the trail bottoms out as you reach the valley floor, and begins to parallel Highway 40. The trail ends at the Wasootch Creek day use area at kilometre 17 (10.6 mi.).

*Barrier Lake*

# 13. Kananaskis Village Trail System

Map pg 178 👪 📷 🌿 🚲

## Trailhead

There are numerous trailheads for this trail system, but the two principle ones are at the Ribbon Creek trailhead and at Kananaskis Village. For Ribbon Creek, head south on Highway 40 (Kananaskis Trail) for 23.8 km (14.8 mi.), and turn right, following signs for Kananaskis Village. After leaving Highway 40, take the first left and an immediate right for the Ribbon Creek day use area.

To make your way to the Kananaskis Village trailhead, avoid the final turn into the Ribbon Creek trailhead, instead following the signs all the way to Kananaskis Village. There are numerous parking areas there.

## Route

| Route | Elevation | | Distance | |
|---|---|---|---|---|
| | metres | feet | km | mi. |
| Trailhead | 1525 | 5,002 | 0.0 | 0.0 |
| Kovach Viewpoint | 1650 | 5,412 | 3.5 | 2.2 |
| Link Junction | 1600 | 5,248 | 4.1 | 2.6 |
| Ribbon Creek day use | 1500 | 4,920 | 6.0 | 3.7 |

Since this is a trail network, there are many options for exploring. Most users create loops by hiking or biking from Kananaskis Village along trails like Kovach or Terrace. Heading south from the village on the Terrace Trail, Kovach Trail forks to the right after approximately 0.6 km (0.4 mi.). It then heads north, traversing the lower slopes of Mount Kidd, and passes a junction with Aspen Trail at kilometre 1.9 (mile 1.2). Kovach climbs up to a pleasant viewpoint after an additional 1.6 km (1 mi.). Beyond the viewpoint, the trail meets a junction with Link Trail at kilometre 4.1 (mile 2.5). You can either go left on Link Trail to access Ribbon Creek Trail at kilometre 4.7 (mile 2.9), or turn right to continue on Kovach Trail. Turning right, you will meet Aspen Trail again at 4.4 km (2.7 mi.). Aspen passes through numerous flowery meadows and offers several picturesque viewpoints. Kovach continues straight to a junction with Terrace Trail at 5.3 km (3.3 mi.). Kovach finally ends at the Ribbon Creek day use area at kilometre 6 (mile 3.7).

The network continues to the north of the Ribbon Creek day use parking lot. There are several trails, the most obvious of which is Hidden Trail, which leaves the parking lot at a trail sign. Hidden Trail climbs to Nakiska at Mount Allan after 0.9 km (0.5 mi.). You can follow Hidden Trail as it passes the ski hill, meeting a junction with Skogan Pass and Ruthie's Trail at 1.6 km (1 mi.). From Ruthie's, you can follow Troll Falls Trail to a small waterfall, or wind around the outside of the network on Hay Meadows Trail. All the junctions are well signed, and the trails are wide and easy to follow.

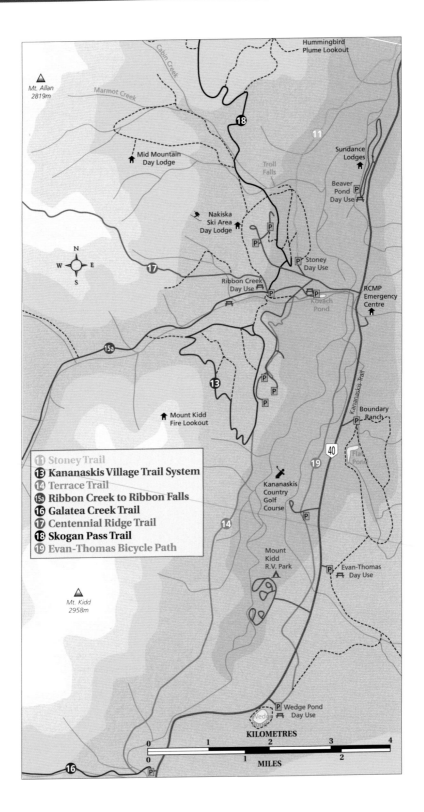

Mt. Allan
2819m

Marmot Creek

Cabin Creek

Hummingbird
Plume Lookout

18

11

Sundance
Lodges

Mid Mountain
Day Lodge

Troll
Falls

Beaver
Pond
Day Use

Nakiska
Ski Area
Day Lodge

N
W    E
S

17

Stoney
Day Use

Ribbon Creek
Day Use

Kovach
Pond

RCMP
Emergency
Centre

15a

Kananaskis Trail

13

Boundary
Ranch

Mount Kidd
Fire Lookout

40

19

**Legend**

- 11 Stoney Trail
- **13 Kananaskis Village Trail System**
- 14 Terrace Trail
- **15a Ribbon Creek to Ribbon Falls**
- **16 Galatea Creek Trail**
- **17 Centennial Ridge Trail**
- **18 Skogan Pass Trail**
- 19 Evan-Thomas Bicycle Path

Kananaskis
Country
Golf
Course

14

Mount
Kidd
R.V. Park

Evan-Thomas
Day Use

Mt. Kidd
2958m

Wedge Pond
Day Use

**KILOMETRES**

0        1        2        3        4

0        1        2

**MILES**

16

*Ribbon Creek Valley*

# 14. Terrace Trail

Map pg 178

## Trailhead

Head south on Highway 40 (Kananaskis Trail) for 23.8 km (14.8 mi.), and turn right following signs for Kananaskis Village. After leaving Highway 40, take the first left and follow this road all the way to the Village. The main access for Terrace Trail is found by following the Rim Trail, which leaves the village between the Lodge at Kananaskis and the Signature Club.

| Route | Elevation | | Distance | |
|---|---|---|---|---|
| | metres | feet | km | mi. |
| Trailhead | 1525 | 5,002 | 0.0 | 0.0 |
| Galatea Trail Junction | 1570 | 5,150 | 9.0 | 5.6 |

This popular hiking and mountain bike trail winds south from the Kananaskis Village to the Galatea trailhead. Along the way, it traverses the lower slopes of Mount Kidd, with fabulous views of the Kananaskis Golf Course and The Wedge on the opposite side of the valley.

From the trailhead at Kananaskis Village, the trail becomes a narrow sidecut along the lower slopes of Mount Kidd. Mountain bikers will enjoy the views, but keep in mind that the trail is narrow, and hikers also share the route. The trail crosses numerous avalanche paths and runoff channels that which drain the winter snows from Mount Kidd. At the southern end of the trail, you'll meet a junction with Galatea Trail. Turn left at this junction, and meet the trailhead parking lot at the 9-km (5.6-mi.) mark. A 24.8-km (15.4-mi.) loop can be made by linking this trail with the Evan-Thomas Bicycle Path.

# 15. Ribbon Creek

Map pg 178

## Trailhead

Head south on Highway 40 (Kananaskis Trail) for 23.8 km (14.3 mi.), and turn right following signs for Kananaskis Village. After leaving Highway 40, take the first left and an immediate right for the Ribbon Creek day use area. Ribbon Creek Trail leaves from the most distant point in this day use area, almost as if the road were to continue up the valley.

| Route | Elevation | | Distance | |
|---|---|---|---|---|
| | metres | feet | km | mi. |
| Trailhead | 1500 | 4,920 | 0.0 | 0.0 |
| Ribbon Falls | 1900 | 6,232 | 11.0 | 6.8 |
| Ribbon Lake | 2100 | 6,888 | 12.8 | 8.0 |
| Lillian Lake via Guinn's Pass | 2020 | 6,626 | 17.7 | 11.0 |

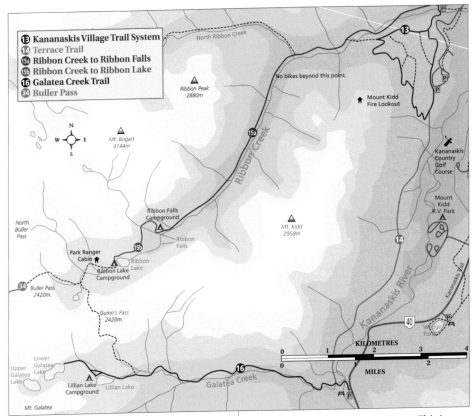

Ribbon Creek Trail begins in a busy picnic area and offers numerous options for wilderness exploration. This trail is exceedingly popular, partly because of its easy access, but also for the diversity of options it provides. The trail follows the winding course of Ribbon Creek as it gradually rises to its headwaters at Ribbon Lake. The scenery along the way is magnificent and the mountain views divine. Mount Kidd looms to the south while Ribbon Peak and Mount Bogart tower to the north.

This route can be linked with routes over to the Smith-Dorrien/Spray Trail via Buller Pass, or over the Lillian and Galatea Lakes via Guinn's Pass. There is one important barrier to completing either of these routes, and that is the cliff hazard between Ribbon Falls and Ribbon Lake. This is a challenging obstacle and will turn most novices. Once you surpass this challenge, though, the options for exploration abound.

# Ribbon Creek to Ribbon Falls

The tranquil waters of Ribbon Creek have en-

ticed countless hikers over the years. This is a very busy hiking area, so mountain bikes are not recommended beyond the point at which the wide trail narrows at around the 4.5-km (2.8-mi.) mark. The flower-lined trail follows the creek up a narrow valley with Mount Kidd to the south and Ribbon Peak and Mount Bogart to the north. Mount Bogart gained its name from Dr. Donald Bogart Dowling, a geologist who examined the coal seams along Ribbon Creek in 1909, and spurred interest in mining. The coal seams are still there, but the mining has long since ended.

Summer hiking up the creek provides a pleasant walk amidst the towering peaks and steep mountain walls. Keep your eyes open for a small bird bobbing up and down on the rocks. The dipper, with its well-earned name, has the magical ability to fly underwater to collect insects from between the rocks. Its drab grey colour tends to make it almost invisible, but it is well worth the challenge.

Link Ski Trail forks off to the left after ap-

*Ribbon Falls*

proximately 2.5 km (1.6 mi.), while Ribbon Creek continues up the valley. The trail crosses the creek numerous times, with only a gradual change in elevation. A rough trail forks to the right shortly after passing an old log pile on the right. This hiker-defined route heads up the North Ribbon Creek towards the Memorial Lakes. After the next creek crossing, the trail passes the remains of an old logging camp. The camp was built by the Eau Claire and Bow River Lumber Company, which operated on this site from 1886 until the early 1940s. Beyond the camp, Ribbon Peak rises above the valley on your right, with Mount Bogart dominating further down the valley.

After leaving the logging camp behind, the trail narrows and signs indicate that mountain bikes are not recommended beyond this point. The intense use of this trail makes it difficult to recommend mountain bikes, and there are better rides available elsewhere. This is also the terminus of the winter cross-country ski trail. Beyond this point, the trail continues up a much narrower valley between Mounts Kidd and Bogart, climbing gradually as the creek becomes constricted by the landscape. After passing numerous old log cabins, also remnants of the valley's former logging activity, the creek emerges from the narrow canyon as the valley begins to close in ahead of you. The cliffs of Mount Bogart now begin to close in with the sheer slopes of Mount Kidd.

The trail enters the Ribbon Falls Camp-

ground after 11 km (6.8 mi.). This rustic back-country campsite has firepits, a pit toilet and a hanging pole. Beyond the campsite, the trail climbs to a great view of Ribbon Falls tumbling down the cliff.

## Ribbon Falls to Ribbon Lake

The falls form a delicate ribbon cascading down the steep face to continue towards the Kananaskis River. At this point, your options are to return on the same trail or ready yourself for adventure. From the falls, the trail takes a turn for the vertical and begins climbing steeply. Over the next 0.8 km (0.5 mi.), the trail climbs 160 m (525 ft.) before dead-ending at a rocky cliff. The trail does continue above the rock face, but to access it you must climb 5 metres (16.4 ft.) up the rock face. To assist you, several chains have been bolted to the cliff to provide solid handholds. This is a serious cliff hazard and it will turn back inexperienced hikers. It is also much easier to climb up than down. It never hurts to have a rope for extra security.

If you do make the ascent, the trail continues to climb towards Ribbon Lake, at approximately 2100 metres (6,888 ft.). This lake mirrors the surrounding peaks. Options here are numerous. You can return on the same trail, climb over the rocky summit of Guinn's Pass, or climb over Buller Pass and descend the western side.

## Ribbon Lake to Lillian Lake

From the Ribbon Lake, continue 1.5 km (0.9 mi.) along the trail to its junction with Guinn's Pass. This rugged trail climbs through prime bear habitat as it traverses some lush growth along its steep avalanche slopes. As you climb, it becomes exposed and rocky, switchbacking back and forth across the exposed scree. A rocky cairn marks the summit of the pass. When I was there, a white cross poked out from above the top of the cairn. Its meaning was unknown to me, but its presence brought on an increased sense of caution.

Ahead of you lies a steep descent along a loose rock trail, toward the junction with the Galatea Trail. Take time to enjoy the views, and watch your footing. As you enter the avalanche slope on the south side of the pass, the vegetation becomes lush and green. Shortly after crossing a bridge, the trail junction leads you upstream to Lillian Lake and the Galatea Lakes.

# 16. Galatea Creek

Map pg 180  👥 📷 🌾 🍃

## Trailhead

Follow Highway 40 (Kananaskis Trail) south for 34 km (21.1 mi.) to the Galatea trailhead.

## Route

| Route | Elevation | | Distance | |
|---|---|---|---|---|
| | metres | feet | km | mi. |
| Trailhead | 1570 | 5,150 | 0.0 | 0.0 |
| Lillian Lake | 2020 | 6,626 | 5.6 | 3.5 |
| Lower Galatea Lake | 2200 | 7,216 | 7.2 | 4.5 |

This trail takes you into remote country and through some enticing grizzly habitat. At the same time, the landscape is divine, and the rewards plentiful. Go prepared, and enjoy an isolated wilderness valley. If you will be on this trail on a weekend, head out early to beat the crowds that descend upon this popular route. Also, keep in mind that there is an annual spring closure on Galatea Creek. While there is no set date for the closure, the trail is kept closed until it begins to dry out. Check with Barrier Information Centre at (403) 673-3985 for more details. The trail is 5.6 km (3.5 mi.) to Lillian Lake, during which it climbs 450 m (1,476 ft.). Continuing to the Galatea Lakes adds an extra 1.6 kilometres (1 mi.) to the distance and 180 m (590 ft.) to the climb.

The trail begins at the Galatea parking lot, 34 km (21.1 mi.) south on Highway 40. From there, it descends quickly to the Kananaskis River, where a high-quality suspension bridge provides easy access to the opposite side. A junction near the far side of the bridge links Terrace Trail with Galatea Creek. Turn left at this junction and begin the slow climb up valley. The trail zigzags back and forth over the creek as it climbs the valley. As you go further, you begin to get some views to the left towards Fortress Ridge and an outlier of The Fortress.

After crossing the creek for the third time, the trail begins to traverse a high cutbank rising to the right. Soon, the trail makes a number of short switchbacks to climb above the creek, and then it quickly rejoins. After crossing back over to the left of the river at bridge 5, the creek drops over a pretty waterfall. At around the 2-

km (1.2-mi.) mark, the trail crosses several runoff channels coming off the cliffs of Mount Kidd to the right of the trail. This brings the trail into a darker, moister section of forest. After several more crossings, the trail begins a very steep section just after crossing bridge 9 at kilometre 4.5 (mile 2.8). This steep section levels out just before joining the junction with Guinn's Pass Trail at the 5-km (3.1-mi.) mark. Keep climbing more gradually past that junction and you will meet the shores of Lillian Lake half a kilometre (0.3 mi.) further.

Lillian Lake Campground is at the far end of the lake, with the trail traversing the north bank of the lake. From the primitive campground, an undesignated trail climbs sharply to ascend towards the Galatea Lakes. The climbing is sudden and unrelenting for 0.6 km (0.4 mi.) until you finally crest a view above the lower Galatea Lake. The lakes are well-known for their cutthroat trout, so don't forget your license and fishing rod.

# 17. Centennial Ridge Trail

Map pg 184  📷 🌾 🍃

## Trailhead

Head south on Highway 40 (Kananaskis Trail) for 23.8 km (14.8 mi.), and turn right following signs for Kananaskis Village. After leaving Highway 40, take the first left and an immediate right for the Ribbon Creek day use area. Centennial Ridge Trail begins on Hidden Trail, which leaves to the right of the entrance to the furthest parking area.

## Route

| Route | Elevation | | Distance | |
|---|---|---|---|---|
| | metres | feet | km | mi. |
| Trailhead | 1500 | 4,920 | 0.0 | 0.0 |
| Olympic Summit | 2450 | 8,036 | 4.4 | 2.7 |
| True Summit | 2819 | 9,249 | 6.3 | 3.9 |
| Alpine Resort Haven | 1310 | 4,297 | 16.8 | 10.4 |

Are you ready for adventure? If so, then this is the trail for you. Climbing straight up the side of Mount Allan, this trail traverses the summit of the mountain at the 2,819-m (9,249-ft.) mark,

*Mushroom Garden on Centennial Ridge*

making it the highest hiking trail in the Canadian Rockies. The trail is 6.3 km (3.9 mi.) to the summit, with an elevation gain of 1,319 m (4,326 ft.). Should you choose to continue the ridge walk to the north trailhead, you'll need to hike an additional 10.5 km (6.5 mi.). To ensure the trail has dried off each spring, the route is closed between April 1 and June 22.

Beginning at the Ribbon Creek parking lot, the trail begins along the gentle path of Hidden Trail. Turn left at the first junction at 0.3 km (0.2 mi.), and left again at a junction at 0.8 km (0.5 mi.). The trail begins climbing after this junction and also narrows down into a more definite single-track route. Stay left at an unmarked junction at kilometre 1.3 (mile 0.8), following a trail marked by an orange diamond and a hiker symbol. Soon, the trail crosses the first of three old access roads. On the first two of these old roads, you follow the trail across and continue climbing. The third time's the charm, though, and this time turn left and follow the road.

As you approach the old coal mine scar on the side of the mountain, the steep climbing begins. Ahead of you lies a climb of 700 metres (2,300 ft.) in less than 2 km (1.2 mi.). It's time to dig in and go for it. The footing is sometimes tricky due to the extreme steepness, but the views keep improving with the elevation. To the south, the sheer face of Mount Kidd dominates, while to the west, Mounts Bogart and Spar-

rowhawk stand defiantly. There are numerous false summits as you climb, with the first at approximately 2.3 km (1.4 mi.) as you emerge on a small outcrop. As you crest the next section, you'll see a large Atomic ski sticking out of a large cairn. Beyond this, there is a short patch of scrambling to get through several sheer rock bands. While you may be tempted to climb up to the left at these bands, an easier route traverses to the right. As you emerge through the final band at around the 3.5-km (2.2-mi.) mark, you approach a smooth ascent to the top of the Olympic Summit at kilometre 4.4 (mile 2.7). Take a nice long rest here and drink in the views. You now get a clear view of the long ridge walk to the true summit.

As you descend momentarily from the Olympic Summit, look down to the valley directly to the west, and notice the tiny tarn at the base of the ridge between Mounts Bogart and Sparrowhawk. This tiny lake is one of the Memorial Lakes, and pays homage to three plane crashes that occurred between June 6 and 14, 1986. On June 6, biologist Orval Pall and pilot Ken Wolff disappeared while doing aerial wildlife surveys. Over the next 8 days, 11 more people lost their lives when, in separate incidents, two of the search planes crashed. In total, 13 people died in that 8-day period, marking one of the darkest periods in recent Kananaskis history.

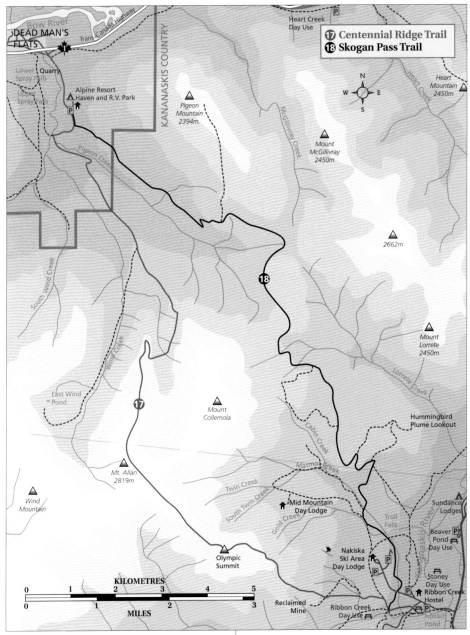

Heart Creek
Day Use

**17 Centennial Ridge Trail**
**18 Skogan Pass Trail**

DEAD MAN'S FLATS
Bow River
Trans Canada Highway
Lower Quarry
Spray Falls
Upper Spray Falls
Alpine Resort Haven and R.V. Park
Pigeon Creek
KANANASKIS COUNTRY
Pigeon Mountain 2394m.
McGillivray Creek
N W E S
Heart Mountain 2450m
Heart Creek
Mount McGillivray 2450m
2662m
18
Mount Lorrete 2450m
South Wind Creek
Wind Creek
East Wind Pond
17
Mount Collemola
Lorrete Creek
Cabin Creek
Hummingbird Plume Lookout
Mt. Allan 2819m
Twin Creek
Marmot Creek
Wind Mountain
South Twin Creek
Gold Creek
Mid Mountain Day Lodge
Troll Falls
Sundance Lodges
Beaver Pond Day Use
Nakiska Ski Area Day Lodge
Stoney Day Use
Ribbon Creek Hostel
Olympic Summit
Kananaskis River
Reclaimed Mine
Ribbon Creek Day Use
Kovach Pond

KILOMETRES
0   1   2   3   4   5
0   1   2   3
MILES

From the summit of the platter, it's a constant but more reasonable climb along the ridge to the true summit. Along the way, you'll pass the mushroom garden at 5 km (3.1 mi.), with its curious collection of rocky sentinels. These hard outcrops of conglomerate are very resistant to erosion and stand in defiance of the elements.

These are a warm-up for the conglomerate pinnacles you'll pass minutes later. Standing like stone giants, they are the guardians of this mountain world. A plaque in the mushroom garden pays tribute to the Rocky Mountain Ramblers Association of Calgary, who built this trail for Canada's Centennial in 1967.

Beyond the mushroom garden, the trail drops down a series of steps to descend through a rock band. After this tricky drop, the trail begins to skirt the west side of the ridge. Just beyond the 6-km (3.7-mi.) mark, it rejoins the ridge top for the final ascent to the summit. As you climb towards the summit, it is easy to find yourself drawn to a sheep trail along the eastern side of the ridge. Avoid the temptation. The correct route stays right on the ridgetop. The wide summit is fully equipped with cairn and summit register. The views are fabulous. To the northwest, the town of Canmore sprawls across the Bow Valley, while Wind Mountain and Mount Lougheed block the western skyline. Mount Collembola rises to the northeast and the views to the south and southwest spread across the Kananaskis valley.

## Summit to Alpine Resort Haven

From the summit, most hikers return to Ribbon Creek, but if you are able to arrange a pickup at the Alpine Resort Haven, near Dead Man's Flats, you can descend from the summit and enjoy one of the best ridge walks in the Rockies. The trail drops quickly along an easy scree descent with less exposure than the northern exit. As you approach the next ridge, the trail traverses to the right with great views down the valley between Mounts Allan and Collembola. After passing through "the black band", a series of dark rock outcrops, the trail continues through what appears to be a solid rock wall. Upon closer approach, a red flag and cairn will guide you through an opening after which the trail winds to the right along a pleasant ridge walk. Enjoy the magic of this ridge as it ends far

## Martin Nordegg and Canadian Coal

Coal played a vital role in the opening of the Bow Valley, but most of the mines were short-lived ventures. Martin Nordegg was a pivotal character in the story of the western Canadian coal industry.

Nordegg arrived from Germany in 1906, and represented a German financing company. His backers were looking to invest in Canada's potentially immense mineral industry. When he discovered a thick coal seam on Mount Allan, he collected a large sample as proof of his find . His backers were very impressed, but wanted a second opinion, and so consulted the world's foremost expert on coal at that time, Professor Pontonie. Upon finding the coals origin, the professor immediately called Nordegg a fraud, for according to Pontonie's book, coal did not exist in rocks of the Rockies age. Despite Nordegg's insistence that there were already more than 2,000 tons/day being mined in places like Canmore and the Crowsnest Pass, the Professor would not alter his assessment. It appeared the only way to change Pontonie's mind would be to personally show him the seams. Nordegg convinced the Canadian Mining Institute to bring Pontonie to the Rockies, and apparently, as the Professor rode up to the base of Mount Allan and hacked off a few pieces of coal for himself he responded with: "I must rewrite my book!" His report on the quality of the coal in the area helped establish Canada's reputation as a coal producing nation.

Convinced of the value of the coal deposits in the Rockies, Nordegg was recalled once more to assist his backers in their final decisions. Although the Mount Allan site was the ideal place to develop, there was another site further north, in the Brazeau area. It would have been far more difficult, and costly, to develop, as it was much further from the railroad. The banker charged with the final decision took one look at the details of the two sites, and stated that his choice was very simple—the most expensive site was the best.

Of course Nordegg protested that the Brazeau site was very poorly located, but the banker insisted that "it is easier, and more profitable for me, to find several millions than a few hundred thousand." In fact he would have been happier had Nordegg found an even less accessible local.

Nordegg returned to Canada sickened by European greed, and never again returned to his homeland. During the first world war, almost everything he had worked so hard to build, was taken from him because he was a German national. He eventually regained most of his losses after the war ended, and died a citizen of Canada.

Although the Mount Allan location was not developed until 1947, the northern site developed by his European backers still bears the name "Nordegg."

*Mountain views from Skogan Pass*

too quickly. At the 9-km (5.6-mi.) mark, you descend sharply off the upper ridge, down towards the lower bench. Soon after this, you meet another conglomerate outcrop, and you'll need to climb down the face to the right of the cliff. Below this, you traverse a very exposed grassy slope, which would be treacherous if snowy. Along this narrow traverse are several sections where you may need to assist one another past very narrow, steep sections.

Eventually, the trail turns sharply to the right and drops off the summit, making a beeline for the valley bottom. As you head back into the trees, the drop is sharp for the next 0.3 km (0.2 mi.) until you bottom out in a meadow between Mounts Allan and Collembola. The trail is easy to follow as it crosses the meadow and then turns left to make its way down the valley towards the north trailhead. The trail passes an Inukshuk-shaped cairn at approximately 11.5 km (7.2 mi.). Beyond this point, it widens out along an old access road. Follow this wide road as it drops towards the boundary with Kananaskis Country, which you pass in 2.5 km (1.6 mi.). As you leave Kananaskis, a road forks off to the left. Ignore this trail and continue straight ahead. After the creek begins to parallel the road down to your right, you meet a junction near several old metal culverts. Go right, over a washed-out crossing with little more than a few rusted culverts lying across the stream. After an additional 0.6 km (0.4 mi.), you'll meet the powerline and the junction with the Skogan Pass Trail. Stay straight and meet the trailhead within a few minutes. The total hike is approximately 16.8 km (10.4 mi.).

# 18. Skogan Pass Trail

Map pg 184

## Trailhead

There are two trailheads for this route. The north one is more heavily used, and is located at the Alpine Resort Haven, near Dead Man's Flats. As you approach the resort, park at the right end of the gravel parking lot. You will see the trail continuing beyond the trailhead.

The south trailhead is at Ribbon Creek day use along Highway 40. Head south on Highway 40 (Kananaskis Trail) for 23.8 km (14.8 mi.), and turn right, following signs for Kananaskis Village. Then take the first left and an immediate right for the Ribbon Creek day use area. Skogan Pass Trail begins on Hidden Trail, which leaves to the left of the picnic shelter in the furthest parking area.

## Route

| Route | Elevation | | Distance | |
|---|---|---|---|---|
| | metres | feet | km | mi. |
| Trailhead | 1310 | 4,297 | 0.0 | 0.0 |
| Skogan Pass Summit | 2073 | 6,799 | 9.7 | 6.0 |
| Ribbon Creek Trailhead | 1500 | 4,920 | 20.9 | 13.0 |

Skogan Pass is a very popular summer hike and mountain-bike ride. Climbing high above the Bow Valley, it offers a convenient link between

*Cyclists on the Evan-Thomas Bicycle Path*

the valleys of the Bow and Kananaskis Rivers. From its summit, the views stretch to the northeast, all the way to Canmore and Cascade Mountain beyond. To the south, you get excellent views of the Olympic ski hill at Mount Allan and the surrounding Kananaskis Valley.

As you leave the Alpine Resort Haven trailhead, stay left at the junction with the Centennial Ridge Trail at kilometre 0.15 (mile 0.1). Stay left at another junction at approximately 0.7 km (0.4 mi.) and begin climbing sharply. The trail climbs through a forest of spruce, aspen and poplar, as it zigs and zags back and forth under the power line access that runs over the Skogan Pass summit. Stay left as another road forks to the right at 1.6 km (1 mi.). The main route remains easy to follow as it climbs at a steady pace. Great views open up at 4.6 km (2.9 mi.) as the trail traverses a meadow of red paintbrush, wild rose, locoweed, and yarrow. To the northeast, you can see all the way to Cascade Mountain in Banff National Park. Stay left at a junction beyond this meadow and begin a series of switchbacks. At 6 km (3.7 mi.), the trail traverses another flower-filled meadow of cow parsnip and alpine forget-me-nots.

You finally crest the pass at the 9.7-km (6-mi.) mark, and soon the views open up to the south towards Nakiska at Mount Allan, site of the downhill events during the 1998 Winter Olympic Games. At this point, mountain bikers and cross-country skiers will rejoice as the uphill grind gives way to a downhill thrill. The trail is easy to follow as it descends, with most junctions signed. After passing a sign indicating the entrance to the recreation area, stay left at a

junction and left again at the next signed junction. The views continue to expand as you drop down the south side of the pass. Soon you can see beyond Mount Allan to the towering face of Mount Kidd. Pass High Level Trail at kilometre 15.2 (mile 9.5), and then Sunburst at 16.2 km (10.1 mi.). All too soon, you pass a metal gate and enter the ski hill area. Stay straight on the gravel road until you pass Ruthie's trail. Continue to follow the Skogan Pass signs and finally drop down to the Ribbon Creek parking lot at 20.9 km (13 mi.).

# 19. Evan-Thomas Bicycle Path

Map pg 178

## Trailhead

Evan-Thomas bike path parallels Highway 40, allowing access at numerous points along its 13-km (8.1-mi.) length. Major trailheads are available at Wedge Pond, Mount Kidd RV Park, Ribbon Creek trailhead, and Kananaskis Village.

## Route

| Route | Elevation | | Distance | |
|---|---|---|---|---|
| | metres | feet | km | mi. |
| Trailhead | 1550 | 5,084 | 0.0 | 0.0 |
| Mount Kidd RV Park | 1500 | 4,920 | 2.2 | 1.4 |
| Kananaskis Golf Course | 1475 | 4,838 | 4.0 | 2.5 |
| Kananaskis Village Road | 1460 | 4,789 | 8.0 | 5.0 |
| Lodge at Kananaskis | 1500 | 4,920 | 11.0 | 6.8 |

This exceedingly popular paved trail attracts families with bicycles, strollers, roller blades, and sneakers. The rolling paved surface makes this trail perfect for just about everyone. Its smooth surface adds to its potential for users with limited mobility. In the winter, it performs double duty as a cross-country ski trail. Along its rolling course, the trail winds from Wedge Pond in the south to Kananaskis Village in the north. The towering slopes of Mount Kidd rise high above the valley to the west.

Along the rolling course of this trail, why not stop in at the Mount Kidd RV Park store for a snack or ice cream? Numerous picnic areas make pleasant stops enroute as well. While the

*Ptarmigan Cirque trail*

trail extends 11 km (6.8 mi.) from Wedge Pond all the way to Kananaskis Village, many trail users take advantage of shorter sections of the trail. An extended loop can be made by linking the Terrace Trail with the Evan-Thomas bike path.

# 20. Ptarmigan Cirque

Map pg 189 👫 📷 🌾 🍃

## Trailhead

Follow Highway 40 (Kananaskis Trail) south for 71 km (44.1 mi.) to the Highwood Pass parking lot. Ptarmigan Cirque trail begins along the wide Highwood Meadows Trail.

## Route

| Route | Elevation | | Distance | |
|---|---|---|---|---|
| | metres | feet | km | mi. |
| Trailhead | 2206 | 7,239 | 0.0 | 0.0 |
| Turnaround Point | 2425 | 7,954 | 2.2 | 1.4 |
| Return to Trailhead | 2206 | 7,239 | 4.5 | 2.8 |

Climbing high above Highwood Pass, the 4.5-km (2.8-mi.) self-guiding loop of Ptarmigan Cirque provides a wonderful way to access the alpine. Park at the Highwood Pass parking lot and follow the signs toward the trail. It crosses Highway 40, and quickly begins climbing through a forest of alpine larch, subalpine fir,

and Engelmann spruce. Before you know it, the views begin to open up.

The trail passes a large avalanche slope whose lush growth testifies to the power of sunlight. With the trees removed, the area explodes into a diverse community of plant life. This variety makes avalanche slopes prime habitat for many high altitude residents including grizzly bear, elk, and bighorn sheep.

When you arrive at the fork in the trail at kilometre 0.9 (mile 0.5), stay left and continue climbing past a fabulous avalanche slope that explodes in wildflowers in July.

Beyond the avalanche slope, the trees begin to exhibit a stunted nature. The effects of altitude take over, and before long, you leave the alpine larch trees behind and enter the true alpine. Low shrubs like heather and hardy wildflowers like the alpine forget-me-not reflect the harshness of this landscape. As you explore the alpine, the views open up to the southwest to the dipping summit of Mount Tyrwhitt. Ahead of you, the bowl of Ptarmigan Cirque begs to be explored. Keep your eyes open for ptarmigan wandering through the meadows. At the base of the bowl, a small waterfall drains the seemingly endless supply of snowmelt, and the straight-walled valleys above you present evidence of the former glaciers that sculpted them. As the cirque begins to wind back upon itself, keep your eyes and ears open for the hoary marmot, which will usually announce its presence with its whistling call. The rocks in the base of the bowl near interpretive marker 10 are a favourite sunning spot for marmots.

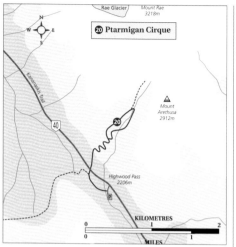

All too soon, the trail heads back into the trees and descends towards the closing of the loop. If you have not had enough exploring, you can spend much time in the upper part of the cirque exploring the alpine and marvelling at the power of the glaciers that carved this bowl.

## Julius Rickert

In 1884, Doctor George Dawson reported seeing anthracite coal in the area of the Sheep River and Rickert's Creek junction. A few years later, a man named Julius Rickert began prospecting in the area, and having read Dawson's report, sought out the coal seam. Julius Rickert was a unique character, a compelling combination of prospector, con artist and fraud. He claimed the title Count de Brabant, and using the prestige that the title brought, began to look for investors to develop the coal seam. In 1909, he managed to convince wealthy rancher Pat Burns to buy his holdings and to pay all expenses for the operation of the mine. Over the next few years, Burns was given numerous land grants in the area, all of which are still registered in his name.

Rickert continued to be involved with the mine, and time and again Burns paid off the debts of Rickert and his wife. By 1932, Burns was tiring of Rickert's demands, and the final straw was a lawsuit Rickert filed against Burns for past mine interest and revenue. In the ensuing battle, it was revealed that Rickert had no right to the title Count de Brabant. In fact, the title rightfully belonged to the Crown Prince of Belgium.

Rickert's name still survives in the name of the pass separating the Sheep River Valley from Mist Creek.

# 21. Mist Creek

Map pg 189 📷 🌾 🐎 🚵

## Trailhead

Head south on Highway 40 for 88.8 km (55.2 mi.) to the Mist Creek parking lot. The trail begins on the north side of the highway, just to the right of the Highway 40 bridge over Mist Creek.

## Route

| Route | Elevation | | Distance | |
|---|---|---|---|---|
| | metres | feet | km | mi. |
| Highway 40 Trailhead | 1767 | 5,795 | 0.0 | 0.0 |
| Rickert's Pass | 2330 | 7,642 | 8.9 | 5.5 |
| Burns Mine | 1785 | 5,855 | 11.9 | 7.4 |

The Mist Creek Trail offers excellent access for hikers, mountain bikers or horseback riders looking for a way to link Highway 40 with the Sheep Trail. A 54.3-km (33.8-mi.) loop can be made by linking highway riding with the Elbow Pass Trail, Sheep Trail and Mist Creek Trails. The views from Rickert's Pass are pleasant, with Mist Mountain and the Misty Range to the southwest, and Mount Burns and the peaks of the Highwood Range to the north. Hot springs are rumoured to exist in the area, and some people believe that the 'mist' in Mist Creek is

*Views from Rye Ridge*

caused by steam rising from these springs on cold days. During the ice age, a glacier cut a low pass between Storm Mountain and Gibraltar Mountain, and today this pass makes for a reasonably easy connection between the Kananaskis and Sheep River Valleys.

Follow Mist Creek as it winds its way to the northwest, towards its headwaters at the base of Rickert's Pass. Local natives referred to this as "Many Porcupines Trail." As you make your way towards the summit, you get periodic views of a prescribed burn set alight in 1990.

As you crest the pass, you are treated to great views towards the Misty Range to the southwest. Beyond the summit, the trail drops sharply towards the Sheep River. It is a steep, switchbacking drop of 545 m (1,788 ft.) in just 3 km (1.9 mi.) along a sometimes muddy track. After bottoming out, the trail passes several old mine relics before joining the wide Sheep Trail.

# 22. Cataract Creek

Map pg 191 📷 🌾 🍁 🐎 🚵

## Trailhead

Travel south on Highway 40, or west on Highway 541 from Longview, to Highwood Junction. Head south on this gravel road. When you pass Etherington Creek Campground, check your odometer. The trailhead to Cataract Creek and Rye Ridge is 4.6 km (2.8 mi.) further south, where a gated road forks off to the right.

## Route

| Route | Elevation | | Distance | |
|---|---|---|---|---|
| | metres | feet | km | mi. |
| Trailhead | 1707 | 5,600 | 0.0 | 0.0 |
| Rye Ridge Summit | 2349 | 7,160 | 14.1 | 8.8 |

The former forestry access roads along Cataract Creek allow easy access into remote country. Beginning along its lazy namesake creek, the wide route is used by hikers, horseback riders, mountain bikers, and in winter, snowmobiles. The Cataract Creek Road has been upgraded over the years to provide access for logging trucks. The wide road crosses Cataract Creek numerous times. After the second crossing at kilometre 2.1 (mile 1.3), a gravel road forks to the right to climb steeply to a fire lookout on Raspberry Ridge. Be sure to stay on the lower road. The views to the west towards the High Rock Range are wide open for much of this trail.

The trail forks again at kilometre 5.8 (mile 3.6) as the Lost Creek Trail branches to the left. Stay to the right at this junction, and again at a junction with Faller's Trail at 7.4 km (4.6 mi.). The route becomes more rustic at this point as it begins to climb towards the head of the valley. At the same time, there are a number of junctions in quick succession. It might appear that you will need to ford the river at 7.9 km (4.9 mi.), but if you look to the right of the main trail, there is a bridge just out of view. Stay left at a junction soon after this bridge and turn right onto a wood-chip-coated trail at a junction at 8.3 km (5.2 mi.). Go straight at a junction at 9.3 km (5.8 mi.) and left at a signed intersection

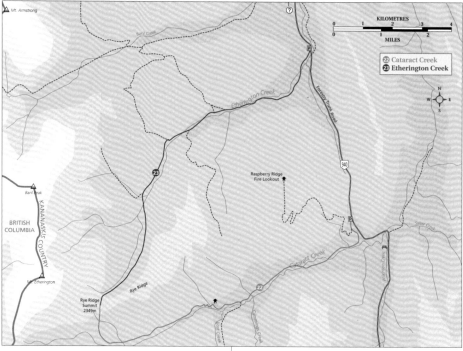

soon after. There is another left at 9.7 km (6 mi.) and a right minutes later.

Higher up the valley, you pass Perkinson's Cabin at kilometre 10.7 (mile 6.7). In days gone by, this cabin allowed range riders to stay with their cattle during their period of summer grazing. The cabin has seen better days, and for cyclists marks the end of easy riding as the trail takes an uphill turn for the final climb to Rye Ridge. This open ridge offers fabulous views of the High Rock Range to the west, and access to a loop option with Etherington Creek trail to the north. Along this climb, stay right at the first junction enroute and straight at the second.

As the trail approaches Rye Ridge, at kilometre 14.1 (mile 8.8), a solid wall of mountains—the High Rock Range—blocks the western skyline. On the opposite side of this mountain barrier is the province of British Columbia. For the 32.8-km (20.4-mi.) loop, drop down the north side of Rye Ridge to link up with Etherington Creek Trail.

# 23. Etherington Creek

Map pg 191  🌲 🏇 🚴

## Trailhead

Travel south on Highway 40, or west on Highway 541 from Longview, to Highwood Junction. Head south to Etherington Creek Campground, and follow the campground road to the far end. Park at a locked gate.

## Route

| Route | Elevation | | Distance | |
|---|---|---|---|---|
| | metres | feet | km | mi. |
| Trailhead | 1596 | 5,235 | 0.0 | 0.0 |
| Rye Ridge Summit | 2349 | 7,160 | 11.2 | 7.0 |

North of Cataract Creek, Etherington provides a less travelled character, along a good quality logging road. It begins gently, as it follows former logging roads along Etherington Creek, and on towards excellent views of the High Rock

Range. It is most commonly used by mountain bikers, equestrians, and winter snowmobilers. If you follow the trail up towards Rye Ridge, you are rewarded with fabulous views of the peaks of the High Rock Range to the west.

The trail follows Etherington Creek, and passes the Baril Connector Trail at kilometre 2.5 (mile 1.5). Beyond this junction, the character of the trail changes as it crosses Etherington Creek numerous times. Stay straight at a junction at 3.5 km (2.2 mi.).

After several more fords, the trail enters a meadow at kilometre 8 (5 mi.). This marks the beginning of the climb towards Rye Ridge. Mountain bikers will find themselves pushing this steep grind, finally cresting at kilometre 11.2 (miles 7). Here you are rewarded with great views to the west and the sheer face of the High Rock Range. If you want, you can descend to the north to Cataract Creek and make a 32.8-km (20.4-mi.) loop.

# 24. Paved Trail

Map pg 194  👫 📷 🍁 🚴

## Trailhead

There are numerous trailheads for this paved path. The northern trailhead is at the Peter Lougheed Provincial Park Visitor Centre. Alternate access points can be found at Canyon Campground, William Watson Lodge, Elkwood Campground, Boulton Campground, Lower Lake Campground and Mount Sarrail Campground.

## Route

| Route | Elevation | | Distance | |
|---|---|---|---|---|
| | metres | feet | km | mi. |
| Kananaskis Visitor Centre | 1650 | 5,412 | 0.0 | 0.0 |
| Elkwood Campground | 1700 | 5,576 | 2.9 | 1.8 |
| Boulton Creek Campground | 1725 | 5,658 | 6.7 | 4.2 |
| Mount Sarrail Campground | 1675 | 5,494 | 10.4 | 6.5 |

Paralleling the highway as it winds towards the Kananaskis Lakes, this is one of the most popular trails in the valley. It links Lodgepole, Wheeler, and Lakeside Trails, beginning at the Kananaskis Visitor Centre. The trail concludes at Mount Sarrail Campground at the south end

of the Lower Kananaskis Lake. Along its winding course, most of the facilities in the Kananaskis Lakes area are accessible by bike, wheelchair, hiking boots, or cross-country skis. For families looking for a summer outing, this trail is ideal. Kids of all ages can mount their bikes or trikes and plug along beside mom and dad. It does get busy, though, so make sure they are wearing a helmet and try to stay to the right-hand side of the trail. Along the way, stop in at the Boulton Creek Trading Post for an ice cream.

From the Visitor Centre, the trail crosses the Kananaskis Lakes Trail (road) to provide access to the Canyon Campground. Beyond Canyon, the trail winds south to parallel the busy roadway. At approximately 2.4 km (1.5 mi.), the trail crosses the road again as it approaches Elkwood Campground. From the campground, it rolls past Marl Lake on the left and then runs to the east of the paved road. After passing Boulton Creek Trading Post at 6.7 km (4.2 mi.), the trail crosses the road again as it enters its final stretch along the Lakeside Trail towards Lower Lake Campground and Mount Sarrail Campground. The trail terminates at Mount Sarrail at kilometre 10.4 (mile 6.5).

# 25. Pocaterra to Kananaskis Fire Lookout

Map pg 194  📷 🌾 🍁 🚴

## Trailhead

Follow Highway 40 to its junction with the Kananaskis Lakes Trail. Turn right onto this popular road and follow it to the Pocaterra day use Area. Park here.

## Route

| Route | Elevation | | Distance | |
|---|---|---|---|---|
| | metres | feet | km | mi. |
| Pocaterra Trailhead | 1620 | 5,314 | 0.0 | 0.0 |
| Whiskey Jack Junction | 1925 | 6,314 | 8.1 | 5 |
| Kananaskis Fire Lookout | 2100 | 6,888 | 12.1 | 7.5 |

Taking its name from George Pocaterra, this

*Lower Kananaskis Lake from Fire Lookout*

trail follows Pocaterra Creek as it climbs towards the Kananaskis Fire Lookout. George Pocaterra prospected up this creek, and placed numerous claim stakes on promising outcrops of coal. He was associated with the MacKay and Dippie Coal Company. None of the deposits was ever mined, but a surveyor later stumbled across one of his claim stakes and named the creek flowing past it Pocaterra Creek.

This is a great point-to-point trail that begins along the marshes adjacent to the Pocaterra day use area and climbs gradually to its junction with Whiskey Jack Trail. From this junction, the trail climbs sharply to the Kananaskis Fire Lookout where panoramic views of the Upper and Lower Kananaskis Lakes await you.

## Pocaterra to Whiskey Jack Junction

Follow the wide path of Pocaterra trail as it passes the marshes behind the Pocaterra day use area. Keep your eyes open for moose in the open marshland. The trail remains quite level for the first kilometre (0.6 mi.), before it begins

to ascend the lower slopes of the Elk Range and Mount Tyrwhitt. Along the way, the wandering course of Pocaterra Creek remains a constant presence until you pass the junction with the Lynx winter ski trail at 2.1 km (1.3 mi.). The climbing remains moderate along the length of Pocaterra Trail. You pass another junction with a cross-country ski trail at 7.4 km (4.6 mi.). At this T-intersection, the Packers Trail drops off to the right. Stay straight and meet the junction with Whiskey Jack Trail at 8.1 km (5 mi.). You can now either take the downhill option at Whiskey Jack, or continue towards the fire lookout.

## Whiskey Jack Junction to Kananaskis Fire Lookout

There are numerous routes to access the Kananaskis Fire Lookout. Whichever route you choose, the view from the summit is worth the work. It can be accessed summer or winter, by foot, ski or mountain bike. It provides the scenic focal point for summer mountain biking within Peter Lougheed Provincial Park, as there is no better park view accessible by two wheels.

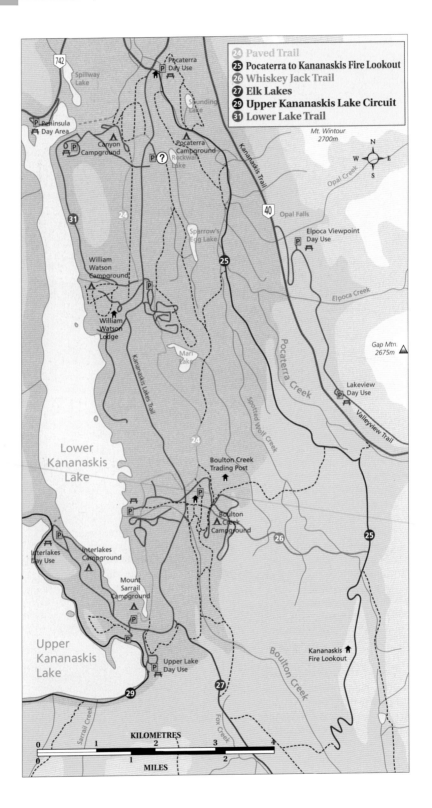

**24** Paved Trail
**25** Pocaterra to Kanaskis Fire Lookout
**26** Whiskey Jack Trail
**27** Elk Lakes
**29** Upper Kananaskis Lake Circuit
**31** Lower Lake Trail

742

Spillway Lake

Pocaterra Day Use

Saunding Lake

Peninsula Day Area

Canyon Campground

Pocaterra Campground

Rockwall Lake

Mt. Wintour 2700m

Kananaskis Trail

Opal Creek

31

24

40

Opal Falls

Sparrow's Egg Lake

Elpoca Viewpoint Day Use

25

William Watson Campground

Elpoca Creek

William Watson Lodge

Mari Lake

Gap Mtn. 2675m

Pocaterra Creek

Spotted Wolf Creek

Lakeview Day Use

Valleyview Trail

Kananaskis Lakes Trail

Lower Kananaskis Lake

24

Boulton Creek Trading Post

Boulton Creek Campground

26

25

Interlakes Day Use

Interlakes Campground

Mount Sarrail Campground

Upper Kananaskis Lake

Upper Lake Day Use

Kananaskis Fire Lookout

29

27

Boulton Creek

Sarrail Creek

Fox Creek

**KILOMETRES**

0     1     2     3     4

0         1         2

**MILES**

**194**

*Mt. Sarrail soars over Upper Kananaskis Lake*

# 26. Whiskey Jack Trail

Map pg 194 🍃 🚲

Whiskey Jack trail meets Pocaterra Trail at a T-intersection. From this junction, the signed trail to the lookout heads almost due south. After just 0.3 km (0.2 mi.), the winter cross-country ski trail called Tyrwhitt continues straight, while the trail to the lookout forks to the right. From this final junction, the trail climbs 220 m (720 ft.) in just the last 1.8 km (1.1 mi.) to crest the summit.

As you reach the lookout, please keep in mind that this is not a public building and the Alberta Forest Service asks that you don't approach the fire lookouts. Please enjoy the view without disturbing the lookout personnel. From this point, the valley to the west is spread below your feet. The Upper and Lower Lakes sit at the base of a wall of mountains. To the northwest, Mount Indefatigable stands defiantly like the battleship it was named after (see 'Battle of Jutland', page 103). Directly west, the imposing face of Mount Lyautey still holds several glaciers, and sits adjacent to the Continental Divide.

From the lookout, cyclists and expert skiers may want to continue, over the summit and descend down to Elk Pass Trail. Hikers will likely wish to return along the same route. The summer trail is dark and wet, and offers little to attract hikers.

## Trailhead

Follow the Kananaskis Lakes Trail (road) for approximately 10 km (6.2 mi.) to the Boulton Creek Trading Post. The trail leaves from the far side of the trading post trailhead.

## Route

| Route | Elevation | | Distance | |
|---|---|---|---|---|
| | metres | feet | km | mi. |
| Whiskey Jack Trailhead | 1700 | 5,576 | 0.0 | 0.0 |
| Pocaterra Junction | 1925 | 6,314 | 3.7 | 2.3 |

Whiskey Jack Trail is usually linked with other trails in the area to provide access to the Kananaskis Fire Lookout or the rolling Pocaterra Trail. The trail is wide and smooth, climbing steadily from the trailhead to its junction with the Pocaterra Trail at kilometre 3.7 (mile 2.3).

Beginning in the parking lot adjacent to the Boulton Creek Trading Post, Whiskey Jack Trail parallels the campground access road for a short distance. The steep climbing begins at kilometre 2.4 (mile 1.5) as the trail enters an old growth forest. The trees appear unhealthy due to stringy lichens hanging from their branches like beards—hence their common name "old man's beard". These lichens don't damage the trees at all, but merely use the tree to get access to sunlight.

After a second crossing of Spotted Wolf Creek, the trail meets a T-junction with Pocaterra Trail at 3.7 km (2.3 mi.). You now have the option of turning right to climb to the Kananaskis Fire Lookout, or left to enjoy a rolling descent along the wide Pocaterra Trail.

# 27. Elk Lakes

Map pg 197  📷  🌿  🍁  🚲

## Trailhead

Follow the winding Kananaskis Lakes Trail (road) for approximately 12 km (7.2 mi.) to the Elk Pass Trailhead.

## Route

| Route | Elevation | | Distance | |
|---|---|---|---|---|
| | metres | feet | km | mi. |
| Trailhead | 1710 | 5,609 | 0.0 | 0.0 |
| Elk Pass | 1960 | 6,429 | 5.7 | 3.6 |
| West Elk Pass | 1925 | 6,314 | 4.8 | 3.0 |
| Upper Elk Lake | 1770 | 5,806 | 8.2 | 5.1 |

This route takes you across the Continental Divide to several glacially-fed lakes in British Columbia's Elk Lakes Provincial Park. Hikers, mountain bikers and cross-country skiers use the route.

The main route to the Elk Lakes follows the Elk Pass Trail. Beginning at the trailhead along the Kananaskis Lakes Trail, follow this wide road as it leaves the parking lot. Stay right at the junction with Boulton Creek Trail just beyond the trailhead, and right again at a junction with Fox Creek at around the 1.5-km (0.9-mi.) mark. At another junction 0.5 km (0.3 mi.) further, stay right again. This is the access trail to the hydro-line. As the trail climbs gradually, it follows the meandering course of Fox Creek. Patterson Trail forks to the left at kilometre 3.8 (mile 2.4).

Stay straight and pass the winter trail to Blueberry Hill 0.5 km (0.3 mi.) beyond. Only a hundred metres or so beyond the Blueberry Hill junction, you'll see a trail fork off to the right with a sign indicating Lower Elk Lake. Hikers will likely want to take this route, which traverses West Elk Pass, while mountain bikers will need to continue towards Elk Pass proper.

## Elk Pass to Elk Lakes Park Headquarters

Mountain bikers and skiers should continue past the West Elk Pass Trail for an additional 1.3 km (0.8 mi.). Just prior to meeting the pass, the trail joins the hydroline, which offers cyclists a loop option back to the trailhead. The pass is quite low, only 1960 m (6,429 ft.), following the hydroline as it enters British Columbia and drops into the Elk Valley. As you roll your way downhill, following the western boundary of Elk Lakes Provincial Park, you will come to the Park Administration Offices after a descent of 3.9 km (2.4 mi.).

## West Elk Pass to Upper Elk Lake

From the junction for West Elk Pass, you leave the wide road of Elk Pass Trail behind and head into the bush on a more rustic route. Follow the trail for a few hundred metres and meet the pass at a T-intersection with a boundary cutline. There is also an information board here.

From West Elk Pass you have two options. You can either continue across the cutline and descend the wide trail towards the Elk Lakes Park headquarters, or turn right up the cutline and take the trail to the Upper Elk Lake.

If you want to hike towards Upper Elk Lake, stay to the right and follow the cutline west for 0.4 km (0.24 mi.) until you see a signed trail forking to the left near a monument marked by "1M". The trail passes through a marshy area on a wooden boardwalk before passing the shoreline of Fox Lake. As you begin to descend towards the Upper Elk Lake, you get periodic views to the Elk Valley to the southwest. After passing a large avalanche slope on the side of Mount Fox, you enter the final approach to Upper Elk Lake. Your first views show the lake with the Castelnau Glacier high above it. Just before you reach the lake, you'll cross a bridge over the outflow from Upper Elk Lake, and then meet a

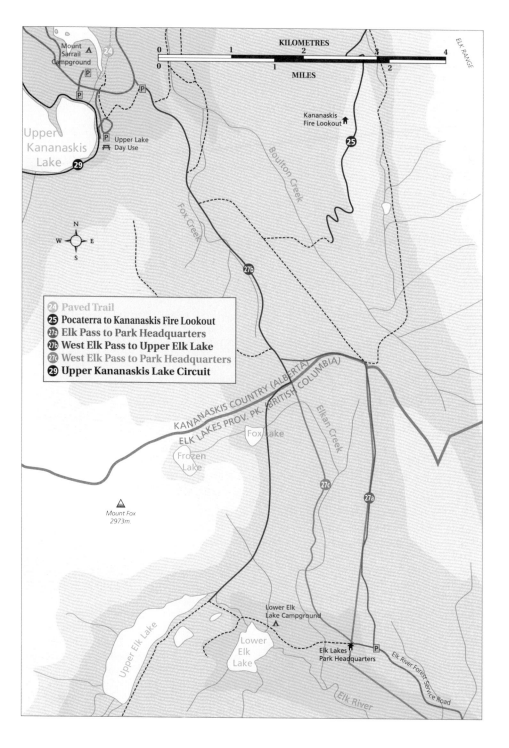

KILOMETRES

MILES

Mount
Sarrail
Campground

24

Kananaskis
Fire Lookout

Upper Lake
Day Use

Upper
Kananaskis
Lake

29

25

27b

Fox Creek

Boulton Creek

**24** Paved Trail
**25** Pocaterra to Kananaskis Fire Lookout
**27a** Elk Pass to Park Headquarters
**27b** West Elk Pass to Upper Elk Lake
**27c** West Elk Pass to Park Headquarters
**29** Upper Kananaskis Lake Circuit

KANANASKIS COUNTRY (ALBERTA)
ELK LAKES PROV. PK. (BRITISH COLUMBIA)

Fox Lake

Frozen
Lake

Elkan Creek

27c

27a

Mount Fox
2973m.

Lower Elk
Lake Campground

Upper Elk Lake

Lower
Elk
Lake

Elk Lakes
Park Headquarters

Elk River Forest Service Road

Elk River

ELK RANGE

*Mt. Indefatigable in autumn*

trail forking to the left at kilometre 8.2 (mile 5.1). This trail goes to Lower Elk Lake and the BC Parks campground. The campground is 1 km (0.6 mi.) from this point and lies near the shoreline of Lower Elk Lake. Beyond, the park entrance and administration buildings lie 1.6 km (1 mi.) past the campground.

If you have several days, you can follow the shore of Upper Elk Lake and head up the valley of Petain Creek 2.6 km (1.6 mi.) to the Petain Creek Campground, or beyond to Petain Falls 1.9 km (1.2 mi.) beyond the campsite.

## West Elk Pass to Elk Lakes Park Headquarters

To take the more direct route to the park headquarters, cross the wide cutline at West Elk Pass and follow the trail as it drops south into the Elk Valley. Soon after crossing the cutline, you'll cross Elkan Creek for the first time. (It's name is a combination of the words elk and Kananaskis) After crossing a long wooden boardwalk across a marshy section, the trail continues towards the park headquarters with great views of the surrounding peaks. The headquarters is 4.2 km (2.6 mi.) from West Elk Pass.

# 28. Mount Indefatigable

Map pg 200 📷 🌿 🍃

### Trailhead

Follow the Kananaskis Lakes Trail to its terminus at the North Interlakes Trailhead. The Mount Indefatigable Trail begins on the opposite side of the Upper Lake dam.

### Route

| Route | Elevation | | Distance | |
|---|---|---|---|---|
| | metres | feet | km | mi. |
| Trailhead | 1700 | 5,576 | 0.0 | 0.0 |
| Upper Lake Viewpoint | 1950 | 6,396 | 1.0 | 0.6 |
| Trail Terminus | 2200 | 7,216 | 2.2 | 1.4 |

If you hike only one trail in Kananaskis Country, make this the trail. It's steep and rocky, but the views are absolutely the best you'll find anywhere. Climbing high above the Upper and Lower Kananaskis Lakes, it provides a panorama that is hard to beat. The trail is short, only 2.2 km (1.4 mi.) one way, but it climbs 500 m (1,640 ft.) in that short distance.

*Hikers at Upper Kananaskis Lake*

died while scrambling towards the summit. Scrambling is best reserved for very experienced hikers.

# 29. Upper Kananaskis Lake Circuit

Map pg 200 🚹🚺 📷 🍃

## Trailhead

Follow the Kananaskis Lake Trail (road) for approximately 12.5 km (7.8 mi.) to the Upper Lakes day use area. Follow the access road to the parking area near the boat launch.

The trail begins at North Interlakes day use area, at the end of the Kananaskis Lakes Trail. After crossing the dam separating the Upper and Lower Lakes, branch off to the right and head north through the trees. The forest is dark and damp for a few minutes, but after crossing a tiny bridge, it climbs out of the trees, and onto the exposed rock slope. As you climb this ridge, the route crosses some loose gravel and you'll find yourself scrambling over numerous rocks, but the trail is well-defined, and the views keep improving with every step. Before you know it, you crest out on a ledge overlooking both lakes, and a seemingly out-of-place bench beckons you to take a load off. This is the scenic highlight of the trail, so take the time to do it justice. While not far from the parking lot, you've done the most difficult part of the trail. As you continue climbing, the Upper Lake slowly disappears from view and the panorama begins to concentrate north, up the Lower Lake and the valley of the Smith-Dorrien/Spray Trail. Near the upper extent of the trail, alpine larch show off their golden plumage each fall, making the trip worthwhile all over again.

It is tempting to keep going, climbing beyond the formal trail end, towards the various outliers of Mount Indefatigable. The mountain was named for a battleship at the Battle of Jutland in WW1, and, like a battleship, it is still taking casualties. In the summer of 1995, a hiker

## Route

| Route | Elevation | | Distance | |
|---|---|---|---|---|
| | metres | feet | km | mi. |
| Trailhead | 1680 | 5,510 | 0.0 | 0.0 |
| Hidden Lake Junction | 1750 | 5,740 | 5.2 | 3.2 |
| Point Campground | 1730 | 5,674 | 7.6 | 4.7 |
| North Interlakes | 1700 | 5,576 | 11.0 | 6.8 |
| Return to Trailhead | 1680 | 5,510 | 14.9 | 9.3 |

The Upper Kananaskis Lake Circuit offers a pleasant, level day trip. It winds 14.9 km (9.3 mi.), circumnavigating the shores of Upper Kananaskis Lake. Point Campground, only 3.4 km (2.1 mi.) from the North Interlakes day use area, offers the chance for an overnight stay, making a nice loop backpacking trip. Along the way, the change in elevation is virtually zero, making this a nice introductory backpacking route.

Beginning at Upper Lake day use area, the wide trail follows the shoreline of the Upper Lake as it winds around the south end of the lake. There are great views across the lake towards Mount Indefatigable. After passing a waterfall at the base of Sarrail Creek, you'll pass a signed junction for Rawson Lake Trail at kilometre 1.2 (mile 0.8). The trail remains level beyond this junction, still hugging the shoreline until you pass an unsigned junction with a trail heading south (left) to Hidden Lake at kilometre 5.2 (mile 3.2).

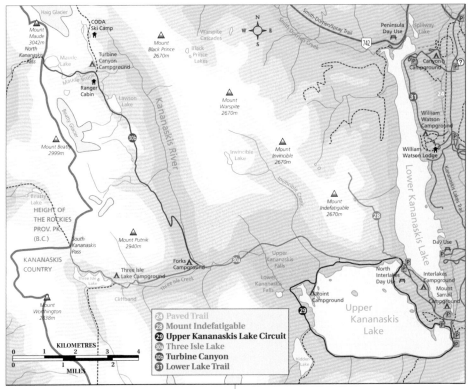

Beyond this rustic junction, the trail leaves the lakeshore behind, heading inland to make a more direct line around an inlet of the Upper Lake. You'll do a bit of uphill at the beginning of this stretch as you traverse the base of Mount Lyautey. As you round the inlet, the trail crosses the Kananaskis River upstream of the Lower Kananaskis Falls. After the crossing, turn right, following the trail downstream to the falls and past a spur trail to Point Backcountry Campground. This small backcountry campsite only 3.4 km (2.1 mi) from the North Interlakes Day-use area and so makes for a great introductory backpack site. Her you will find 20 sites with picnic tables, firepits, firewood and lockers for your food.

As you continue beyond the campsite, the trail begins to wind to the right after half a kilometre or so. This marks the beginning of a field of boulder debris that has tumbled down the side of Mount Indefatigable. As you pick your way through the rocks, you will pass an exit trail that offers the option of climbing up to the wide access road to Forks Campground. Staying on the lower trail will eventually allow you to join

with this route anyway. There are some impressive views as you wander along the north shore of the Upper Kananaskis Lake with Mounts Sarrail and Foch to the south and Mount Lyautey mirroring the western shore of the lake. Standing alone in the lake is tiny Hawke Island. It is now one of only a few islands in a lake that once contained many. The raising of the water level for hydro generation has submerged the majority of the historic islands. Join the wide fire road at kilometre 10.2 (mile 6.3), and dig in for the flat grind towards North Interlakes. Just before you meet this busy day use area, you'll pass a signed junction for Mount Indefatigable Trail. This fabulous trail heads to the left. Stay straight on the wide gravel, and after climbing over the dam spillway, meet North Interlakes at kilometre 11 (mile 6.6).

To continue along this circuit, follow the trail from North Interlakes. The final 3.9 km (2.4 mi.) follows the east shoreline of the Upper Kananaskis Lake with great views reflecting the snowy summits of Mounts Lyautey and Sarrail. As you approach the Upper Lake day use area, a short spur trail to the right continues onto the point where many years ago Geoffrey Gaherty had a cozy little cabin. Today a crumbling chimney is all that remains. Finally, you rejoin civilization at kilometre 14.9 (mile 9.3).

# 30. Three Isle Lake and Turbine Canyon

Map pg 200  📷  🌾  🍃

## Trailhead

Follow the Kananaskis Lakes Trail (road) to its terminus at the North Interlakes Trailhead. The Three Isle Lake Trail begins on the opposite side of the Upper Lake dam.

## Route

| Route | Elevation | | Distance | |
|---|---|---|---|---|
| | metres | feet | km | mi. |
| Trailhead | 1700 | 5,576 | 0.0 | 0.0 |
| Forks Campground | 1780 | 5,838 | 7.0 | 4.4 |
| Forks to Three Isle Lake | 2200 | 7,216 | 9.8 | 6.1 |
| South Kananaskis Pass | 2310 | 7,478 | 11.6 | 7.2 |
| Forks to Turbine Canyon | 2210 | 7,249 | 14.8 | 9.2 |
| North Kananaskis Pass | 2368 | 7,767 | 16.5 | 10.3 |

This route offers two of the most popular backpacking routes in Peter Lougheed Provincial Park—the route to Three Isle Lake and the South Kananaskis Pass, or, as an alternative, Turbine Canyon and North Kananaskis Pass. Beginning at North Interlakes day use, the trail follows the shoreline before leaving the lake behind and heading up the valley of the Kananaskis River. Forks Campground at kilometre 7.2 (mile 4.5) forms the juncture between the two routes. Three Isle lake continues to the west, and Turbine Canyon branches to the north.

The Three Isle Lake Trail leaves the Kananaskis River behind and follows the winding course of Three Isle Creek towards its source at Three Isle Lake. Keep in mind that the headwall beneath Three Isle Lake is very steep and has significant exposure. Novices and younger hikers may find it more than they bargained for.

When I was here, many hikers were turned away by the intensity of the climb. The rewards, though, are great, as you cook your breakfast on the shore of this pleasant tarn on the Continental Divide.

Turbine Canyon offers different challenges, with greater distances but equally spectacular scenery. After attaining the bench on the side of Mount Putnik, the trail crosses numerous meadows and stands of larch. There are several lakes and great views of the Haig Glacier. The canyon is fabulous and the area around the pass offers endless potential for exploration.

## North Interlakes to Forks Campground

From North Interlakes Campground, cross over the dam and drop down the steps on the opposite side of the spillway. The trail immediately winds left as it passes the start of the Mount Indefatigable Trail. Drink in the views across the Upper Lake as you pound your way along the hard gravel surface. Stay right at a Y-junction at kilometre 0.8 (mile 0.5). The trail to the left takes you across the debris slope to the Point Campground. For a while, the two trails parallel each other, and there is an alternate exit to Point Campground at kilometre 2.2 (mile 1.4). Stay right again at this fork and begin to leave the views of the Upper Lake behind as the trail heads up the valley along the base of Mount Indefatigable.

Invincible Creek tumbles down from the right at approximately 3.7 km (2.3 mi.). This junction marks the end of the mountain bike trail, and cyclists will need to park their bikes to continue. Cross the creek on a high-quality bridge and enjoy the now soft carpet beneath your feet as you leave the hard, rocky gravel behind. As you head into a much darker spruce and alpine fire forest, there is an understory of false azalea, bunchberry, bearberry and grouseberry. Soon after rejoining the Kananaskis River, there is another high-quality bridge that crosses this large stream just above the Upper Kananaskis Waterfall. As you follow the stream (now on your right), you get good views towards Mount Invincible to the north. In the spring, keep your eyes open for the delicate white-flowered rhododendron.

Half a kilometre (0.3 mi.) past the Upper Kananaskis Waterfall, the trail emerges at the base of a huge rock debris slope on the base of Mount Lyautey. As you walk along the edge of this slope, note the contrast between the rocky boulder field to the left and the horsetail-lined river to the right. Leave the boulder field behind at 6.2 km (3.9 mi.) and head back into a needle carpeted forest. After crossing the river several times, you enter Forks Campground at kilometre 7 (mile 4.4). This popular backcountry campsite has 15 sites boasting all the amenities, including picnic tables, firepits, outhouses and a food hanging rack.

## Forks Campground to Three Isle Lake

As you arrive at Forks Campground, turn left at the entrance to the campground to continue to Three Isle Lake. Soon after leaving Forks Campground, the trail begins to wind along the outflow of Three Isle Creek. As it joins the creek, it begins with a short traverse up a narrow sidecut

to the right of the stream. As you climb this short section, be sure to stay to the right, as it is easy to get off the main trail here. The correct route leaves the river briefly to climb high above the river. This uphill trend continues for the remainder of the trip to the lake.

As you climb, the understory becomes a lush mixture of cow parsnip and bracted honeysuckle, along with a mixture of other wildflowers. As you pass a series of stone steps at kilometre 8.6 (mile 5.4), the climbing gets steeper. Beyond this, you'll cross a bridge over a runoff channel, and as you cross the avalanche slope, you get a clear view of the headwall. It is sheer, steep and brutal. From this point you'll climb 270 m (886 ft.) in just 0.8 km (0.5 mi.). As you approach the base of the headwall there is a set of wooden cribwork steps with a chain handrail, marking the beginning of the very steep climb. Beyond these steps, you'll need to scramble up a small cliff band that will intimidate novices. From this point, you begin to head up towards

## Beaver Fever

**Picture this.** You're out hiking on one of Kananaskis Country's many hot summer days. You reach down into a pristine stream and splash a few handfuls on your face to cool down. A few weeks later you begin to notice an unpleasant change. It begins with a little diarrhea and progresses to include abdominal cramps, nausea, loss of appetite, weight loss, bloating, and abnormal amounts of

*Don't blame it on the beaver*

gas. Chances are you've been chosen as a host for a tiny, single-celled animal known as *Giardia* ("gee-ARD-ee-uh") *lamblia*. This tiny parasite causes a malady known as giardiasis, commonly referred to as "Beaver Fever."

*Giardia* are so small that more than 15,000 can fit on the head of a pin, but it only takes a dozen or so to bring on giardiasis. Once ingested, they make their way to your small intestine and eventually leave your body, hidden within cysts, in your wastes. In a full-blown case of giardiasis, you may excrete hundreds of millions of cysts per day.

The cure involves a few-weeks-worth of the drug

Flagyl. This bombards your intestinal tract with chemicals designed to kill *Giardia*. While it is true that beaver do carry the disease, so do many other animals, including man. Man must take some of the responsibility for the recent spread of this disease into more and more areas. Poor sanitary practices and the inclusion of "man's best friend" in the outdoor experience have allowed *Giardia* to move into areas not frequented by beaver. Dogs are even less particular than some hikers about where they do their business.

Proper treatment of drinking water can help make sure the little guys are not allowed into your intestines. There seems to be some dispute as to the effectiveness of various chemical treatments, so the two best remedies remain boiling for at least five minutes, or filtration. You will need a filter capable of filtering *Giardia* as small as 10–20 microns across.

*Stairs on Three Isle Lake trail*

the draw that will take you to the top of the headwall. There are fabulous views to the east down the valley of Three Isle Creek as you climb, and finally, at approximately 9.6 km (6 mi.), you reach the top of the headwall.

From the headwall, the trail drops slightly to meet the campground junction at kilometre 9.8 (mile 6.1) and the lake is just slightly ahead. Three Isle Lake is surrounded by alpine larch and is set amidst the backdrop of Mount Worthington on the west and Mount Putnik to the northeast. A short hike from the campground will bring you to the South Kananaskis Pass and the British Columbia boundary after an additional distance of 1.8 km (1.1 mi.) and 106 m (348 ft.) of elevation.

## Forks Campground to Maude and Lawson Lakes

Turbine Canyon likely welcomed the first non-native travellers within the Kananaskis Valley in 1854, and provides some of the most elegant backpacking in the park. The trail begins along the same route as Three Isle Lake; however, at Forks Campground, at kilometre 7 (mile 4.4), the route heads north, up the valley of the Upper Kananaskis River. This wide, glacial valley leads the hiker into an alpine wonderland with numerous options for exploration.

When James Sinclair travelled this route in 1854, along with 15 non-native families, 100 Cree, and 250 cattle, the route was so difficult the cattle had to be slaughtered. Sinclair described a harrowing expedition, but he and the

group of settlers he led were the first non-natives (though some, including Sinclair, were Métis) known to have travelled through the rugged Kananaskis valley.

Beyond Forks, the Maude-Lawson trail follows the Upper Kananaskis River for a short while before climbing sharply up the lower slopes of Mount Putnik. After climbing approximately 400 m (1,312 ft.) in just over 2 km (1.2 mi.), it eventually levels out along a bench on the side of Mount Beatty. The trail follows this elevated bench through a series of alpine meadows and stands of alpine larch. After passing a tiny pond, the views open towards the Haig Glacier to the north. Lawson Lake is at kilometre 13.5 (mile 8.4). The trail skirts the western shoreline before heading on towards Turbine Canyon and the North Kananaskis Pass. After leaving the lake, you'll pass a ranger's cabin before descending towards Turbine Canyon backcountry campsite at kilometre 14.8 (mile 9.2). Turbine Canyon is a sheer, narrow canyon carved by the meltwater from the Haig Glacier and the runoff from Maude Brook. The campground has 12 rustic sites, but lacks firepits or picnic tables.

If you want to continue towards Maude Lake and the North Kananaskis Pass, follow the trail as it climbs to the west, bringing you to the frigid shoreline of the lake at kilometre 16.5 (mile 10.3). The actual pass is at kilometre 17 (mile 10.6), at an elevation of 2368 m (7,767 ft.). Unlike the South Kananaskis Pass, this is a rugged, wind-blasted glacial landscape of rock and snow.

*The Elk Range*

# 31. Lower Lake Trail

Map pg 194 👫 📷 🌾 🍂

## Trailhead

Follow the Kananaskis Lakes Trail (road) for several kilometres to the Canyon Campground. Turn into the campground and follow the signs for the boat launch. The trailhead is at the boat launch parking lot.

| Route | Elevation | | Distance | |
|---|---|---|---|---|
| | metres | feet | km | mi. |
| Trailhead | 1650 | 5,412 | 0.0 | 0.0 |
| William Watson Lodge | 1680 | 5,510 | 3.5 | 2.2 |

This trail can be hiked in either direction, but will be described in a north-south direction here, beginning at Canyon Dam and finishing at William Watson Lodge. It is a pleasant 3.5-km (2.2-mi.) hike that skirts the shoreline of the Lower Kananaskis Lake. Across the Lake, the steep faces of Mounts Invincible and Indefatigable are reflected in the deep blue water of the Lower Lake. In early summer, low water levels reveal the bleached bones of the long-flooded forest that once lined the original lake. Like the Upper Lake, its level was raised significantly when the lake was dammed in 1954.

Following the lakeshore, take the time to relax along the quiet waters of the lake and forget the worries of city life. All too soon, the trail turns inland as it approaches the south trailhead at William Watson Lodge. As you meet the paved interpretive trail that radiates out from the lodge, turn left near Interpretive Stop 5. Signs will guide you to either to William Watson Lodge, or on towards Elkwood Campground. You can also make a loop with the Lodgepole section of the paved bike path. The loop option is around 6.3 km (3.9 mi.) long.

# 32. Elbow Lake

Map pg 205 👫 📷 🌾 🍂 🐎 🚴

## Trailhead

Elbow Lake trailhead is located on Highway 40, 12.9 km (8 mi.) south of the winter gate and the junction with Kananaskis Lakes Trail.

| Route | Elevation | | Distance | |
|---|---|---|---|---|
| | metres | feet | km | mi. |
| Trailhead | 1960 | 6,429 | 0.0 | 0.0 |
| Elbow Lake | 2080 | 6,822 | 1.3 | 0.8 |

Elbow Lake trail is used by families looking for a nice summer walk to a picturesque lake, as well as by horseback riders using it as an access into the Elbow-Sheep Wildland Park. It is the only trail in Peter Lougheed Provincial Park that allows horses, and the trail is merely used as a travel corridor by equestrians. You may also see hikers lugging their skis with them, as the trail is

*The Goat Range*

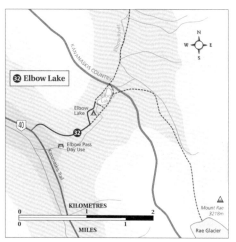

32 Elbow Lake

often used to access the Rae Glacier for some summer turns.

From the trailhead, the wide trail winds westward, passing beneath the summits of Elpoca Mountain to the north and Mount Rae to the south. The trail is wide and smooth, but after approximately 1 km (0.6 mi.), there is an unmarked junction with a more rustic trail forking to the right. The main trail continues left to meet the shoreline at 1.3 km (0.8 mi.). There is a campsite at Elbow Lake with 15 sites.

Elbow Lake is a fabulous pond that reflects the snow-capped summits above it with remarkable clarity. A trail skirts the shoreline, making for a pleasant loop walk. Options include continuing over Elbow Pass to link with the trails of the Elbow-Sheep Wildland Park, or following a hiker-defined route, that continues to the Rae Glacier some 2.7 km (1.7 mi.) further.

# 33. Goat Creek

Map pg 171 🚶👫 🚲

## Trailhead

The trailhead is along the Smith-Dorrien/Spray Trail (road), at a signed trailhead 5.4 km (3.4 mi.) south of the Canmore Nordic Centre.

## Route

| Route | Elevation | | Distance | |
|---|---|---|---|---|
| | metres | feet | km | mi. |
| Trailhead | 1675 | 5,495 | 0.0 | 0.0 |
| Spray Loop Junction | 1430 | 4,690 | 18.5 | 11.5 |
| Banff Springs Hotel | 1384 | 4,538 | 19.8 | 12.3 |

This trail is one of the most popular mountain bike and cross-country ski routes in the Rockies. Providing easy access to Banff, its 19.8 km (12.3 mi.) take you along the west side of Mount Rundle's sloping face. For hiking, there are other options that offer more in the way of scenery, and you don't reach any alpine vantage points on this trail, but it does offer a nice route to explore.

The scenery along this trail is pleasant, though not spectacular. Paralleling the length of Mount Rundle, you are treated to numerous views of its steeply bedded slopes. This mountain, one of the most photographed in the Rockies, is a classic example of a Front Range peak. Although more of a range than a single peak, its rock layers have been thrust upwards at steep angles. Mount Rundle takes its name from one of the first non-natives to set foot in this area way back in 1845. Reverend Robert T. Rundle was a Methodist missionary who worked extensively with the local Stoney Indians.

On numerous occasions, you will encounter well-bridged stream crossings as the trail follows Goat Creek, and later, the Spray River. Thus the sound of water is a common and pleasant addition to this trip. From the trailhead along the Smith-Dorrien/Spray Trail, the trail begins dropping right away. It will maintain this trend throughout most of its route. After approximately 0.9 km (0.6 mi.), the trail leaves Kananaskis Country and enters Banff National Park. After rolling for 6.8 km (4.2 mi.), the trail crosses a bridge over Goat Creek, followed by crossings at 7.4 and 7.9 km (4.6 and 4.9 mi.) respectively. There is a sharp climb following this last crossing of Goat Creek.

At kilometre 9.8 (mile 6.1), there is a final bridge crossing after a sharp, winding drop to meet the Spray River. A short climb after the bridge brings you to a junction with the Spray Fire road. Turn right and follow this wide road as it makes its way towards Banff. At kilometre 18.5 (mile 11.5), you have the option of crossing the Spray River and riding the opposite bank or remaining on the main road and continuing to the Banff Springs Hotel. Staying on this main route will bring you to the Springs at kilometre 19.8 (mile 12.3).

# 34. Buller Pass

Map pg 207

*Hiker on the Buller Pass trail*

## Trailhead

Follow the Smith-Dorrien/Spray Trail (road) from Canmore to the Buller Pass day use area. The trail begins on the opposite side of the dusty Smith-Dorrien/Spray Trail.

## Route

| Route | Elevation | | Distance | |
|---|---|---|---|---|
| | metres | feet | km | mi. |
| Trailhead | 1800 | 5,904 | 0.0 | 0.0 |
| Buller Pass | 2470 | 8,102 | 6.5 | 4.0 |
| Ribbon Lake | 2100 | 6,888 | 9.1 | 5.7 |

This 6.5 km (4 mi.) point-to-point trail provides an alternate access route to the Ribbon Creek area, and panoramic views of the Spray Valley to the west and beyond, all the way to Mount Assiniboine. Beyond the pass, the trail descends into the valley of Ribbon Lake, where options include exiting over Guinn's Pass or descending the Ribbon Creek valley.

Beginning at Buller Mountain day use area, along the dusty Smith-Dorrien/Spray Trail, the trail begins by that road. After traversing a good quality bridge, the trail begins climbing gradually through an alpine fir and Engelmann Spruce forest. At 0.9 km (0.6 mi.), the trail crosses Buller Creek over a high-quality bridge, bringing you onto the left side of the creek. Beyond this, the trail continues to climb gradually and the views begin to open up towards the

jagged summit of Mount Engadine on your right. Soon, the view is balanced with periodic views to the left, towards Buller Mountain.

At kilometre 2 (mile 1.2), the trail begins to pass alongside a steep dogtooth summit on the slopes of Mount Engadine. Cross the creek again at kilometre 2.7 (mile 1.7) and begin a steep uphill section. With this gain in elevation, the views open up. As you cross a rocky outcrop you get good views to the rear, all the way to the Smith-Dorrien/Spray Trail.

After joining the creek again, the trail emerges at the base of a scree slope with great views towards the sheer face of an unnamed ridge up to the right. Just beyond this, you'll pass a plunge pool on the left, into which a delicate waterfall pours, in two steps.

After crossing another bridge over the creek, the trail enters a beautiful, open, subalpine forest. There is a massive ridge above you with a sharp summit that almost looks like a sharkfin. At kilometre 4.1 (mile 2.6), the trail makes a left to traverse a small canyon that is carved across your path. It is only about 15 m (49 ft.) deep, but makes for an impressive sight in such a splendid setting.

You get your first views towards the actual pass at kilometre 4.8 (mile 3). As you cross this wide alpine meadow, there is plenty of evidence

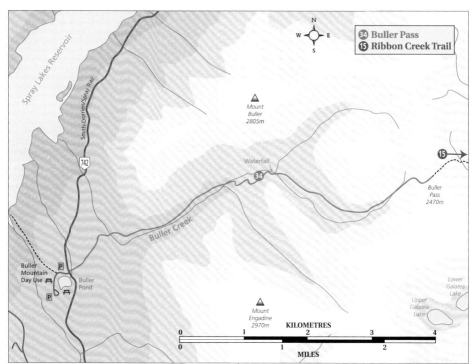

of grizzly bear diggings. In summer and fall, grizzlies like to dig up ground squirrel dens for a quick hit of protein. They also dig for the underground roots of plants like the hedysarum. Some of these excavations can be immense, as evidenced by the diggings through this section of trail.

As you begin to approach the steep scree slope that guards the pass, there is a pretty little waterfall beside the trail. Beyond this, the climbing begins in earnest as you zigzag your way up the steep face towards the pass. Just before you summit, look back to the west and get a fabulous view of the towering summit of Mount Assiniboine. This is one of the few places in Kananaskis Country from which you can see this immense mountain. You reach the pass at kilometre 6.5 (mile 4).

If you are planning on continuing to Ribbon Lake and beyond, descend the east side of the pass. The trail drops rapidly until you reach the base of the pass and the T-intersection with Guinn's Pass trail at kilometre 7.9 (mile 4.9). Stay left and reach Ribbon Lake after an additional 1.2 km (0.8 mi.).

# 35. Mount Shark to Mount Assiniboine

Map pg 209

## Trailhead

From Canmore, follow the Smith-Dorrien/Spray Trail south for 39 km (24.2 mi.) to the south end of the Spray Lakes. At the Mount Shark turnoff, turn right and follow this road to its conclusion at the Mount Shark trailhead.

## Route

| Route | Elevation | | Distance | |
|---|---|---|---|---|
| | metres | feet | km | mi. |
| Trailhead | 1763 | 5,785 | 0.0 | 0.0 |
| Watridge Lake | 1800 | 5,904 | 3.8 | 2.4 |
| Karst Springs | 1820 | 5,970 | 4.6 | 2.9 |
| Assiniboine Pass | 2180 | 7,152 | 22.0 | 13.7 |
| Lake Magog | 2072 | 6,800 | 25.5 | 15.9 |

## Mount Shark Trailhead to Watridge Lake

How does one describe the route to Mount Assiniboine? This is an area that must be experienced to be believed. Although the main access is through Kananaskis Country, this route also passes through parts of Banff National Park before entering Mount Assiniboine Provincial Park in British Columbia. Culminating at Lake Magog, beneath the towering horn of Assiniboine, this trail should be near the top of anyone's list.

Winter and summer, the access to Assiniboine is varied. Travel options include horseback, helicopter, cross-country skis or even foot. The last two are by far the most difficult, requiring a backpack and enough gear for several days. The distance from Mount Shark to Lake Magog tops out at 25.5 km (15.9 mi.).

As you leave the trailhead at Mount Shark, the Spray Lakes are visible to the north and Mount Shark stands fast to the south. Following the winter ski trail, the trail takes you past Watridge Lake.

### Pika Paradise

**The pika is** one of the most amazing residents of the alpine. If you've never seen one, relax, you're not alone. Generally found only in desolate debris slopes, they blend perfectly with their rocky surroundings. Often, the first sign of a pika (pronounced "pee-kuh") is its strange call. It's this call that gives the animal its name, and it can be described as a sort of bleating "Peeek."

The sound generally comes from the middle of a seemingly lifeless rock slide, and before long it becomes a chorus that surrounds you. This is complicated by the nature of the rock slope, which causes the sound of a single call to seems like it comes from all directions—almost like a ventriloquist throwing his voice. This works very well to confuse predators.

Usually your first sighting begins with a flash of movement out of the corner of your eye. Upon further examination, you'll find a small grey animal that resembles a guinea pig and blends in so well with the limestone that you'll almost lose it in the rocks. It is about 18 cm (7 in.) long, with short, rounded ears

*Pika*

*Pika tracks*

and no visible tail.

Pikas are not rodents, but are actually part of the rabbit family. Their body temperature is quite high, around 40°C (104°F), and a rise of between four and six degrees can be fatal. This narrow range forces them to live in cooler areas, usually at elevations above 2,100 m (6,930 ft.).

Unlike most other small members of the alpine community, the pika does not hibernate. It spends most of the summer months collecting plants and building large hay piles (some of which may be as large as a bushel) and leaving them to season, much like a farmer leaving out his bales. These stores will feed it through the eight or nine months of winter.

To collect its supply of plants, it must leave the security of its rock or talus slope. Recognizing its vulnerability, it spends as little time in the meadow as possible. Quickly gathering plants, it places them crossways in its mouth and returns to the talus.

There are many great spots to view pikas, but Rock Glacier is the very best I have ever found. Bring along your binoculars and your patience, as they are not easy to spot. It is definitely worth the effort.

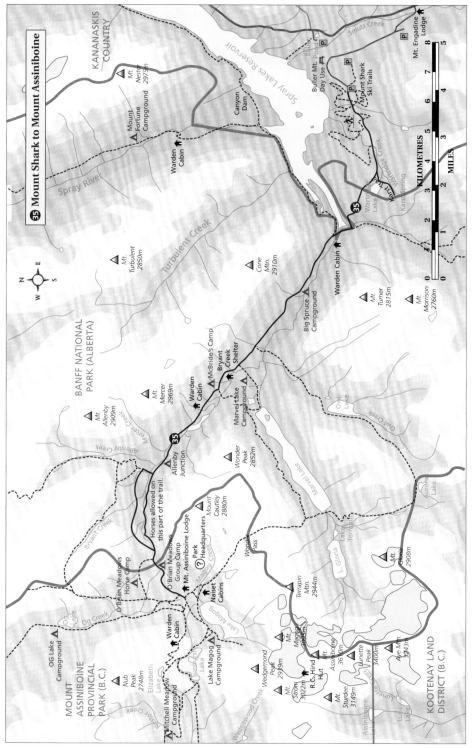

**35 Mount Shark to Mount Assiniboine**

KANANASKIS COUNTRY

BANFF NATIONAL PARK (ALBERTA)

MOUNT ASSINIBOINE PROVINCIAL PARK (B.C.)

KOOTENAY LAND DISTRICT (B.C.)

Spray Lakes Reservoir

Smuts Creek

Mt. Engadine Lodge

Mount Shark Ski Trails

Buller Mt. Pond Day Use

Karst Spring

Watridge Creek

Warden Lake

Spray River

Mount Fortune Campground

Mt. Nestor 2975m

Canyon Dam

Warden Cabin

Turbulent Creek

Mt. Turbulent 2850m

Cone Mtn. 2910m

Warden Cabin

Big Spruce Campground

Mt. Turner 2815m

Mt. Morrison 2760m

Mt. Mercer 2969m

Warden Cabin

McBride's Camp

Bryant Creek Shelter

Marvel Lake Campground

Mt. Allenby 2909m

Mercer Creek

Allenby Creek

Allenby Junction

Wonder Peak 2852m

Marvel Lake

Owl Creek

Owl Lake

Turbine Lake

Bryant Creek

Horses allowed on this part of the trail.

O'Brian Meadows Horse Camp

O'Brian Meadows Group Camp

Mt. Assiniboine Lodge

Park Headquarters

Naiset Cabins

Mount Cautley 2880m

Wonder Pass

L. Gloria

Terrapin Lake

Mt. Gloria 2908m

OG Lake Campground

Nub Peak 2748m

Mitchell Meadows

Lake Elizabeth

Warden Cabin

Sunburst Lake

Cerulean Lake

Lake Magog

Lake Magog Campground

Wedgewood Creek

Mt. Wedgemond Peak 2939m

Mt. Strom 3022m

Mt. Magog 3611m

R.C. Hind Hut

Mt. Assiniboine 3618m

Sturdee Peak

Lunette Peak 3400m

Mt. Sturdee 3149m

Aye Mtn. 3243m

Terrapin Mtn. 2944m

Lake Terrapin

Lunette Lake

Assiniboine Creek

Nestor Creek

Og Creek

Og Lake

N W E S

KILOMETRES
0 1 2 3 4 5 6 7 8

MILES
0 1 2 3 4 5

*Mt. Assiniboine over Lake Magog*

## Watridge Lake to Karst Springs

If you have time, be sure to plan a short side trip to the shore of Watridge Lake, and the adjacent Karst Springs. Karst is a 0.8-km (0.5-mi.) side trip that takes you through the woods, along a brilliant green, moss-carpeted spring. Following the trail, you leave the lakeshore and head into the woods, staying to the right side of the stream. Along the upper extent of the trail, a wooden boardwalk allows you to move around a resistant rock outcrop and witness the source of the stream—a spring bursting forth from the rock face itself.

## Watridge Lake to Lake Magog

Beyond Watridge Lake, the trail drops suddenly at kilometre 5 (3.1 mi.) to join with the Bryant Creek Trail at kilometre 6.6 (mile 4.1). A pleasant fire road will take you to the Bryant Creek Warden's Cabin at the 14 km (8.7 mi.) mark. From the junction with Allenby Pass Trail at kilometre 19.1 (miles 11.9), head left and choose either the hiking or the horse path towards Assiniboine Pass. The trail narrows at this point, and after some moderate climbing, you crest the pass at kilometre 22 (mile 13.7). From the pass, the trail widens out again and the final 2.5 km (1.6 mi.) to Lake Magog are wide and smooth.

Accommodation at the lake is varied. At one extreme, you can go in style and stay at Assiniboine Lodge, a privately operated wilderness lodge near Lake Magog. At the other extreme are numerous campsites within Mount Assini-boine Provincial Park. Somewhere in the middle, and generally just right, are the Naiset Cabins. Operated by the park, they are simple cabins with wood stoves for heat. They provide excellent winter camping opportunities, and are worth utilizing. They are operated on a first-come, first-served basis during the summer, but in winter, reservations are required to ensure space. Reservations can be made by calling (604) 422-3212 or by mail to B.C. Parks, Box 118, Wasa BC V0B 2K0.

# 36. Burstall Pass

Map pg 212 📷 🌾 🍁 🚲

Map pg 212

## Trailhead

From Canmore, follow the Smith-Dorrien/Spray Trail south for 45 km (28 mi.) to the Burstall Pass trailhead. From the Kananaskis Lakes Trail, head north for approximately 20 km (12.4 mi.) to reach the trailhead.

## Route

| Route | Elevation | | Distance | |
|---|---|---|---|---|
| | metres | feet | km | mi. |
| Trailhead | 1920 | 6,298 | 0.0 | 0.0 |
| Dryas Flats | 2000 | 6,560 | 3.6 | 2.2 |
| Burstall Pass | 2380 | 7,806 | 7.1 | 4.4 |
| Return to Trailhead | 1920 | 6,298 | 14.2 | 8.8 |

This 7.5-km (4.7-mi.) trail offers easy access to a magnificent larch-lined mountain pass with

*Mt. Birdwood from Burstall Pass*

endless opportunities for wilderness wandering. From the pass, there are fabulous views of Mount Birdwood, Pig's Tail and Commonwealth Peak. To the west, Leman Lake glistens and Mount Queen Elizabeth straddles the Continental Divide. During winter, Burstall Pass provides a challenging destination for advanced backcountry skiers looking for some fresh powder.

The trail begins rather modestly, with 3 km (1.9 mi.) of former logging road. This is a great place to use your mountain bike to take time off the approach and increase the time for playing at the pass. From the trailhead, stay right at an unsigned junction at kilometre 0.2 (mile 0.12) and begin climbing towards the Burstall Lakes. At kilometre 1.7 (mile 1.1), an unmarked trail forks off to the right, heading towards the first Burstall Lake. Beyond this, at 2.1 km (1.3 mi.), a limestone boulder sits in the middle of the trail, having long ago tumbled from the slopes of Mount Burstall.

Along the road, three small lakes, one for each of the high summits above, are passed in succession. The logging road ends at kilometre 3.4 (mile 2.1), marking the end of the bike trail. Beyond this, the trail narrows as it enters a dark forest of alpine fir and Engelmann spruce. After a short wander through the woods, the trail crosses several small bridges as it approaches the Dryas flats. These open flats take their name from the small yellow flower that forms a carpet across sections of the gravel wash. Commonly known as the yellow mountain avens, its Latin name is Dryas drummondii.

As you cross the flats, Burstall Creek is braided into dozens of small channels that change almost daily. Add to this the runoff from the Robertson Glacier, visible to the south as you cross the flats, and you get an ever-changing trail. Pick your way across the flats towards the trees on the far side. The trail is dotted with periodic bridges, but you may have to ford some of the channels. Also, keep in mind that on hot summer days the water level of these channels can rise dramatically. I have found myself almost stranded on return trips on such days.

At the far side of the flats, the trail re-enters the forest and the climbing begins in earnest. After 0.6 km (0.4 mi.), the trail crests the lower bench into a meadow of western anemone, paintbrush, valerian and lousewort. The next 1.1 km (0.7 mi.) wander across the meadow through stands of alpine larch. The views to the rear improve with every step, and at kilometre 6 (mile 3.7), you reach the far end of the bench and begin climbing towards the pass. At 6.4 km (4 mi.), the trail winds to the right to climb a bleached limestone outcrop. Stop and look back to the triple-summited panorama and enjoy one of the best views along the route. In September, the route turns gold as the needles of the alpine larch take on their fall colours.

The trail soon begins to traverse the base of Snow Peak up to the right as it makes its way towards the pass. A boundary sign indicates the border of Banff National Park at kilometre 7.1 (mile 4.4). From here, the trail continues down to the Palliser valley. For day hikers, the high

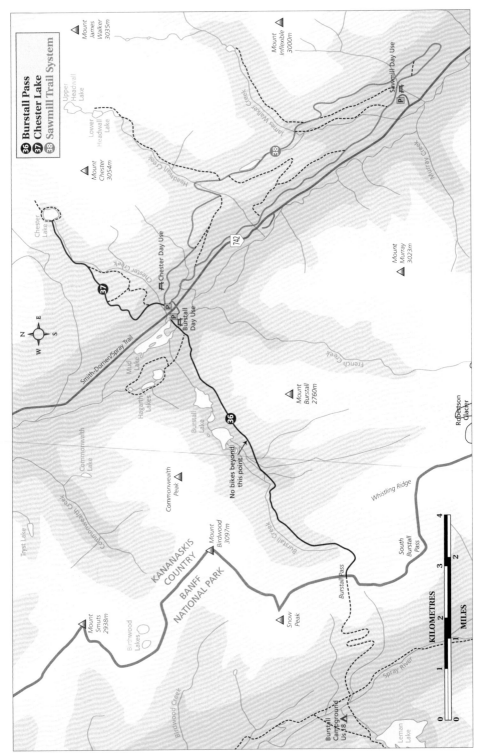

*Autumn colours on the Chester Lake trail*

slopes above this low pass beg for exploration. You don't get views down to the Palliser valley and Leman Lake without scrambling up the higher summit ridges above the trail at this point.

# 37. Chester Lake

Map pg 212  🚻 📷 🌿 🍂 🚲

From Canmore, follow the Smith-Dorrien/Spray Trail south for 45 km (28 mi.) to the Chester Lake trailhead. From the Kananaskis Lakes Trail (road), head north for approximately 20 km (12.4 mi.) to reach the trailhead.

## Route

| Route | Elevation | | Distance | |
|---|---|---|---|---|
| | metres | feet | km | mi. |
| Trailhead | 1920 | 6,298 | 0.0 | 0.0 |
| End of Road Hiking | 2130 | 6,986 | 2.1 | 1.3 |
| Chester Lake | 2240 | 7,347 | 3.9 | 2.4 |
| Return to Trailhead | 1920 | 6,298 | 7.8 | 4.9 |

This 3.9-km (2.3-mi.) point-to-point trail follows a winding logging road and then a pleasant single track, bringing you to a tiny lake beneath an imposing rock face. This trail is equally pleasant in winter, where it makes a nice back-country ski trip. It is not maintained for skiing, but is generally well packed by large numbers of skiers heading up towards the lake. Once in the

trees, though, the skiing can be quite tight, especially on the way down. You'll need to be a confident tree skier to enjoy this downhill slalom.

From the busy trailhead, follow the wide road, staying left at a junction at kilometre 0.2 (mile 0.12). The trail to the right is part of the Sawmill Trail network. The road meets another junction at kilometre 0.5 (mile 0.3). You can take either direction at this junction; however, turning left makes for a more moderate climb, although it is slightly longer. Head left at this junction and follow the wide road as it begins a steady uphill trend. As the road climbs, the views to the south open up. You get good views of Mount Burstall and Commonwealth Peak, and even periodic views of the French Glacier.

There is an important signed junction at kilometre 2 (mile 1.2). The two earlier loop options meet here and the trail to Chester Lake continues climbing up to the left. After approximately 100 m (330 ft.), the trail leaves the wide road and heads left into the woods on a narrower trail. At 2.2 km (1.4 mi.), you get your first real views towards the unusual summit of Mount Chester. This towering peak has layers tilted almost straight up, making it somewhat resemble Mount Rundle in Banff National Park. After climbing past some wooden cribwork placed to help reduce erosion on the trail, you approach a wide meadow with more great views towards Mount Chester. The elevation is revealed by the presence of alpine larch as you pass a huge snag. Beyond this is a fabulous meadow that in spring explodes in wildflowers, and in fall is rimmed with the golden needles of alpine larches. Across the meadow, Chester Creek drains the meltwater from the lake.

You reach the lake at kilometre 3.7 (mile 2.3). Mount Chester towers directly overhead, making it hard to fit the entire scene into a camera frame. Chester Lake is a popular spot for anglers, so be sure to bring your license and rod. From the lake, there are numerous options for off-trail exploration.

# 38. Sawmill Trail System

Map pg 212 🚲

## Trailhead

There are two main trailheads for the Sawmill Trail System. The north one is at the Chester Lake trailhead, 45 km (28 mi.) south of Canmore along the Smith-Dorrien/Spray Trail. An alternate trailhead is located at the Sawmill day use area approximately 6 km (3.7 mi.) further south.

## Route

| Route | Elevation | | Distance | |
|-------|-----------|------|----------|------|
| | metres | feet | km | mi. |
| Chester Lake Trailhead | 1925 | 6,314 | 0.0 | 0.0 |
| Green Trail Junction | 1875 | 6,150 | 3.2 | 2.0 |
| Sawmill Day Use | 1850 | 6,068 | 7.2 | 4.5 |
| Small Pond | 2060 | 6,757 | 13.4 | 8.3 |
| Back to Trailhead | 1925 | 6,314 | 18.4 | 11.4 |

This winding network of trails is most popular as a summer mountain biking and winter cross-country ski network. In winter, the trails are no longer trackset, but there is often a good skier-defined track available. The trails are colour-coded, and offer a wide variety of terrain. To maximize the distance, begin at the Chester Lake Trailhead and climb the wide access road to the first junction. Turn right and follow the Blue trail. The Blue trail parallels the Smith-Dorrien/Spray Trail for 1.1 km (0.7 mi.). Stay right at a junction with the Yellow trail to continue south for an additional 1.8 km (1.1 mi.). Stay on Yellow as the Green trail forks to the left at 3.2 km (2.0 mi.). The Green trail rejoins the Yellow at 5.4 km (3.4 mi.), and together they

meet Sawmill day use at 7.2 km (4.5 mi.).

From the Sawmill day use, the Red trail continues south and makes a 2 km (1.2-mi.) loop before winding back to the north. The Red trail takes the high line, climbing the lower slopes of Kent Ridge. As it rolls northward, you'll pass a small pond between crossings of James Walker Creek and Headwall Creek. The pond is at approximately 13.4 km (8.3 mi.). Soon after the pond, a hiker-defined trail forks to the right to climb up to the Headwall Lakes. Beyond this junction, the Red trail drops to a crossing of Headwall Creek and a junction with the Orange trail at 15.3 km (9.5 mi.). Turning right onto Orange, you will climb over a small shoulder on the base of Mount Chester before dropping to join the Blue trail at 16.7 km (10.4 mi.). Turn right and return to Chester trailhead at approximately 18.4 km (11.4 mi.).

This is only one possible loop option, and there are many ways to explore this trail network. As a general rule, southward directions gradually drop in elevation, while heading north takes you uphill. Also, the trails that follow the higher lines along Kent Ridge have a more rolling character than the trails closer to the road.

# 39. Black Prince Cirque

Map pg 215 🚻 📷 🌿

## Trailhead

From Canmore, head south on the Smith-Dorrien/Spray Trail for approximately 52 km (32.2 mi.) to the Black Prince Cirque trailhead. Alternately, head north from the Kananaskis Lakes Trail on the Smith-Dorrien/Spray Trail for approximately 8 km (5 mi.).

## Route

| Route | Elevation | | Distance | |
|-------|-----------|------|----------|------|
| | metres | feet | km | mi. |
| Trailhead | 1760 | 5,773 | 0.0 | 0.0 |
| Warspite Lake | 1830 | 6,002 | 1.8 | 1.1 |
| Return to Trailhead | 1760 | 5,773 | 4.0 | 2.5 |

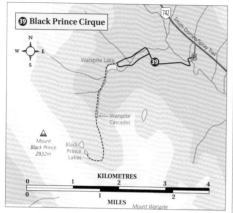

*Warspite Lake on Black Prince trail*

From the trailhead parking lot, the trail begins beside a sign reading "Welcome to Black Prince Trail". The trail quickly crosses a high-quality bridge over Warspite Creek. After passing the post for Interpretive Stop 2, the trail begins climbing on a wide former logging road. Drainage channels have been cut across the old road to help reduce erosion. At the 0.8-km (0.5-mi.) point, there is a bench offering a break where you can take in the great views across the valley to Mount Kent and the Kananaskis Range.

Beyond the viewpoint, the trail begins a downhill trend that brings you to a fork in the trail at kilometre 1.7 (mile 1.1). This fork marks the beginning of the loop section of the trail. Take the right fork at this Y-junction, and after approximately 100 m (328 ft.), cross Warspite Creek again over a high-quality bridge. The trail resumes climbing after the bridge, passing an open area strewn with limestone boulders, and emerges on the shores of Warspite Lake at kilometre 1.8 (mile 1.1). This pleasant tarn sits in a perfect bowl carved by ancient glaciers on the slopes of Mount Black Prince. The shoreline is lined with a lush growth of cow parsnip, which adds its pungent aroma to this pleasant panorama. Beyond the lake, Warspite Cascade tumbles down the slopes of Mount Black Prince from the Black Prince Lakes hidden from view on the upper slopes.

From Warspite Lake, the trail continues its counter-clockwise progress, crossing the creek two more times after leaving the shoreline. As you wander this rhododendron-lined trail, the loop finally closes at kilometre 2.3 (mile 1.4). Turn right at this junction and follow the wide roadway back to the trailhead at kilometre 4 (mile 2.5).

# 40. Many Springs Trail

Map pg 216 🏃‍♂️ 📷 🌿 🍃

## Trailhead

Follow the Bow Valley Provincial Park access road until it forks soon after passing Middle Lake on your left. Turn left at this junction and park in the Middle Springs trailhead parking lot.

## Route

| Route | Elevation | | Distance | |
|---|---|---|---|---|
| | metres | feet | km | mi. |
| Trailhead | 1340 | 4,395 | 0.0 | 0.0 |
| Wooden Viewing Platform | 1340 | 4,395 | 0.6 | 0.4 |
| Boil Springs | 1340 | 4,395 | 0.9 | 0.5 |
| End of Loop | 1340 | 4,395 | 1.5 | 0.9 |

This should be one of the first trails you hike in Bow Valley Provincial Park, especially if you like wildflowers. While numerous park trails offer a plethora of colourful flowers, none can compete with the diversity found along this short trail. The self-guided route circumnavigates a tiny spring-fed pond.

Turn right at a junction at kilometre 0.3 (mile 0.2) that marks the beginning of the loop. The trail circles the springs in a counter-clock-

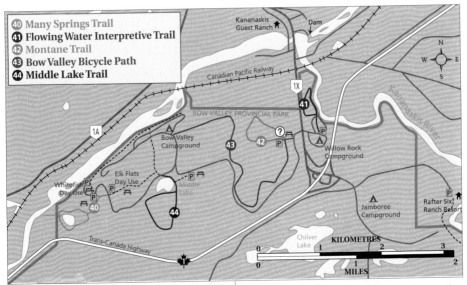

40 Many Springs Trail
41 Flowing Water Interpretive Trail
42 Montane Trail
43 Bow Valley Bicycle Path
44 Middle Lake Trail

wise direction, past western wood lilies and yellow lady's slipper orchids. As you make your way to the far side of the pond, boardwalks guide you through pleasant wetlands. Along the margin, a seemingly endless variety of flowers bloom. The elephant head stands taller than most, and the tiny individual pink flowers along the spike-like head reveal the secret of its name. Lower down, delicate blue butterworts survive in the nitrogen-poor soils of the marsh by curling up their leaves and digesting unsuspecting insects that land on their sticky surface.

At a small wooden platform at kilometre 0.9 (mile 0.5), you get a great view of the Boil Spring, and the mud literally bubbles as if it were boiling. Feel the water. It may not be warm enough to swim in, but it does stay above freezing throughout winter. This helps create a

## Cold Water that Boils

**The Many Springs** area in Bow Valley Provincial Park is a unique combination of geology and luck. More than 12,000 years ago, a glacial river flowed across this site, depositing thick layers of gravel. The river has long since disappeared, but the dry gorge remains as a low wetland at the base of a giant basin. Water falling on the surrounding mountains percolates into the rocks and flows downhill, funnelling much of this water towards the area of Many Springs.

The water flows from the springs at a rate of 100 litres (22 gallons) per second. This is higher than the rainfall the basin receives. In addition, the temperature remains a balmy 6°C (42°F) all year. This is warmer than both the Bow River and nearby wells. It is also chemically different, with higher calcium, sulphur and carbon dioxide levels, and lower levels of oxygen. What does this all mean? Quite simply, the water must have a different origin than that

flowing in the river.

If you look to the north at the towering face of Mount Yamnuska, you are looking at the official start of the Front Ranges of the Rocky Mountains. At the base of the sheer cliff a major geological fault exists, and along this fault the rocks of the upper cliffs have been pushed several kilometres over the much younger rocks below the cliff. This sliding fault also formed the mountains to the north and south of the springs. As a result of the fracturing that has taken place during this piling up of the mountains, water that falls as rain is able to penetrate deep into the Earth's surface, where it is heated. The water also picks up dissolved minerals as it travels underground, only to emerge as springs. Some of the water can be seen surfacing at Many Springs and at the Boil Springs. You can watch the mud bubble as if it were actually boiling.

*Mt. Yamnuska looms over Bow Valley Provincial Park*

unique microclimate around the pond. Just beyond this point, keep your eyes open for one last look at the floral highlight of the trail—the bright colours of the yellow lady's slipper.

## Prehistoric Life

**Many Springs** in Bow Valley Provincial Park is well-known as a location where one can see rare and unusual plants. Its birdlife is equally spectacular, with a great diversity of birds attracted to the year-round source of open water. One thing most visitors are unaware of is a tiny resident known as an isopod. These tiny creatures live beneath the rocks in total darkness. They don't even have eyes.

This species of isopod can only be found in a few other locations in western Canada, and as a group dates back almost 400 million years. They have long since disappeared from most of their original range, but persist in a few isolated sites. One theory is that they were more common during warmer periods after the end of the last ice age. As climates cooled, they died off in most areas of the Rockies, managing to survive only in sites such as this, where the water temperature remains above freezing all year long.

# 41. Flowing Water Interpretive Trail

Map pg 216

### Trailhead

The trail begins at a signed trailhead in Willow Rock Campground.

### Route

| Route | Elevation | | Distance | |
| --- | --- | --- | --- | --- |
| | metres | feet | km | mi. |
| Trailhead | 1340 | 4,395 | 0.0 | 0.0 |
| End of Loop | 1340 | 4,395 | 2.0 | 1.2 |

From Willow Rock Campground, this 2-km (1.2-mi.) self-guided trail takes you down to the Kananaskis River, where it describes the power of moving water. On the way, the trail crosses an iron-rich stream, and wanders along a bench above the river for about half of its length. The views down the Kananaskis River are quite open here; occasionally you can see rafters or other paddlers plying the swift waters of the river. After descending steeply to water level, the trail emerges on the gravelly banks of the Kananaskis River, following the shoreline briefly before climbing back upward to return to the trailhead.

*Views from Montane trail*

# 42. Montane Trail

Map pg 216 👫 🌾 🍃

## Trailhead

The trail begins directly behind the Bow Valley Provincial Park Information Centre.

### Route

| Route | Elevation | | Distance | |
|---|---|---|---|---|
| | metres | feet | km | mi. |
| Trailhead | 1340 | 4,395 | 0.0 | 0.0 |
| End of Loop | 1340 | 4,395 | 2.2 | 1.42.2 |

Behind the information centre, the Montane Trail takes you past a wildflower-laden meadow before traversing a forest of aspen and Douglas fir, and then returning to the visitor centre. Along the route of this fairly level 2.2-km (1.4-mi.) trail, you pass numerous points of interest. The meadow behind the Park Information Centre is an excellent place to look for some of the first wildflowers of spring. Early each May, the prairie crocus pokes its head through late snowfalls. Beyond, the trail passes a series of sinuous ridges known as eskers, which were left behind by the Bow Valley Glacier. Eskers are formed when tunnels within the glacier become choked with debris. When the ice melts, this debris is deposited in linear ridges.

The trail takes its name from the Douglas fir forest that it passes. This tree is indicative of the montane forest. It survives well in wind-blasted sites like this one. It has become less common over the years as stands of ancient trees have fallen victim to the axe.

# 43. Bow Valley Bicycle Path

Map pg 216 👫 🍃 🚲

## Trailhead

The trail begins at the Bow Valley Provincial Park Information Centre. Park opposite this building. The paved trail leaves from the southeast corner of the parking lot.

### Route

| Route | Elevation | | Distance | |
|---|---|---|---|---|
| | metres | feet | km | mi. |
| Trailhead | 1340 | 4,395 | 0.0 | 0.0 |
| Yamnuska Viewpoint | 1340 | 4,395 | 2.2 | 1.4 |
| Bow Valley Campground | 1340 | 4,395 | 4.1 | 2.6 |

Like the paved paths in other parts of Kananaskis, this sinuous route provides pleasant access between the park's visitor centre and Bow Valley Campground. It winds through a mixture of open meadow and stands of trembling aspen and Douglas fir. Many of the aspen look low and stunted, a direct result of being blasted by the high winds that prevail in this valley. The mountains lining the Bow Valley act like a wind funnel, and the trees at the entrance to the valley show the effects of these winds.

There is an excellent viewpoint, with a bench, at kilometre 2.2 (mile 1.4). The open meadow provides fabulous views of the sheer face of Mount Yamnuska to the north. Whether you walk, blade or ride this trail, do take the time to explore some of the meadows and marvel at the many different types of flowers. The Bow Valley information centre can help you with questions you may have on identification, or see if you can find a few on pages 20-21 of this book. While the trail is tame, please wear a helmet whenever riding your bike.

The trail parallels Bow Valley Campground

*Mt. Yamnuska*

for a few minutes before emerging at the campground store. If you're returning along the same route, this is a great place to stop for an ice cream before you head out again.

# 44. Middle Lake

Map pg 216 👫 📷 🌿 🍁

## Trailhead

Follow the Bow Valley Provincial Park road for several kilometres to the Middle Lake oarking lot. The trail begins here.

## Route

| Route | Elevation | | Distance | |
|---|---|---|---|---|
| | metres | feet | km | mi. |
| Trailhea | 1340 | 4,395 | 0.0 | 0.0 |
| End of Loop | 1340 | 4,395 | 2.5 | 1.6 |

Shhh! Hiking the shores of Middle Lake is a good place to stay very quiet and watch for some of the plentiful birdlife of this slough pond. The lake is fed by underground springs and surface runoff, so it has no river source. There are no fish to catch, but the birdlife is diverse. I've seen red-necked and horned grebes swimming in the water while red-winged blackbirds perched atop the reeds.

The trail is designed so that you circle the lake in a clockwise direction, going along the shoreline first. During June, the trail boasts large numbers of western wood lilies. Be careful if you stop to sniff them. They have tendency to deposit dark brown pollen on the tip of your nose if you get too close—and of course nobody will tell you how silly you look. As you travel the loop, you'll see numerous Douglas fir stumps, left behind during operations of the Eau Claire logging company (see "Logging" on page 107). If you're lucky, you may get to see some of the elk that make the park home; if not, you do get to see the signs of one of the other park residents, the black bear. The trail passes some trees scarred by the action of black bears climbing. Aspen trees hold such scars for life, as their bark is easily marked.

# 45. Jumpingpound Loop

Map pg 220 👫 📷 🌿 🍁 🐎

## Trailhead

From Highway 40, head east along the Sibbald Creek Trail (Highway 68) for approximately 24.5 km (15.2 mi.) to the Pine Top day use area. Park here to begin the loop. Alternatively, from the Trans-Canada Highway, follow the Sibbald Creek Trail for approximately 15.5 km (9.6 mi.) to the Pine Top day use area.

Alternate trailheads can be found at Jumpingpound day use and Pine Grove Group Campground.

## Route

| Route | Elevation | | Distance | |
|---|---|---|---|---|
| | metres | feet | km | mi. |
| Pine Top Day Use | 1350 | 4,428 | 0.0 | 0.0 |
| Jumpingpound Link Junction | 1450 | 4,756 | 2.5 | 1.6 |
| Pine Grove Group Camp | 1350 | 4,428 | 5.1 | 3.2 |
| Pine Top Day Use | 1350 | 4,428 | 9.0 | 5.6 |

If you're looking for a good early-season trail, Jumpingpound Loop may fit the bill. It receives lots of sun with its south-facing exposure, so it clears of snow earlier than many other trails. It

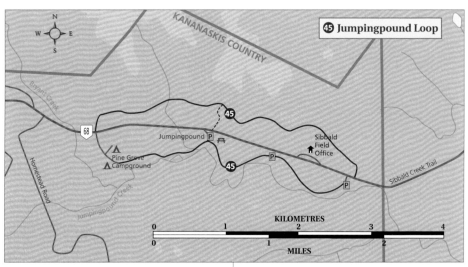

also has a very moderate gradient, allowing the legs to work their way back into shape. There are numerous access points, but the Pinetop day use area makes for an easily-located trailhead. The entire loop is 9 km (5.6 mi.) long, but it can be broken down into shorter lengths.

Beginning at Pinetop day use, cross Highway 68 and begin climbing through the open slopes on the north side of the road. Along this section of trail, there are great views of Moose Mountain to the south. Also, in early spring, keep your eyes open for the prairie crocus, usually one of the first wildflowers to appear along this sunny trail. The trail varies between open Douglas fir forest and sun-baked meadow. As you wander along this upper bench, the trail rolls up and down until it meets a junction with a trail offering an early exit to Jumpingpound day use. If you are doing the entire route, stay straight at this junction. After an additional 2.1 km (1.3 mi.), the trail winds left to meet Highway 68.

Cross the highway into the Pine Grove Group Campground and follow the access road for 0.5 km (0.3 mi.). The trail continues just beyond the end of the campground access road. From this point, the trail begins to turn east towards the Jumpingpound day use area. Along the way, you'll cross a grassy road that once led to Charlie Logan's "Last Chance Cabin". The trail soon winds to the left of Jumpingpound Creek to the junction with the Jumpingpound day use area.

Beyond the day use area, the trail continues

its downstream course as it makes its way towards the east trailhead at Pinetop.

# 46. Eagle Hill

Map pg 225  📷  🍁  🐎

## Trailhead

Follow the Sibbald Creek Trail (Hwy. 68), either from the Trans-Canada Highway or from the Kananaskis Trail (Hwy. 40), until you see Sibbald Lake day use area. There, you will find numerous trail access points. The easiest way is to drive into the day use, stay left at a three-way junction, and follow this to the road's end at a trailhead parking lot.

The main challenge of hiking this trail is the network of access points in and about the Sibbald Lake day use area. Alternate accesses can be found along the Sibbald Lake Interpretive Trail, at Dawson Equestrian Campground, and along the gated road to Camp Adventure.

In the day use parking area, the Sibbald Lake Interpretive Trail leaves from the southwest corner of the lot.

| Route | Elevation | | Distance | |
|---|---|---|---|---|
| | metres | feet | km | mi. |
| Sibbald Lake Trailhead | 1500 | 4,920 | 0.0 | 0.0 |
| Summit of Eagle Hill | 1722 | 5,648 | 5.0 | 3.1 |

From Sibbald Lake day use area, Eagle Hill climbs the divide between the Jumpingpound and Bow River drainages. The 5 km (3.1 mi.) trail climbs 222 m (728 ft.) before providing a great view of the Bow Valley to the west and the Sibbald area to the south.

Beginning on the Sibbald Lake Interpretive Trail, stay left as the trail forks, and then right at a T-intersection. Almost immediately, the access trail from Deer Ridge and Dawson Equestrian Campground joins in from the left. Stay straight at this junction. Within moments, the trail begins to follow the northeast shore of Moose Pond. Stay straight (left) as the interpretive trail joins in from the right again, just beyond Interpretive Stop 7. The trail then becomes much more straightforward as it traverses an aspen hillside, staying above a wetland down to the left. After approximately 1.7 km (1.1 mi.), the trail crosses a cutline before the access trail from the Camp Adventure road joins in from the right. The trail winds left to skirt the base of a small knoll.

The trail eventually turns towards the northwest, and after approximately 3.6 km (2.2 mi.), the Deer Ridge Trail joins in from the left. The trail begins climbing Eagle Hill and joins a cutline access road that heads towards the summit.

The summit marks the boundary between Kananaskis Country and the Stoney Indian Reserve. A fence runs along the boundary and provides the limit to northerly travel on this route. The Stoney Reserve runs from the summit of the Scott Lake Hill on the Trans-Canada Highway west to the Kananaskis River. To the north it extends well beyond the Bow River and the 1A Highway.

The Stoneys traditionally preferred the mountains to the plains. On the plains, the Blackfoot were very aggressive, and the Stoneys were generally peaceful. With the coming of missionaries like Reverend Robert T. Rundle and his successors, Reverends George and John McDougall, many Stoneys were converted to Christianity. Culturally, they are related to the eastern Sioux and Assiniboine Indians.

# 47. Tom Snow Trail

Map pg 223  🛶 🐎 🚲

## Trailhead

**West Trailhead:**
Head south on Highway 40 for 7.7 km (4.8 mi.) and turn left onto the gravel of Highway 68/Sibbald Creek Trail. Follow this road for 4 km (2.5 mi.) and turn right onto the Jumpingpound Demonstration Forest Road. Pass through an open gate and follow this road for 3.6 km (2.2 mi.) to the Spruce Woods trailhead. Park here.

**East Trailhead:**
As Highway 22 approaches the community of Bragg Creek, take the right fork at the entrance to the hamlet. This will take you past the shopping mall with the grocery store. Continue over the Bragg Creek bridge and turn left after the crossing. This will wind for 6.3 km (3.9 mi.) where the pavement will end. Keep going on the gravel for another 1.1 km (0.7 mi.) to the West Bragg Creek trailhead. The Tom Snow Trail begins at the point at which this road is blocked to vehicle traffic.

## Route

| Route | Elevation | | Distance | |
|---|---|---|---|---|
| | metres | feet | km | mi. |
| Trailhead | 1400 | 4,592 | 0.0 | 0.0 |
| Barbed Wire Gate | 1550 | 5,084 | 8.1 | 5.0 |
| Moose Loop Junction | 1490 | 4,887 | 11.4 | 7.1 |
| West Bragg Creek Trailhead | 1425 | 4,674 | 15.6 | 9.7 |

From the west trailhead, descend from the Spruce Woods trailhead on a wide trail. There are numerous unmarked trail junctions, so be sure to watch the route description carefully. Beyond your first bridge crossing over Moose Creek, take the right fork along a nice trail carpeted with spruce needles. Beyond Interpretive Marker 1, the trail forks. Take the left fork, and soon after passing Interpretive Marker 2, you'll meet another T-junction with an unmarked trail. Avoid the temptation to turn right onto this wide trail, and rather continue on the same route, following the Moose Creek Loop signs. The trail begins to climb sharply as it parallels a road off to the right. Soon after passing Interpretive Marker 3, you will meet another junction. At this point the trail leaves the Moose

Creek Loop behind as you turn right onto the single track of the Tom Snow Trail. The trail continues to climb gradually, paralleling the gas well access road off to your right. Once you leave the Moose Creek Loop, the trail has the potential to hold water in wet weather, so save this for a dry spell. By kilometre 2 (mile 1.2), you leave civilization behind as the trail wanders through a secondary growth of lodgepole pine. Along the trail, periodic orange diamonds nailed onto trees mark the route.

Cross a small bridge at 2.2 km (1.3 mi.), followed by a left turn at an unsigned junction. If you look, you'll see an orange diamond marking the correct route. There is a shallow ford at 3.9 km (2.4 mi.). Mountain bikers should be able to make it through without dismounting, but hikers will likely get wet feet. There are several large mudholes along this section, which ends as the trail enters an old clearcut at kilometre 5.7 (mile 3.6). As you cross the clearcut, stay left at an unsigned junction, following a large red arrow sign. Take a few minutes to admire the twin summits of Moose Mountain, clearly visible as you cross this clearing. As you leave the clearcut, stay left again at another diamond marked junction.

After a nice smooth section, the trail descends back into a muddy stretch before meeting a closed barbed wire fence at kilometre 8.1 (mile 5.0). When you go through the gate, be sure to close it again behind you. The trail trends slightly downhill after the gate, descending towards a culverted crossing at kilometre 9 (mile 5.6) and a major washout at 9.2 km (5.7 mi.). The washout is indicated by a large orange roadblock, and can be bypassed by a ford to the right.

From the ford, the trail climbs above Bragg Creek to begin paralleling a marshy pond on your right at 10 km (6.2 mi.). This marks the start of some nice single track, marred only by a few large mudholes. The trail enters an aspen meadow at 10.8 km (6.7 mi.). Strike out across the meadow and you will find the trail continuing on the opposite side, bringing you to a T-junction with Moose Loop Trail at kilometre 11.4 (mile 7.1). Turn left here and follow a wide fire road. There is a picnic bench at 12.1 km (7.5 mi.), offering a sunny spot for a short pause to take in the view. At a fork in the trail at 12.8 km (8.0 mi.), turn right and then left on the Blue

*Marshy pond on Tom Snow trail*

cross-country ski trail. This will wind its way to meet a junction with the Telephone Trail at 13.5 km (8.4 mi.). Stay straight on the wide road as you begin the final stretch towards the West Bragg Creek terminus.

As you approach a crossing with Bragg Creek at 14.5 km (9.0 mi.), you'll find the bridge has been washed away, making for one final challenge. It can be difficult to find a method for crossing, so be cautious. Beyond the creek, the trail joins a wide road coming in from the right. Follow this road as it passes through several locked gates to meet the West Bragg Creek trailhead at 16.5 km (10.3 mi.).

This 16-km (10.0-mi.) loop makes for a great mountain bike ride or a nice cross-country ski (snow permitting). Hikers will need to keep in mind that it is a long trail, and should prepare accordingly. Also, the trails are not maintained in the summer, so be prepared for some large mud holes along the way.

From the trailhead at the parking lot, the climb begins along a nice single-track trail. Stay straight at a junction with the Hostel Loop at 0.7 km (0.4 mi.) and again at 1.5 km (0.9 mi.). Beyond this junction, a sign warns hikers of the extended nature of this hike. This next stretch holds water in the summer, so you will need to negotiate numerous mud holes. By the 4-km (2.5-mi.) mark, the trail improves as it winds around the north end of the loop. Soon after-

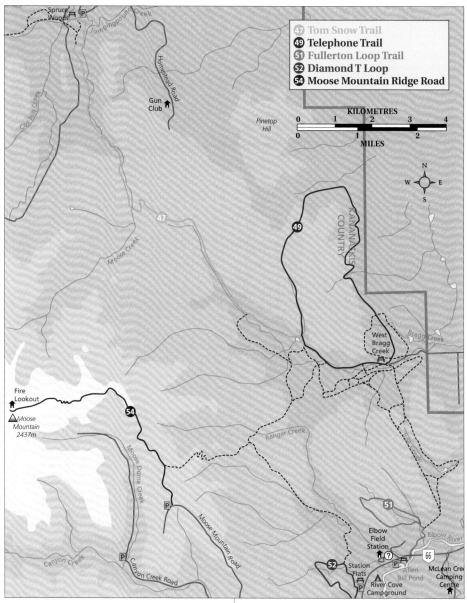

**47** Tom Snow Trail
**49** Telephone Trail
**51** Fullerton Loop Trail
**52** Diamond T Loop
**54** Moose Mountain Ridge Road

wards it takes a downhill turn, passing through a barbed wire gate at 4.6 km (2.9 mi.).

A rough trail crosses the Telephone Trail at 6.5 km (4.0 mi.) as you enter a recently logged area. You cross a high-quality bridge at 9.4 km (5.9 mi.), making a right-hand turn soon after. This marks another wet section, as you make your way through a marshy area before passing another barbed wire fence gate at 11 km (6.8 mi.). The quality of the trail improves again by 12.5 km (7.8 mi.), before meeting a winter sign indicating ice flows at 12.9 km (8.0 mi.). From this sign, the trail drops down to a junction with the Moose Loop and Tom Snow Trails.

At this signed junction, go left to continue on the Telephone Trail. The bridge over Bragg Creek is out at kilometre 14 (mile 8.7), but once you get past this challenge, the trail meets a wide road and rolls through several gates to return to the trailhead at 16 km (10.0 mi.).

# 48. Jumpingpound Ridge to Cox Hill

Map pg 225 📷 🌿 🍁 🐎 🚴

## Route

| Route | Elevation | | Distance | |
|---|---|---|---|---|
| | metres | feet | km | mi. |
| South Trailhead | 1738 | 5,700 | 0.0 | 0.0 |
| Jumpingpound Summit Junction | 2140 | 7,019 | 6.0 | 3.7 |
| Jumpingpound Ridge Exit | 2050 | 6,724 | 9.5 | 5.9 |
| Cox Hill Summit | 2180 | 7,150 | 12.7 | 7.9 |
| Dawson Equestrian Campground | 1500 | 4,920 | 19.3 | 12.0 |
| Back to South Trailhead (along road) | 1738 | 5,700 | 36.7 | 22.8 |

## Canyon Creek Trailhead to Junction with Jumpingpound Summit Trail

This is the primary entry point for this long ridge ride or hike. From the trailhead along Powderface Trail Road, ride along a smooth trail as it leaves the road behind. At kilometre 0.7

(mile 0.4), turn left at the junction for Jumpingpound Ridge Trail. At this point, the climbing begins, and cyclists will find themselves pushing for much of the next kilometre or so as the trail switches back and forth towards the ridge. As you gain in elevation, the views improve dramatically. By kilometre 3.7 (mile 2.3), the views to the north open up. You can also see numerous clear-cuts from recent logging activity in the area, paying testament to the multiple-use mandate of Kananaskis Country.

Also by this point, the climbing has moderated and becomes a pleasant uphill trend, making its way towards the summit of Jumpingpound Ridge. Stay to the right at a signed junction at kilometre 6 (mile 3.7). To the left, Jumpingpound Summit Trail offers a steep exit option, but mountain bikers will want to continue along the summit ridge.

Just 0.4 km (0.2 mi.) beyond this junction, there is a spur trail that climbs a short distance to the true summit of Jumpingpound Ridge. Why not park your bike and take a short hike to the summit? As you continue climbing, the views open up in all directions. To the south are the towering peaks of Mounts Glasgow, Cornwall and Banded Peak. To the east, the summit of Moose Mountain dominates the view.

The gradient soon eases, and cyclists will en-

## Trailhead

While this route can be done in either direction, the south-to-north route is more popular. There are also numerous access points. They are listed here from south to north. For the full experience, begin at Canyon Creek and continue all the way to Dawson Equestrian Campground. This is one of the classic mountain bike rides in the Rockies, but is also popular with equestrians riders and the occasional hiker. All distances are given in two directions, either heading north on the Powderface Trail (road) from the Elbow Valley Trail (Hwy. 66) or south from the Sibbald Creek Trail (Hwy. 68).

### South trailhead at Canyon Creek:
Follow Powderface Trail (road) north from the Elbow Valley Trail (Hwy. 66) for 15.2 km (9.5 mi.) to a trailhead just north of Canyon Creek. From the Sibbald Creek Trail (Hwy. 68), head south for 20 km (12.4 mi.) On the west side of the road is a parking area with a memorial for those lost in a WWII training crash. The trail rolls across the meadow on the

east side of the road.
### Jumpingpound Summit trailhead:
This is 18.1 km (11.3 mi.) north of Elbow Valley Trail (Hwy. 66), or 17 km (10.6 mi.) south of Sibbald Creek Trail (Hwy. 68). This rustic trailhead has a parking area on the west side of Powderface Trail (road), and the Jumpingpound Summit Trail rolls across the meadow on the west side of the road.
### Jumpingpound Ridge north trailhead:
This is 24.4 km (15.2 mi.) north of the Elbow Valley Trail (Hwy. 66) or 10.7 km (6.7 mi.) south of the Sibbald Creek trail (Hwy. 68). Parking is again on the west side of the road, with the trail rolling away to the east and crossing a bridge right away.
North trailhead at Dawson Equestrian Campground: This is 32.1 km (20 mi.) north of the Elbow Valley Trail (Hwy. 66) or 3 km (1.9 mi.) south of the Sibbald Creek Trail (Hwy. 68). Park at the Dawson Equestrian Campground.

joy a bit of downhill beginning around kilometre 8.4 (mile 5.2). At this point, the trail begins a gradual descent towards a junction with Jumpingpound Ridge Trail. Meet this junction at kilometre 9.5 (mile 5.9). If you are only doing the Jumpingpound Ridge section of the trail, turn left here; otherwise stay to the right and continue towards Cox Hill. The exit trail drops through the trees for 3.5 km (2.2 mi.) to meet with Powderface Trail Road. If you don't have a vehicle shuttle, you'll turn left onto the road and return to the trailhead at kilometre 22.3 (mile 13.9).

## Jumpingpound Ridge Trail to Cox Hill Summit

After staying right at the Jumpingpound Ridge Trail and Cox Hill junction, the trail continues to drop for approximately 1 km (0.6 mi.), before the gradient changes. The sharp climb begins towards the summit of Cox Hill. The trail drops to 1950 m (6,396 ft.) before beginning an ascent of 230 m (754 ft.) in just over 2 km (1.2 mi.).

The magic of this trail lies in the open panoramas visible in all directions. Few trails open to mountain bikes offer such high-elevation splendor. This has helped to make this trail one of the classic rides in the Rockies. Hikers and equestrians are equally rewarded by the climb towards Cox Hill. As you crest the summit at kilometre 12.7 (mile 7.9), you'll experience a 360∞ panorama. To the northwest, Mount Yamnuska marks the official start of the Front Ranges. To the west, the peaks of the Fisher Range rise high above the

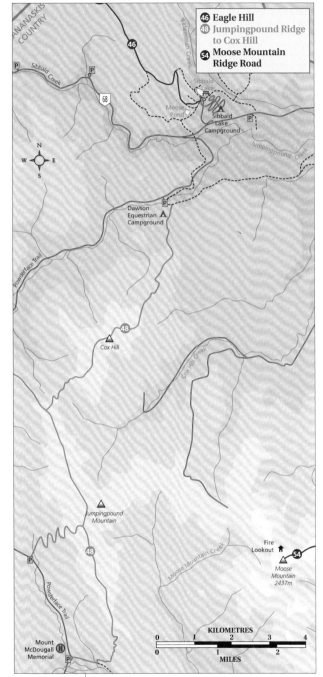

valley. The southern skyline is guarded by the summits of Banded Peak, as well as Mounts Glasgow, Cornwall, and Threepoint Mountain. Moose Mountain rises to the southeast, and to

*View from Jumpingpound Ridge*

the east and northeast the rolling foothills gradually give way to the prairies.

While you sit on the summit, you'll notice that recent logging activity in the area has left behind a telltale patchwork of square-cut blocks in various stages of regeneration. Once you have had sufficient time to take in the views, begin the descent via the north side towards Dawson Equestrian Campground. From the summit, the trail drops sharply, and quickly heads back into the forest canopy. While it stays generally downhill, it emerges onto a lower outlier of Cox Hill at approximately 14.8 km (9.2 mi.). From here, the trail descends steeply, finally meeting Dawson trailhead at kilometre 19.3 (mile 12). Cyclists will need to be cautious as the trail drops very steeply at times, and also may show signs of rutting and horse damage.

# 49. Telephone Trail

Map pg 223

## Trailhead

As Highway 22 approaches the community of Bragg Creek, take the right fork at the entrance to the hamlet. This will take you past the shopping mall with the grocery store. Continue over the Bragg Creek bridge and turn left after the crossing. This will wind for 6.3 km (3.9 mi.) where the pavement will end. Keep going on the gravel for another 1.1 km (0.7 mi.) to the West Bragg Creek trailhead.

## Route

| Route | Elevation | | Distance | |
|---|---|---|---|---|
| | metres | feet | km | mi. |
| Trailhead | 1425 | 4,674 | 0.0 | 0.0 |
| Outside of Loop | 1400 | 4,592 | 4.0 | 2.5 |
| End of Loop | 1425 | 4,674 | 16.0 | 10.0 |

**Mountain bikers on Telephone trail**

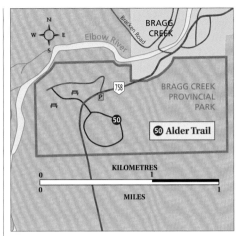

This 16-km (10.0-mi.) loop makes for a great mountain bike ride or a nice cross-country ski (snow permitting). Hikers will need to keep in mind that it is a long trail, and should prepare accordingly. Also, the trails are not maintained in the summer, so be prepared for some large mud holes along the way.

From the trailhead at the parking lot, the climb begins along a nice single-track trail. Stay straight at a junction with the Hostel Loop at 0.7 km (0.4 mi.) and again at 1.5 km (0.9 mi.). Beyond this junction, a sign warns hikers of the extended nature of this hike. This next stretch holds water in the summer, so you will need to negotiate numerous mud holes. By the 4-km (2.5-mi.) mark, the trail improves as it winds around the north end of the loop. Soon afterwards it takes a downhill turn, passing through a barbed wire gate at 4.6 km (2.9 mi.).

A rough trail crosses the Telephone Trail at 6.5 km (4.0 mi.) as you enter a recently logged area. You cross a high-quality bridge at 9.4 km (5.9 mi.), making a right-hand turn soon after. This marks another wet section, as you make your way through a marshy area before passing another barbed wire fence gate at 11 km (6.8 mi.). The quality of the trail improves again by 12.5 km (7.8 mi.), before meeting a winter sign indicating ice flows at 12.9 km (8.0 mi.). From this sign, the trail drops down to a junction with the Moose Loop and Tom Snow Trails.

At this signed junction, go left to continue on the Telephone Trail. The bridge over Bragg Creek is out at kilometre 14 (mile 8.7), but once you get past this challenge, the trail meets a wide road and rolls through several gates to return to the trailhead at 16 km (10.0 mi.).

# 50. Alder Trail

Map pg 227 👫 🌿 🍃

## Trailhead

Follow Highway 22 to the hamlet of Bragg Creek. Stay straight at the stop sign at the entrance to Bragg Creek and follow Highway 758 as it passes through town. Soon after leaving the community, a signed trailhead on the left indicates Alder Trail. Park here.

## Route

| Route | Elevation | | Distance | |
|---|---|---|---|---|
| | metres | feet | km | mi. |
| Trailhead | 1325 | 4346 | 0.0 | 0.0 |
| Return to Trailhead | 1325 | 4,346 | 1.5 | 0.9 |

This short interpretive walk within Bragg Creek Provincial Park makes for a pleasant summer stroll. Approximately 1.5 km (0.9 mi.) long, this loop passes through a moist forest of lodgepole pine and white spruce that create a dense canopy beneath which a unique habitat has formed. It has been many years since fire has touched this area, and the old rotting stumps and vegetation make this a great trail for spotting mushrooms and other fungi. Overall, this is a pleasant walk, and best of all, it's close to town.

*View from Fullerton Loop trail*

# 51. Fullerton Loop Trail

Map pg 223 🚻 🍃 🐎 🚲

## Trailhead

Along the Elbow Valley Trail (Hwy. 66), the trailhead is located at the Allen Bill Pond day use area. Turn off the highway and stay left, parking at the west end of the day use area.

## Route

| Route | Elevation | | Distance | |
|-------|-----------|------|----------|------|
| | metres | feet | km | mi. |
| Trailhead | 1430 | 4,690 | 0.0 | 0.0 |
| Viewpoint | 1585 | 5,198 | 3.2 | 2.0 |
| End of Loop | 1430 | 4,690 | 5.0 | 3.1 |
| Return to Trailhead | 1430 | 4,690 | 6.1 | 3.8 |

Fullerton Loop offers a wonderful family hike that provides excellent views of the Elbow Valley and the nearby foothills. For almost a century, the Fullerton family has ranched in the Bragg Creek area. Ernest "Jake" Fullerton opened a ranch near Bragg Creek in 1914, and Mount Fullerton was later named in his honour. The ample south-facing exposure of this loop makes a great early season hike as the snow melts and the crocuses burst into bloom.

From the trailhead at Allen Bill Pond, the trail parallels Highway 66 as it heads towards the Elbow River. As the highway crosses over the river on a wide bridge, the trail crosses under the that bridge, staying on the left bank of the river. As the trail leaves the highway behind, heading north along the river, it passes by a high cutbank off to the left as the while following a wide access road. At a junction at kilometre 0.7 (mile 0.4), turn left, following signs for Fullerton Loop. Beyond this point, squeeze your way through a V-shaped gate. The trail then begins winding away from the Elbow River. Stay left at a signed junction at kilometre 0.9 (mile 0.5). After crossing a small bridge, the trail forks. The preferred option is to do the loop in a counter-clockwise direction.

After another creek crossing, the trail begins to climb gradually, and soon traverses a hillside up to the right. In summer, these grassy slopes explode in wild bergamot, paintbrush and nodding onion. The trail begins to roll left at 2.8 km (1.7 mi.), and within a few minutes it winds left again to emerge onto the lip of Ranger Ridge. Take a load off at a perfectly located bench, the Elbow Valley spread beneath you. The trail follows the edge of the ridge, slowly losing elevation as it heads towards the ridge's southeast end.

You leave the ridge behind at kilometre 4.1 (mile 2.6), and the trail rapidly loses elevation as it drops to its junction with the end of the loop at kilometre 5 (mile 3.1). Retrace your route back to the trailhead at kilometre 6.1 (mile 3.8).

# 52. Diamond T Loop

Map pg 231 👫 🍃 🐎 🚲

## Trailhead

The trailhead is at Station Flats day use, 0.8 km (0.5 mi.) west of the Elbow Ranger Station. The trail leaves the parking lot from the far side of the loop road.

## Route

| Route | Elevation | | Distance | |
|---|---|---|---|---|
| | metres | feet | km | mi. |
| Trailhead | 1400 | 4,592 | 0.0 | 0.0 |
| Tom Snow Junction | 1450 | 4,756 | 0.7 | 0.4 |
| Viewpoint | 1525 | 5,002 | 2.8 | 1.7 |
| Complete Loop | 1400 | 4,592 | 3.7 | 2.3 |

Diamond T Loop is a short loop that makes for a pleasant afternoon hike, or, for equestrians, can be used to access the southern extension of the Tom Snow Trail. From the day use area, Diamond T Loop branches off the Sulphur Springs almost immediately. From this junction, it climbs through an aspen and lodgepole pine forest for 0.7 km (0.4 mi.) to its junction with Tom Snow Trail. Equestrians may use that trail to link with the West Bragg Creek trail system.

Beyond this junction, the trail winds westward and then south. There is a particularly pleasant viewpoint just after the trail makes another sharp turn and briefly heads east. This open hillside provides clear views of the rolling Elbow Valley and Forgetmenot Ridge to the west.

The trail drops from the viewpoint to rejoin with the Elbow Valley Trail at the 3.3-km (2-mi.) mark. Turn left, and reach the trailhead at kilometre 3.7 (mile 2.3).

# 53. Elbow Valley and Sulphur Springs Loop

Map pg 231 📷 🌾 🍃 🐎 🚲

## Trailhead

The trailhead is at Station Flats day use, 0.8 km (0.5 mi.) west of the Elbow Ranger Station. The trail leaves the parking lot from the far side of the loop road.

## Route

| Route | Elevation | | Distance | |
|---|---|---|---|---|
| | metres | feet | km | mi. |
| Trailhead | 1400 | 4,592 | 0.0 | 0.0 |
| Sulphur Springs Junction | 1550 | 5,084 | 6.2 | 3.9 |
| Return to Trailhead | 1400 | 4,592 | 13.0 | 8.1 |

The combination of Elbow Valley Trail and Sulphur Springs Trail makes a fabulous 13-km (8.1-mi.) loop that showcases the rolling character of the Elbow River Valley. Beginning at the Station Flats trailhead, the trail parallels Highway 66 eastward, passing two junctions for the Diamond T Loop at kilometres 0.1 and 0.4 (miles .06 and .25). After the second junction for Diamond T, the trail begins climbing briefly before dropping down to the junction with the Sulphur Springs Trail. You can do this loop in either direction, but we will describe it in a clockwise manner by suggesting you stay left on Elbow Valley Trail at this junction and later return on Sulphur Springs Trail. At this four-way junction, go straight to continue on Elbow Valley Trail, and soon cross a bridge over an unnamed creek. The trail begins climbing once you cross the bridge, and mountain bikers will find themselves huffing along the steady uphills of this section of the trail. With the climb, the views open up. By the 3-km (1.9-mi.) mark, there are numerous openings with clear views west all the way to Forgetmenot Ridge. At 4.3 km (2.7 mi.) the trail begins a rocky, sharp descent towards its junction with Moose Mountain Road.

Cross Moose Mountain Road at 5.4 km (3.4 mi.), and immediately begin climbing a short

*Livestock are common on the Sulphur Springs Loop*

uphill stretch that takes you away from the road. After the trail levels out in a pleasant aspen meadow at 6.2 km (3.9 mi.), a signed junction for the Sulphur Springs Trail marks your departure from the Elbow Valley Trail. Turn right and begin climbing steeply across a meadow lined with owl clover, locoweed and sage. This steep climb crests at 7.2 km (4.5 mi.) just before crossing Moose Mountain Road for the second time.

After crossing the road, the trail continues a pleasant downhill trend, passing through a variety of habitats. Beginning in an open aspen forest, it descends to a wet, marshy area where there are some badly eroded and wet sections of trail. These are short-lived, though, and after a short climb out the valley bottom, the trail drops to the junction with Elbow Valley Trail at 11.6 km (7.2 mi.). Turn left and return to the trailhead at kilometre 13 (mile 8.1).

# 54. Moose Mountain Ridge Road

Map pg 223 📷 🌱 🍃 🚲

## Trailhead

From Bragg Creek, head west on the Elbow Falls Trail (Hwy. 66). From the Kananaskis Country entrance sign, head west for 9.5 km (5.9 mi.) to the Moose Mountain Ridge Road. Climb this gated road for 7.5 km (4.7 mi.). At this point you will see a gated road forking off to the right.

## Route

| Route | Elevation | | Distance | |
|---|---|---|---|---|
| | metres | feet | km | mi. |
| Trailhead | 1960 | 6,429 | 0.0 | 0.0 |
| Moose Mountain Summit | 2437 | 7,995 | 7.1 | 4.5 |
| Return to Trailhead | 1960 | 6,429 | 14.2 | 8.8 |

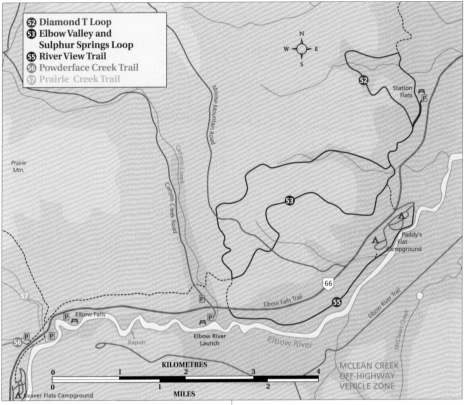

(see 'Moose Mountain' on page 142)

52 Diamond T Loop
53 Elbow Valley and
   Sulphur Springs Loop
55 River View Trail
56 Powderface Creek Trail
57 Prairie Creek Trail

Moose Mountain fire road takes you to the summit of Alberta's highest fire lookout, while providing a 360° panorama. The 7.1-km (4.4-mi.) trail can be covered either as a hike or as a combination of 5.6-km (3.5-mi.) mountain bike ride, followed by 1.4 km (0.9 mi.) of hiking the final switchbacks to the summit.

The trail begins 7.5 km (4.7 mi.) along the Moose Mountain Ridge Road, which allows you to cover much of the elevation gain in your vehicle. However, there is still 477 m (1,565 ft.) left for you. Lookouts have been located here since around 1929, but this structure was built in 1974 (see 'Moose Mountain' on page 142). When you reach the building, please don't approach it, as it is not a public facility. It is a residence, and as such, hikers are asked to respect the privacy of the tower staff.

The trail follows a wide former access road. Keep in mind that both cyclists and hikers use this route, and there may be fast-moving mountain bikes on some of the downhill sections. The trail begins with a moderate uphill trend, and

the views towards your distant objective rapidly open up. At kilometre 0.7 (mile 0.4), the trail begins a sharp drop for just over half a kilometre. During this descent, you lose approximately 60 m (200 ft.) of elevation, all of which must be regained before the summit. At the bottom of this drop, the unmarked junction with Packers Trail joins in from the right.

The climbing begins again, although moderately for the next kilometre, beyond which the trail steepens. By kilometre 2.5 (mile 1.6), the trail begins to approach the upper levels of the subalpine. Treeline is visible in the distance, and there is still a short drop before the final climb to the summit. At the bottom of this short drop, the trail winds west to climb a tight group of seven switchbacks towards the lower summit, cresting at approximately 5.7 km (3.6 mi.).

From the first summit, you are faced with the exposed climb towards the final summit. Now, completely above treeline, the exposed trail snakes across the ridge, winding below the final summit before swinging back to the east

**231**

for the final climb. From the lookout, the views to the east stretch all the way to Calgary, while the western skyline is dominated by the transition from foothill to mountain. To the south stands another former lookout site, Forget-menot Ridge.

# 55. River View Trail

Map pg 231

*Hikers on Moose Mountain Ridge Road*

## Trailhead

There are numerous access points for the River View Trail. One of the best ways to access it is to begin along the Paddy's Flat Interpretive Trail. Turn into the Paddy's Flat Campground. Turn left following signs for loops B and C, and then right into loop C. There is a small pull-off on the right to access the campground amphitheatre. The trail begins just to the left of the stage. Go left onto the interpretive trail. Alternate access points can be found on loops A, D and E.

The western access is along the Elbow Falls Trail (Hwy. 66). Look for a trail branching off to the left just prior to where the highway drops down to meet Canyon Creek.

## Route

| Route | Elevation | | Distance | |
|---|---|---|---|---|
| | metres | feet | km | mi. |
| Paddy's Flat Trailhead | 1450 | 4,756 | 0.0 | 0.0 |
| River View Trail | 1450 | 4,756 | 1.0 | 0.6 |
| Highway 66 Junction | 1450 | 4,756 | 4.0 | 2.5 |

## Paddy's Flat Interpretive Trail

This 2.2-km (1.4-mi.) self-guided interpretive trail allows for pleasant foothill views, river views and diverse wildflowers. It also demonstrates the terraced nature of the Elbow Valley. The valley contains thick layers of material that were deposited by meltwaters of the receding Elbow Valley glacier. Later, as water levels fluctuated, the river cut into the material to varying depths. This created the terrace that this trail follows. In June, watch for western wood lilies along the upper section of the trail where it winds through a pleasant aspen forest, and especially where it drops down to the river. A small sandy beach has formed where the river has created a small, shallow pool. From here,

the trail follows the Elbow through numerous wildflower habitats, covering the spectrum from dry gravel washes to wet marshy areas. Each supports a different wildflower. In moist areas in June, watch for sparrow's-egg orchids.

## River View Trail

As the Paddy's Flat Interpretive Trail climbs away from the river to begin looping back along the upper terrace, the River View Trail forks off to the left approximately halfway up the embankment. The trail follows the winding course of the Elbow River, with numerous views of the river and the rolling landscape to the west. The trail gradually climbs higher above the river itself, and as it does so, the views improve. Before long, the trail begins winding away from the river to join Highway 66 at approximately 4 km (2.5 mi.). If you want to make a nice loop, the trail continues on the opposite side of Highway 66. Here you can link the River View Trail with either the Elbow Valley or the Sulphur Springs Trails to make extended loops.

*Banded Peak from Powderface Summit*

# 56. Powderface Creek Trail

Map pg 234

Map pg 234

## Trailhead

From Bragg Creek, follow signs to the Elbow Valley. Head west on Highway 66. After passing the Kananaskis Country sign, continue west for 14.3 km (8.9 mi.) to the Powderface trailhead. Park here.

## Route

| Route | Elevation | | Distance | |
|---|---|---|---|---|
| | metres | feet | km | mi. |
| Trailhead | 1500 | 4,920 | 0.0 | 0.0 |
| Powderface Pass | 2000 | 6,560 | 6.2 | 3.9 |
| Powderface Trail Road Junction | 1750 | 5,740 | 9.1 | 5.7 |

Mountain bikers and horseback riders use Powderface Creek Trail more heavily than hikers. The trail remains in the trees for much of its length, and offers few real vantage points to attract hikers. On the other hand, it makes for a great trail ride. As it approaches Powderface Creek Pass, you get great views of Banded Peak and Mounts Cornwall and Glasgow, the three peaks that form the western terminus of the Elbow River Valley. The trail also offers excellent loop options with Prairie Creek Trail, allowing horseback riders and mountain bikers to have a nice long ride without backtracking.

From the trailhead, Powderface Creek Trail begins climbing immediately along a wide, loose gravel surface. In early season, the trail holds snow, and much of its length has muddy and rocky stretches. Shortly after the 2-km (1.2-mi.) mark, the creek occasionally begins to run right down the centre of the trail, making for some wet conditions. This is followed by your first views towards Powderface Ridge high and to the west.

Pass the junction with Prairie Link Trail at kilometre 2.8 (mile 1.7). A 12.3-km (7.7-mi.)

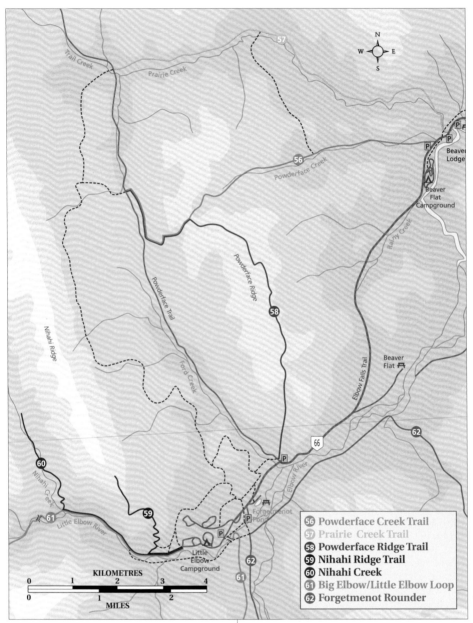

KILOMETRES
0 — 1 — 2 — 3 — 4

0 — 1 — 2
MILES

56 **Powderface Creek Trail**
57 Prairie Creek Trail
58 **Powderface Ridge Trail**
59 **Nihahi Ridge Trail**
60 **Nihahi Creek**
61 Big Elbow/Little Elbow Loop
62 **Forgetmenot Rounder**

loop can be made by turning right at this junction and climbing for 2.9 km (1.8 mi.) to Prairie Creek Trail. To continue on Powderface Creek, stay straight (left) at this junction. The trail condition beyond this junction varies between good, wide track and muddy, rutted track. The gradient also gradually increases until kilometre 4.2 (mile 2.6), where the trail begins to climb

sharply. After a long switchback at kilometre 4.7 (mile 2.9), the climbing moderates briefly, allowing mountain bikers a little break. The views to the east open up as you continue climbing towards the pass. The foothills undulate towards the east, and you begin to get a feel for the elevation gained so far.

The climbing quickly resumes and the trail

*Mountain biker on Prairie Creek trail*

finally crests at kilometre 6.2 (mile 3.9). To the left, the trail to Powderface Ridge continues climbing to a windswept summit with panoramas in all directions. Ahead of you, Powderface Creek begins dropping off of this low pass to join with Powderface Trail Road.

From the pass, the trail suddenly takes a downhill turn and becomes narrow and rooty. There are several low areas where water collects into large mud holes, so mountain bikers will need to exercise caution. The trail begins to wind right at kilometre 7.8 (mile 4.9) to parallel the wide gravel of Powderface Trail Road. Along this next section, the ride becomes a winding drop with some sharp turns and the occasional mud hole. After leveling out, the trail joins with Powderface Trail Road at kilometre 9.1 (mile 5.7).

To make a loop with Prairie Creek, turn right and follow this wide gravel road for 2.7 km (1.7 mi.) to the trailhead for Prairie Creek.

# 57. Prairie Creek Trail

Map pg 234

## Trailhead

From Bragg Creek, follow signs to the Elbow Valley. Head west on Highway 66 for approximately 32 km (19.9 mi.) to a junction with the gravel surface of Powderface Trail Road. Follow this road north for 10 km (6.2 mi.) to an unmarked trailhead. There is a pull-off on the west side of the road, and you can see the trail heading east away from the road, to cross a bridge over the creek.

## Route

| Route | Elevation | | Distance | |
|---|---|---|---|---|
| | metres | feet | km | mi. |
| Trailhead | 1700 | 5,576 | 0.0 | 0.0 |
| Prairie Link Trail Junction | 1725 | 5,658 | 3.8 | 2.4 |
| Powderface Day Use | 1500 | 4,920 | 10.4 | 6.5 |

*Elbow Peaks from Powderface Ridge trail*

Prairie Creek Trail follows the winding course of its namesake creek, along a watercourse that has been heavily impacted by beavers. Numerous dams and lodges offer the opportunity to examine the amazing architectural structures these intelligent rodents are able to build. The trail remains largely in the trees, with a few elevated viewpoints of the foothills. It is most popular with mountain bikers and equestrians and makes a great loop with Powderface Creek Trail. For this reason, it is described in an west to east direction.

The trail winds to the east, leaving Powderface Trail Road behind. After crossing a bridge near the trailhead, there is a short, sharp climb to traverse high to the left of the first of numerous beaver marshes. As the trail rolls alongside the creek, it passes through a mixed forest of white spruce and lodgepole pine. After a steep climb at kilometre 2.4 (mile 1.5), it passes another beaver marsh—this time, with a beaver lodge as well as a large dam. Soon, the trail opens into a small aspen meadow, before returning to the protection of the trees.

The junction with Prairie Link Trail is at kilometre 3.8 (mile 2.4) after a muddy, rooty stretch. The combination of horses and cattle in this area has caused significant damage to sections of the trail. Stay straight at the signed junction and continue to bounce your way along the muddy trail. After climbing high above the river to traverse a narrow sidecut above the creek, you'll descend back to the creek as it passes another large beaver pond. There is plenty of evidence of the beavers having cut down some of the local aspen and alder trees. Beyond the dam, the climbing resumes. Pass a gated fence at 7 km (4.4 mi.). When I passed this gate, there was a "Keep Closed" sign, but the gate had been wired in the open position.

Soon after the gate, the trail emerges beneath an overhanging sandstone cliff. This marks the beginning of a very steep climb. The trail slimbs up a loose scree and the trees begin showing signs of the high winds whipping over this exposed ridge. Some of the lodgepole pines and aspen trees have taken on a low, twisted character. Finally, at kilometre 8 (mile 5.0), you crest the top of this climb. From this mini-summit, the trail begins the final drop towards its junction with Highway 66. Mountain bikers will love this winding slalom section that mixes a moderately steep drop with sharp corners and small rock ledges. The trail joins Highway 66 at kilometre 9.9 (mile 6.2). Turn right and follow the pavement to Powderface trailhead at kilometre 10.4 (mile 6.5).

# 58. Powderface Ridge Trail

Map pg 234 📷 🌾 🐎 🚴

## Trailhead

From Bragg Creek, follow signs to the Elbow Valley. Head west on Highway 66 for approximately 32 km (19.9 mi.) to a junction with the gravel surface of Powderface Trail Road. Park at this junction, and just beyond the cattle guard you'll see the trail climbing the hillside to the right side of this gravel road.

## Route

| Route | Elevation | | Distance | |
|---|---|---|---|---|
| | metres | feet | km | mi. |
| Trailhead | 1600 | 5,248 | 0.0 | 0.0 |
| Powderface Ridge Summit | 2190 | 7,183 | 4.5 | 2.8 |
| Return to Trailhead | 1600 | 5,248 | 9.0 | 5.6 |

Beginning in a dark lodgepole pine forest, this trail climbs steadily to the summit at kilometre 4.5 (mile 2.8). The focus of this trail is the high, windswept summit of Powderface Ridge. From this lofty viewpoint, the contrasts between foothill and mountain are spread out before you. To the southwest, the three main peaks of the Elbow Valley—Banded, Cornwall, and Glasgow—form the focus. Westward, the knife-like Nihahi Ridge marks the official start of the Front Ranges of the Rocky Mountains. To the east, watch the gradual shrinking of the foothills in the distance. Once you've enjoyed the view, you can either return along the same route or continue down Powderface Creek slightly to the north of the summit.

The climbing is unrelenting. In the first 2 km (1.2 mi.), the trail climbs approximately 440 m (1,443 ft.) before cresting a lower outlier of Powderface Ridge. After a bit more climbing, the trail begins to traverse a grassy sidecut with good views down to the right towards the Elbow Valley. From this vantage point, if you look south towards Forgetmenot Ridge, you can see how the rock layers of this foothill summit were once continuous with the slopes of Powderface Ridge. Over time, though, the Elbow River has

carved its way through this rock face and separated the two summits.

At kilometre 2.6 (mile 1.6), the trail emerges at what almost appears to be a low pass. To the right, another outlier of Powderface Ridge seems to beckon you upward from this cairn-marked junction. The actual trail winds to the left at this point and re-enters the forest as it makes its way towards the true summit of Powderface Ridge. Over the next 1.2 km (0.8 mi.), the trail winds around through the forested eastern slopes of Powderface Ridge, gradually dropping approximately 41 m (134 ft.), before it begins climbing towards the true summit.

Soon after you pass a marshy section with a white drainage pipe sticking out of the ground, the final 0.7-km (0.4-mi.) summit climb begins. It is approximately 156 m (512 ft.) to the wind-blasted summit of Powderface Ridge. From here, the trail stays in the open for a short distance, and the open slopes provide wonderful options for a sunny picnic. Generally the true summit, although dramatic, is far too wind-blown for lengthy relaxation.

# 59. Nihahi Ridge Trail

Map pg 234 👫 📷 🌾

## Trailhead

From Bragg Creek, follow signs to the Elbow Valley. Head west on Highway 66 for approximately 32 km (19.9 mi.) to the Little Elbow Campground. Stay left in the campground, following signs for Loops C, D and E. As you see the suspension bridge to your left, you will see the trailhead parking lot on your right.

## Route

| Route | Elevation | | Distance | |
|---|---|---|---|---|
| | metres | feet | km | mi. |
| Trailhead | 1625 | 5,330 | 0.0 | 0.0 |
| Nihahi Ridge Terminus | 2135 | 7,002 | 3.8 | 2.4 |
| Back to Trailhead | 1625 | 5,330 | 7.6 | 4.7 |

"Nihahi" is a Stoney Indian word meaning "rock". Appropriately, the trail climbs from the

*Nihahi Ridge*

Little Elbow Campground towards the official start of the Front Ranges of the Rocky Mountains. I once watched a peregrine falcon soar above the ridge before disappearing from view in a steep dive. It may be hard work for humans to gain the ridge, but for the area's birds of prey, it's a simple flight.

From the parking lot at the Little Elbow Campground, follow the campground access road to the west, and after 1 km (0.6 mi.), leave the campground behind as you make your way through a series of three metal gates. Follow the wide course of the Little Elbow Trail until kilometre 1.5 (mile 0.9), and turn right, following an access trail to the Ford Creek Trail, which you meet at a T-intersection after just 0.1 km. Turn left on this wide horse trail and than right onto the actual Nihahi Ridge Trail at another signed junction.

The Nihahi Ridge Trail leaves the Ford Creek Trail behind and winds through a lodgepole pine forest with an understory of buffaloberry, nodding onion and a few patches of one-sided wintergreen. The climbing starts immediately as the trail begins a section of switchbacks along the lower slopes of Nihahi Ridge. While you climb, the lodgepole pine forest shows plenty of evidence of its fiery genesis in the charred remains of old trees. The lodgepole pine uses the heat of forest fires to open its cones. This makes

it one of the first trees to colonize these fire scarred locations.

Finally, at kilometre 2.3 (mile 1.4), the climbing levels out as you emerge atop a pleasant subalpine meadow. You can see the trail snake across the meadow towards the base of the summit ridge. Follow this path across the meadow, and enjoy the splash of colour provided by the spring and summer wildflowers that make this meadow home.

As you reach the far side of the meadow at kilometre 2.7 (mile 1.7), you rapidly approach the base of the summit ridge. As you begin climbing, there is a cable railing placed at kilometre 3.1 (mile 1.9) to help you pull your way up the slope. As you climb above the railing, you'll come across an unmarked junction. Both trails soon rejoin, so you can select either option. At this point, the trail begins climbing straight along the edge of Nihahi Ridge. There are excellent views to the east towards the rolling foothill summits of Powderface and Forgetmenot Ridges. To the south and west, the valleys of the Big and Little Elbow Rivers stand beneath Mounts Glasgow and Cornwall, along with Banded Peak.

At kilometre 3.6 (mile 2.2), you must scramble up a short cliff face. As you climb the final, easier section of the trail, it makes its way towards the base of a cliff at kilometre 3.8 (mile

*Nihahi Creek*

2.4). This is the end of the actual hike. Beyond this, it becomes technical scrambling beyond the scope of this book. The actual summit of Nihahi Ridge is still some 210 m (690 ft.) above you, but this point is the turnaround point for most day hikers. To finish the hike, retrace your steps, returning to the trailhead at kilometre 7.6 (mile 4.7).

# 60. Nihahi Creek

Map pg 234 👫 📷

## Trailhead

From Bragg Creek, follow signs to the Elbow Valley. Head west on Highway 66 for approximately 32 km (19.9 mi.) to the Little Elbow Campground. Stay left in the campground, following signs for Loops C, D and E. As you see the suspension bridge to your left, you will see the trailhead parking lot on your right.

## Route

| Route | Elevation | | Distance | |
|---|---|---|---|---|
| | metres | feet | km | mi. |
| Trailhead Parking Lot | 1625 | 5,330 | 0.0 | 0.0 |
| Nihahi Creek Junction | 1675 | 5,494 | 2.6 | 1.6 |
| Return to Trailhead | 1625 | 5,330 | 5.2 | 3.2 |

This wonderful trail is best left to the latter part of the season, when Nihahi Creek is largely devoid of water. Why? Because half the fun of this hike is exploring the intricately carved canyon formed within the streambed itself. This becomes more difficult when spring runoff is filling the canyon and hiding its polished walls. This is the kind of hike where you follow the trail for sections, and then drop down to the channel to explore a little. Keep in mind that it is impossible to follow the channel bed downstream to its junction with the Little Elbow Trail, as there is a high waterfall drop that will prevent this.

Beginning at the Little Elbow Campground, follow the campground roads west for 1 km (0.6 mi.), where the Little Elbow Trail leaves the campground after passing through a series of three metal gates. A mountain bike helps make short work of the 1.6 km (1 mi.) that you'll need to follow this wide track before meeting the junction with Nihahi Creek.

Just before you cross the (often dry) bed of Nihahi Creek, a signed junction on the right marks the start of the climb. The trail climbs sharply at this point to crest the hanging valley in which the majority of Nihahi Creek is located. Finally, at kilometre 2.9 (mile 1.8), the climbing moderates and soon the dry channel of Nihahi Creek appears down to the left. As you continue upstream on the wide trail, there are numerous points from which you can access the dry channel. The narrow canyon seems to end at kilometre 3 (mile 1.9) where it widens into a gravel wash. The formal trail continues 2 km (1.2 mi.) further up the valley of Nihahi Creek, but most hikers tend to use this hike merely as an excuse to explore the dry river channel. You can head down to the gravel wash here, follow the channel downstream a short distance, and explore the narrow canyon. Don't go too far or you'll find yourself stranded above the high cliff at the downstream end of this hanging valley.

When you have explored enough, head back upstream until you either return to this location or find another spot where you can scramble up to the formal trail. Retrace your route back to the trailhead at the Little Elbow Campground.

*Misty Range from Elbow Pass*

# 61. Big Elbow/Little Elbow Loop

Map pg 241 📷 🌿 🍃 🐎 🚲

## Trailhead

From Bragg Creek, follow signs to the Elbow Valley. Head west on Highway 66 for approximately 32 km (19.9 mi.) to the Little Elbow Campground. Stay left in the campground, following signs for Loops C, D and E. As you see the suspension bridge to your left, you will see the trailhead parking lot on your right.

## Route

| Route | Elevation | | Distance | |
|---|---|---|---|---|
| | metres | feet | km | mi. |
| Trailhead | 1625 | 5,330 | 0.0 | 0.0 |
| Tombstone Creek Junction | 2000 | 6,560 | 19.4 | 12.1 |
| Tombstone Pass | 2250 | 7,380 | 23.0 | 14.3 |
| Romulus Campground | 1800 | 5,904 | 31.5 | 19.6 |
| Little Elbow Campground | 1625 | 5,330 | 44.2 | 27.5 |

This long, wild loop takes you toward the headwaters of the Elbow River, in a circuit around the Big Elbow and Little Elbow Rivers. The loop is 44.2 km (27.5 mi.) along former fire access roads and wide single-track. The route can be done in either direction, but the clockwise route is described here.

From the Little Elbow Campground, cross the bridge over the Little Elbow, and follow the Big Elbow River south between the round face of Forgetmenot Ridge and the glacier-scarred face of Mount Glasgow. The trail begins by following the dividing line between rolling foothills to the left and the craggy peaks of the Rocky Mountains to your right. During the first 10 km (6.2 mi.), the trail trends south on a wide road surface. At kilometre 10.5 (mile 6.5), it winds west as the valley of the Elbow River cuts a gap in the mountain wall to the west. After a bridge crossing at kilometre 10.6 (mile 6.6), there is a sharp uphill, and the next section of trail periodically narrows. Mountain bikers will find numerous technical sections through this part of the route, while hikers will enjoy the narrower trail. By 11 km (6.8 mi.), the trail has climbed above the river, but it soon begins a rapid descent back down to another bridge over the Elbow. At an unmarked junction at kilometre 15.9 (mile 9.9), stay right on the more obvious track. The next section varies between old growth forest and open slopes, until you meet the signed junction for Tombstone Creek Trail. Turn right at this junction and begin climbing almost immediately.

Turn right at another junction at kilometre 20.7 (mile 12.9) and begin the steep grind towards Tombstone Pass. You will pass two side junctions that go to the Tombstone Lakes. These lakes are a worthwhile side trip, but cyclists will need to park their bikes and hike to them. The two tiny tarns sit beneath the glacial bowl of Tombstone Mountain. They earned their name from the large slabs of rock along their shores, which almost resemble grave

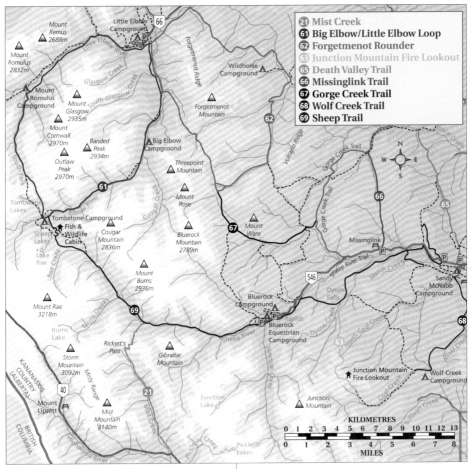

21 Mist Creek
61 Big Elbow/Little Elbow Loop
62 Forgetmenot Rounder
63 Junction Mountain Fire Lookout
65 Death Valley Trail
66 Missinglink Trail
67 Gorge Creek Trail
68 Wolf Creek Trail
69 Sheep Trail

markers. The first junction is passed at kilometre 20.8 (mile 12.9), and the second is beyond the pass at kilometre 24.8 (mile 15.4). From either of these junctions the lakes are less than a 2-km (1.2-mi.) side trip.

The pass is crested at kilometre 23 (mile 14.3), and sits in a beautiful landscape of glacier-scoured peaks. The summit is blanketed with alpine larch, and a wide variety of wildflowers, including alpine forget-me-not, cow parsnip, sulphur hedysarum, and red paintbrush. From the pass, the gradient changes to one of steady elevation loss. The force of gravity takes over as the trail drops along the beginnings of what will become the Little Elbow River. Along the next 7 km (4.4 mi.), the trail crosses numerous avalanche slopes, revealing the lush growth made possible in these moist, open areas.

The trail approaches Romulus Campground at kilometre 31.5 (mile 19.6). This backcountry site has 14 tent sites, each with firepit and firewood supplied. By now, the Little Elbow River has become a wide channel, and the gradient levels out as you follow its meandering course towards the trail's end at the Little Elbow Campground. Soon after crossing the Little Elbow on a good bridge at kilometre 38.5 (mile 23.9), a signed junction marks the beginning of the Nihahi Creek trail on the left. Stay straight, passing the junction for Nihahi Ridge Trail at kilometre 40.9 (mile 25.4). This marks the final roll to the Little Elbow Campground entrance at 42.4 km (26.4 mi.) and the trailhead at 44.2 km (27.5 mi.).

*Forgetmenot Mountain over the Big Elbow River*

# 62. Forgetmenot Rounder

Map pg 241 📷 🌾 🐎 🚲

## Trailhead

From Bragg Creek, follow signs to the Elbow Valley. Head west on Highway 66 for approximately 32 km (19.9 mi.) to the Little Elbow Campground. Stay left in the campground, following signs for loops C, D and E. As you see the suspension bridge to your left, you will see the trailhead parking lot on your right.

## Route

| Route | Elevation | | Distance | |
|---|---|---|---|---|
| | metres | feet | km | mi. |
| Trailhead | 1625 | 5,330 | 0.0 | 0.0 |
| Threepoint Trail Junction | 1660 | 5,445 | 4.3 | 2.7 |
| Threepoint Mountain Pass | 2075 | 6,806 | 8.5 | 5.3 |
| Volcano Creek Junction | 1975 | 6,478 | 13.6 | 8.5 |
| Volcano Ridge Junction | 1950 | 6,396 | 19.7 | 12.3 |
| Hog's Back Trail Junction | 1650 | 5,412 | 28.2 | 17.5 |
| Wildhorse Junction | 1700 | 5,576 | 30.5 | 19.0 |
| Back to Trailhead | 1625 | 5,330 | 46.4 | 28.8 |

Many of the Elbow Valley's longer routes are designed to circumnavigate mountain ranges or peaks, and this trail is no exception. It completely circles Forgetmenot Ridge, travelling 46.4 km (28.8 mi.) through rugged terrain that will entice the equestrian and challenge the mountain biker. Hikers also use this as a backpacking route.

From the Little Elbow Campground, cross the Little Elbow River on the suspension bridge, staying right at the first junction at kilometre 0.5 (mile 0.3). You will return along this trail to finish the ride. Follow the wide Big Elbow Trail south to an easily-missed junction at kilometre 4.3 km (mile 2.7), where a nondescript trail branches off to the left. The junction is marked with an orange diamond with "Threepoint Mountain" written on it. There are several junctions over the next kilometre (0.6 mi.). Stay right at the first, and left at two more. After several shallow fords, the trail begins climbing sharply towards a low pass. You reach the summit at kilometre 8.5 (mile 5.3), and at this elevated position are treated to fabulous views of Banded Peak and Mounts Cornwall and Glasgow to the west, and Threepoint Mountain to the southwest.

The trail condition deteriorates beyond the summit, and becomes muddy and sloppy from the free-ranging cattle. This sloppy section continues until the junction with Volcano Creek Trail at 13.6 km (8.5 mi.). Look for a sign indicating Threepoint Campground. Cattle hooves may also chew up Volcano Creek Trail, but the conditions tend to improve as you reach the junction with Volcano Ridge Trail at kilometre 19.7 (mile 11.8). Turn left at this junction, where mountain bikers will puff their way up a steep climb away from the mucky valley bottom. The trail conditions improve with this gain in elevation and portions of several old seismic lines are

*Horses in the foothills*

followed. After crossing Threepoint Creek, the trail follows the rim of the magnificent Threepoint Gorge to its junction with Hog's Back Trail. Turn left at this junction at kilometre 28.2 (mile 17.5).

You have two options when you reach the junction with Wildhorse Trail. One option is to follow the wide Quirk Creek exploration road downhill, ford the Elbow River, and follow Highway 66 back to the Little Elbow Campground. The preferred option, however, is to turn left onto the singletrack of Wildhorse Trail which winds through the trees, dropping steadily until it bottoms out along the south side of the Elbow River. Follow the now-level trail as it parallels the river and makes its way towards the Little Elbow Campground. You will have to ford the Elbow River at kilometre 44.6 (mile 27.7, but the ford is often dry in late season. Cross the suspension bridge and finish at the Little Elbow Campground at kilometre 46.4 (mile 28.8).

## Lookout

**A fire lookout** was built in 1954 atop the slopes of Forget-me-not Ridge. This was part of a general expansion of forest-fire protection programs during this period. It was a tiny, 12 x 12-ft. cabin, but each summer, lookout personnel formed the front line against fire. In 1975 it was abandoned, and two years later the building was burned. Eventually even the access road was reclaimed, leaving little evidence of its presence. Why was it removed? It had become redundant—other lookouts covered its area. During its heyday, motorcycles enjoyed roaring up the road to the lookout, and this provided part of the impetus for the road being reclaimed.

## Forget-me-nots

*The delicate alpine forget-me-not*

**When hiking** in the mountains, the alpine forget-me-not is one of the most pleasant flowers of the high country. Delicate, yet unmistakable, its sky blue petals and bright yellow centre are one of the rewards of climbing to the subalpine. Like most high altitude flowers, it is a perennial—there's just not enough time to grow from seed each year. They often stay very low to the ground, protected within, or beneath, a rock slope. When you encounter forget-me-nots, keep your eyes open for some of the other common alpine wildflowers.

*Taking a break on Junction Mountain*

# 63. Junction Mountain Fire Lookout

Map pg 245 📷 🌿 🍃 🐎 🚵

From Turner Valley, follow signs for Kananaskis Country. As you pass the Sheep River Information Centre, continue west for 16.9 km (10.5 mi.) to the Indian Oils trailhead. Park here, and follow an access road to a bridge over the Sheep River.

## Route

| Route | Elevation | | Distance | |
|---|---|---|---|---|
| | metres | feet | km | mi. |
| Trailhead | 1543 | 5,060 | 0.0 | 0.0 |
| Green Mtn Trail Junction | 1585 | 5,200 | 4.1 | 2.6 |
| Dysan Creek Ford | 1570 | 5,150 | 4.7 | 2.9 |
| Junction Mtn. Trail Junction | 1585 | 5,200 | 4.9 | 3.1 |
| Junction Mtn. Lookout | 2225 | 7,298 | 14.2 | 8.8 |
| Back to Trailhead | 1543 | 5,060 | 24.4 | 15.1 |

The 14.2-km (8.8-mi.) point-to-point trail to the fire lookout tends to be a mountain bike or horseback route due to the extended distance and lack of camping facilities along the route. However, those that do travel to the summit of this 2225-m (7,298-ft.) vantage will be rewarded with excellent views of the surrounding ranges.

From the Indian Oils trailhead, the trail drops down to the Sheep River to cross on a good-quality bridge. The river is confined to a narrow canyon as it drops over Tiger Jaw Falls. Go left at a junction with the Sheep Trail immediately across the bridge. The trail begins to climb gradually as it passes through an area that may be badly churned by the hooves of free-ranging cattle. There are periodic views of the pleasant landscape of the surrounding foothills as the trail rolls eastward. Stay right at a junction with the Green Mountain Trail at 4.1 km (2.6 mi.). Prepare yourself for wet feet, because you will need to ford Dysan Creek soon after this junction. The ford is about knee-deep in July, but the current is very strong. Dysan Falls drops over a rock outcrop only 50 m or so (164 ft.) downstream from this ford.

Climb up from Dysan Creek and stay right at the junction with Junction Mountain Fire Lookout Trail at kilometre 4.9 (mile 3.1). As the trail climbs up from the valley bottom, it shows some bad gouging and rutting from cattle in the area. The trail climbs steadily, and at kilometre 6.7 (mile 4.2), the road passes a nice meadow with a marshy pool to the left. Beyond this meadow, the trail makes several switchbacks before the steep climbing begins. Both the trail condition and the views improve with rising elevation. By the 9-km (5.6-mi.) mark, the views begin to open up as you leave the trees behind. Each summer, the sun-baked hillsides explode with wildflowers such as early yellow locoweed,

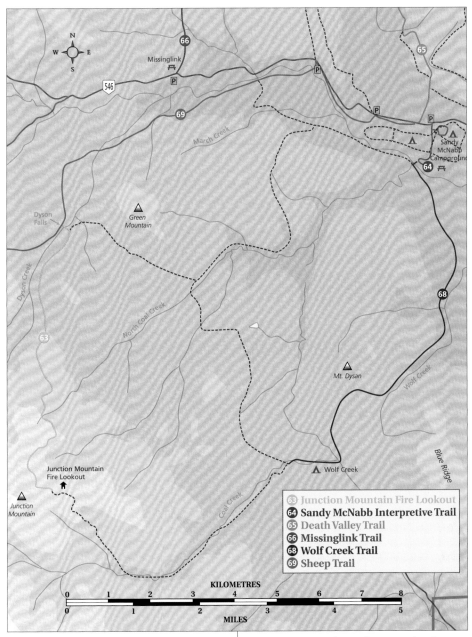

**KILOMETRES**

0 1 2 3 4 5 6 7 8

0 1 2 3 4 5

**MILES**

**63** Junction Mountain Fire Lookout
**64** Sandy McNabb Interpretive Trail
**65** Death Valley Trail
**66** Missinglink Trail
**68** Wolf Creek Trail
**69** Sheep Trail

buttercup, and mouse-eared chickweed.

The trail consistently climbs towards the isolated lookout, making a shallow crossing of North Coal Creek as it tumbles down the hillside. As you near the final ridge, the views open up in all directions. Junction Mountain dominates the southwestern skyline, Bluerock Mountain rises to the northwest, and to the east, the foothills roll away, gradually giving way to the prairies. On a clear day, you may be able to see all the way to Calgary. You reach the lookout at kilometre 14.2 (mile 8.8). While here, please avoid the temptation to approach the lookout building, as it is a private residence.

*Viewpoint on the Sandy McNabb Interpretive trail*

# 64. Sandy McNabb Interpretive Trail

Map pg 245

From the Sheep River Trail (Hwy. 546), turn into the Sandy McNabb Campground. Stay on the main campground road, passing the entrance to both the equestrian and regular camping loops. Just before the road begins dropping towards the Sheep River, there is an access road on the left. This offers access to one of the group campgrounds, but if you stay to the right, there is a parking lot that forms the trailhead for the interpretive trail.

### Route

| Route | Elevation | | Distance | |
|---|---|---|---|---|
| | metres | feet | km | mi. |
| Trailhead | 1430 | 4,690 | 0.0 | 0.0 |
| End of Loop | 1430 | 4,690 | 1.8 | 1.1 |

When Sandy McNabb (see 'Sandy McNabb', page 151) first headed up the valley of the Sheep River, he had the choice of locating his campsite anywhere he wanted. He chose this bench above the Sheep River. His location is as appropriate today as it was then. This short, 1.8-km (1.1-mi.) interpretive trail takes you through open forest and past a wonderful rest spot over the river.

As the trail opens up above the river, the grassy slope explodes into a colour during early June. The three-flowered avens, shooting star, sticky purple geranium, and western wood lily all make an appearance. Its difficult to hike this trail during flower season and not spend a few minutes admiring these colourful characters.

At the viewpoint, a bench provides a place to take a load off and admire the river as it passes beneath your feet. Keep your eyes open for kayakers testing their luck in the currents.

The rolling character of the lower Sheep River Valley is evident from the views of the surrounding area. The river has its headwaters on Mount Rae, the same mountain that spawns the Elbow River to the north.

# 65. Death Valley Trail

Map pg 241

### Trailhead

The trailhead is located on the north side of Sheep River Trail (road) near the entrance to the Sandy McNabb Campground.

### Route

| Route | Elevation | | Distance | |
|---|---|---|---|---|
| | metres | feet | km | mi. |
| Trailhead | 1430 | 4,690 | 0.0 | 0.0 |
| Windy Point Junction | 1370 | 4,494 | 7.0 | 4.4 |
| Ware Creek Junction | 1355 | 4,444 | 11.9 | 7.4 |

*Sheep River and Valley*

Long Prairie Loop forks to the right, marking the first of several junctions over the next 0.5 km (0.3 mi.) or so. Follow the signs for Death Valley Trail. As you leave the cross-country ski trails behind, you begin to descend towards Death Valley Creek.

Death Valley Creek is lined with aspen trees that have attracted generations of beaver. They have renovated the valley repeatedly, leaving behind numerous dams and ponds. In dry weather, it is quite a pleasant walk through this beaver-modified landscape to the junction with Windy Point Trail at 7 km (4.4 mi.).

## Windy Point Trail

Most hikers will turn left at the T-intersection with Windy Point Trail to create a loop. From the Death Valley junction, the trail winds south and crosses Death Valley Creek twice. After passing through numerous meadows, it begins to climb towards the divide between Death Valley Creek and the Sheep River drainage. From this high point, it drops into a mucky section that continues until you pass the boundary sign indicating the entrance to the Sheep River Wildlife Sanctuary. Near this junction you have the option of taking the Foran Grade Trail or continuing on Windy Point down to the highway. The final descent brings you back to Highway 546 at the 13-km (8.1-mi.) mark.

## Windy Point Junction to Ware Creek Junction

Trail users wishing to continue beyond the Windy Point junction should stay straight at the T-intersection and continue along a section that takes you back and forth across the river several times. Hidden along this stretch is the grave marker of a young Stoney Indian named Muriel Dixon who died here more than 30 years ago.

Beyond this wet section, the trail leaves the creek behind, staying to the left of a small knoll. It eventually crosses another tributary of the creek and continues on its northward quest. After approximately 11 km (6.8 mi.), the trail joins with Ware Creek and follows this winding creek to its junction with Ware Creek Trail at 11.9 km (7.4 mi.). At this junction, Ware Creek Trail goes left and 9999 Trail goes right.

The winding trail up Death Valley Creek is best left for very dry weather; otherwise, horse and cattle hooves can leave it terribly chewed up and muddy. It is most popular with equestrians heading out for day trips or extended wilderness forays. Hikers and mountain bikers will likely make a loop with Windy Point or Foran Grade Trails, finishing up on the Sheep Trail.

The name of this valley may have been taken from a local story about a herd of horses and cattle being trapped during the harsh winter of 1906-07. Back then, most ranchers did not put up hay for winter, as they believed that the warm chinook winds would always keep enough forage open. On this fateful winter, the chinooks did not appear, and many cattle and horses died. Ever since then, ranchers have been putting up hay.

From the trailhead in Sandy McNabb Campground, the trail crosses the campground access road and then crosses Highway 546. The trail is wide and smooth as it heads north away from the paved roadway. In winter, numerous cross-country ski trails branch off this summer route.

# 66. Missinglink Trail

Map pg 241 🍃 🐎 🚲

### Trailhead

The Missinglink trailhead is located 7.4 km (4.6 mi.) west of Sandy McNabb Campground, on the north side of the highway. It is well-signed, with a parking area.

### Route

| Route | Elevation | | Distance | |
|---|---|---|---|---|
| | metres | feet | km | mi. |
| Missinglink Trailhead | 1500 | 4,920 | 0.0 | 0.0 |
| End of Trail | 1475 | 4,838 | 7.4 | 4.6 |

Missinglink Trail is a popular equestrian route, offering linkage with Link and Ware Creek Trails. It can form one leg of an extended wilderness ride or mountain bike ride. The route is not exceedingly picturesque, though, remaining largely within a dense canopy of lodgepole pines. The surface varies from soft to former access road and cutline. There are many confusing junctions, so you will want to watch for signs and follow the red markers that guide you along the correct route.

From the trailhead, Missinglink Trail climbs gradually to leave the Sheep River drainage behind. As you leave the Sheep River Wildlife Sanctuary, the trail drops into the drainage of Ware Creek. The remainder of the trail crosses cutline after cutline, all the while maintaining a northward direction. Eventually the trail meets a T-intersection with Link Trail and Ware Creek Trail. Ware Creek winds east, following Link Creek, and offers a loop option with Death Valley Trail after 6.2 km (3.9 mi.). Link Trail heads west for 6.6 km (4.1 mi.) to join up with Link Creek and Gorge Link Trails.

# 67. Gorge Creek Trail

Map pg 241 📷 🌿 🍃 🐎 🚲

### Trailhead

The Gorge Creek day use area forms the primary access point for this winding trail. To get there, head north on the gravel road of Gorge Creek Trail (road), which leaves the highway 9.9 km (6.2 mi.) west of Sandy McNabb Campground. Follow this gravel road for just over 4.2 km (2.6 mi.) and turn into Gorge Creek day use.

### Route

| Route | Elevation | | Distance | |
|---|---|---|---|---|
| | metres | feet | km | mi. |
| Trailhead | 1610 | 5,208 | 0.0 | 0.0 |
| Bluerock Creek Junction | 1775 | 5,822 | 8.7 | 5.4 |
| Volcano Creek Junction | 1970 | 6,462 | 11.8 | 7.3 |

Gorge Creek Trail offers many attractions. It is a major trail linking numerous other routes together, and at the same time it follows a beautiful river valley with numerous tiny waterfalls and magnificent views to the west towards Bluerock Mountain.

After leaving the trailhead, follow Gorge Creek west to its junction with Volcano Ridge Trail. Volcano Ridge heads north, offering options that can take you all the way to the Elbow Valley, should you desire. Stay straight for Gorge Creek Trail, and after a few hundred metres, wade across Gorge Creek. Pass the junction with South Gorge Creek and begin a gradual climb as the trail crosses the lower shoulder of Mount Ware before dropping down again to rejoin Gorge Creek. The sheer face of Bluerock Mountain gradually gets closer until, at 6.2 km (3.9 mi.), Indian Oils Trail forks to the south, meeting Highway 546 in 6.3 km (3.9 mi.).

Beyond the Indian Oils Trail, you will need to ford Gorge Creek three times in quick succession. Gradually, the trail begins winding towards the north until it meets Bluerock Creek Trail at 8.7 km (5.4 mi.). Beyond this junction, the trail heads directly north towards the opening between the rolling summit of Mount Ware

*A prairie storm rolls into Sheep River country*

and the steep face of Bluerock Mountain. It begins climbing, to crest a small shoulder on the base of Bluerock Mountain. This elevated vantage offers great views towards Mount Rose and the valley separating it from Bluerock Mountain. All too soon, you leave Gorge Creek behind and begin the gradual descent towards the final junction with Volcano Creek Trail at kilometre 11.8 (mile 7.3).

# 68. Wolf Creek Trail

Map pg 245

## Trailhead

The trailhead is located at the Sandy McNabb Campground picnic area off Sheep River Trail (road). Down at river level, red diamonds nailed to trees mark the start of the trail.

## Route

| Route | Elevation | | Distance | |
|---|---|---|---|---|
| | metres | feet | km | mi. |
| Trailhead | 1430 | 4,690 | 0.0 | 0.0 |
| Phone Line Trail Junction | 1575 | 5,166 | 11 | 6.8 |

Wolf Creek Trail follows an old roadbed south from Sandy McNabb Campground, offering loop access with the Phone Line and Green River Trails, or, for a more extended trip, with Junction Mountain Trail. One caveat: it starts with a ford of the Sheep River, which may be quite dangerous before mid-July. The trail is well-defined as it winds south on a combination of logging road and cutline, gradually climbing towards a low divide between Blue Ridge and Mount Dyson. It is important to keep an eye on the trail signs, as numerous junctions along the way can tease you with remarkably good cutlines while the trail remains more rustic.

As you approach the pass, the dark shales of Coal Creek Gorge offer an unexpected surprise. The combination of black shale gorge and great views of the summit of Green Ridge make this the highlight of the trip. From the pass, the trail drops to the Wolf Creek Backcountry Campsite. This small campsite has only five sites, but is fully equipped with picnic tables, firepits and outhouses. Soon after passing the campsite, the trail meets a signed junction. You have the option of taking the Phone Line Trail, which forks to the right, or continuing up the Junction Mountain Trail for an additional 7.6 km (4.7 mi.) to the Junction Mountain Fire Lookout.

# 69. Sheep Trail

Map pg 241 🌱 🍃 🐎 🚲

There are numerous access points for the Sheep Trail. The eastern access is at the day use area at the end of the Sandy McNabb Campground road. Alternate access can be found at Windy Point, Indian Oils and Junction Mountain day use Areas, as well as within Bluerock Campground at the western end of the Sheep River Trail (Hwy. 546).

### Route

| Route | Elevation | | Distance | |
|---|---|---|---|---|
| | metres | feet | km | mi. |
| Sandy McNabb Trailhead | 1430 | 4,690 | 0.0 | 0.0 |
| Indian Oils | 1545 | 5,068 | 16.2 | 10.1 |
| Bluerock Campground | 1600 | 5,248 | 19.2 | 11.9 |
| Burns Mine | 1785 | 5,855 | 29.7 | 18.5 |
| Tombstone Campground | 2000 | 6,560 | 42.2 | 26.2 |

The Sheep Trail begins at Sandy McNabb Campground and parallels the Sheep River all the way to its headwaters at the base of Mount Rae. For visitors to the Sheep River Valley, the trail offers a major east-west thoroughfare, providing access for the many trails radiating south from the Sheep River. The impact of cattle wandering along the soft valley bottom can be seen, as sections of the trail are badly damaged.

The trail begins in the foothills, and follows the change in landscape as the foothills give way to the Rocky Mountains. While many of the eastern sections of the trail remains in the trees, as you wander the western sections you are treated to panoramic views of the peaks of the Highwood and Misty ranges.

## Sandy McNabb Campground to Windy Point

This first leg of the Sheep Trail begins at the equestrian parking lot in Sandy McNabb Campground. Cross over the campground access road and follow the wide Sheep Trail. Stay straight as the Death Valley Trail forks off to the right. The trail wanders through pleasant aspen groves, where open slopes are often awash with flowers like the sticky geranium, prairie cro-cuses, and early yellow locoweed.

After just over 1 km (0.6 mi.), you'll pass another junction. The trail forking to the right offers access to Highway 546 and the Foran Grade Trail. Stay straight on the Sheep Trail and enjoy endless views down towards the narrow canyon of the Sheep River, as it winds its way east towards the prairies. After 3.2 km (2.0 mi.), the trail meets a junction that provides access to Highway 546 and the Windy Point trailhead.

## Windy Point to Indian Oils

From the Windy Point junction, the trail passes through a varying landscape of aspen groves and open meadow as it follows the winding course of the Sheep River. Some sections have been damaged by free-ranging cattle and may be wet and mucky. The views are pleasant, however, and the landscape rolling. One of the limiting factors on this trail is a ford of the Sheep River near the beginning. You'll need to save this section for later in the season when the water levels are lower. Beyond the ford, the trail climbs up to a bench that once held a logging camp.

You now wind to the right to cross a cutline. Beyond this, turn left to follow another cutline that trends NE-SW. The trail follows the cutline, wandering in and out of the trees for several kilometres until it meets a ford with Dyson Creek. While not very deep, it is knee-deep and can be challenging in high water. After crossing the river, climb up to a four-way junction with the old Teskey Road. Turn left and follow this road, staying right at an unsigned junction above Dyson Creek. Stay straight until you join a wide fire road. Stay right at this junction. The trail to the left fords Dyson Creek, and provides option to the Green Mountain Trail and the Junction Mountain fire lookout.

Just downstream of the Dyson Creek ford is Dyson Falls. In the 1940s, one of the companies logging along the creek used a cave behind Dyson Falls as a walk-in pantry. Animals taken by hunters would be field-dressed and the meat kept safe from scavengers in this cool recess.

Staying on the Sheep Trail, you leave the creek behind and begin to wind to the west to squeeze between a small knoll to the right and the lower slopes of Mount Hoffman on the left. Finally, you meet a junction above a bridge over the Sheep River. To exit at Indian Oils, turn right, cross the bridge and climb up to the day use area on the access road.

## Indian Oils to Bluerock Campground or Junction Mountain Day Use

As you approach the bridge over the Sheep River, stay left and take the gated trail. This section of the Sheep Trail parallels the Sheep River, just slightly out of view to the right. Along the way, you are treated to occasional views to the west towards Gibraltar Mountain. There is a ford of the Sheep River just to the west of the bridge over Bluerock Creek on Highway 546. To exit, go straight at a junction on the opposite side of the ford. If you want to continue towards Burns Mine, go left at this junction and follow the narrow trail as it makes its way to Junction Mountain day use at kilometre 19.2 (mile 11.9). You can exit the trail at Junction Mountain day use, or continue on towards Burns Mine, or even all the way to the Elbow Valley if you wish.

## Bluerock Campground to Burns Mine

From Bluerock Campground, take the signed trail that leaves Junction Mountain day use near the upper portion of the loop road. The trail follows an old access road to the Burns Mine and provides an airy, open change from the more enclosed nature of the trail to this point. In the distance looms the sheer, vertical face of Gibraltar Mountain. The slopes of Mount Shunga-la-she tower to the south, while Mount Burns rises to the northwest.

The road begins to the north of the Sheep River, but over the next 10.4 km (6.5 mi.) it will cross the Sheep River many times over shallow fords. During the first few kilometres, there are several trail junctions. The first branches to the right almost immediately and provides trail users with a shortcut to the Bluerock Creek Trail. Stay straight and follow the road as it climbs above the valley bottom. Along this well-marked road, the main route is always easy to follow as it winds beneath the summits of the Highwood Range.

At kilometre 29.7 (mile 18.5) the trail meets a slowly rotting fence and several old piles of coal. These are remnants of the Burns Coal Mine (see 'Coal Mining', page 154), which operated on this site from 1903 until 1923. It was again

worked briefly in 1944, but this venture also failed. Near the mine site, a trail branching to the south heads over Rickert's Pass to provide access to Highway 40 along the Mist Creek Trail.

## Burns Mine to the Elbow Pass Junction

Beyond the junction, the trail begins trending northwest beneath the Misty Range and towards the headwaters on Mount Rae. It finally joins the Elbow Pass Trail. From this point, trails radiate towards all four compass points, providing numerous options.

As you leave the mine site behind and continue towards Tombstone Campground, you'll need to accept the fact that you will get wet feet. Over the next 7.2 km (4 mi.) you will repeatedly cross the meandering course of the Sheep River.

After several fords, you will notice Harry Denning's cabin alongside the trail. Harry Denning was a rancher who obtained grazing rights in this area back in the 1930's. Each year he would bring his cattle up the Sheep River Valley to graze. When the old Burns Mine buildings became too dilapidated to use, he built this cabin in 1947, using locally cut logs and materials scavenged from the old Burns buildings. It was used until the last cattle drive in 1971. A sign still reads, "You are welcome to use this cabin. Leave things as you found them with a little food and dry firewood."

After several fords over the course of half a kilometre or so, the Burns Creek Exploration Road forks to the left. Stay straight at this junction.

As you approach the headwaters of the Sheep River you will cross Rae Creek, and then begin to climb towards the divide between the Elbow and Sheep drainages. Along this stretch there are numerous junctions, most heading down to the Sheep Lakes, but finally, at the 42.2-km (26.2-mi.) mark, you meet the junction with the Elbow Pass Trail to the west and the options for continuing to the Elbow Valley via The Big Elbow or Little Elbow Trails.

# Index

# Index

# Reference

## Information

### Emergency Contacts

Kananaskis Country 24 Hour Emergency Response: (403) 591-7767

R.C.M.P. 24 Hour Emergency Response: 911

Reporting Forest Fires (Call Collect) (403) 427-FIRE (3473)

Report a Poacher: 1–800–642–3800

### Tourist Information

Kananaskis Country, Box 280, Canmore, Alberta, T0L-0M0: (403) 678-5508. This office can answer most specific inquires, but for trail information contact the following information centres:

Kananaskis Valley Area Barrier Lake Visitor Information Centre: (403) 673-3985

Peter Lougheed Provincial Park: (403) 591-6322

Smith–Dorrien/Spray Trail Information Centre: (403) 591-6322

Bow Valley Provincial Park: (403) 673-3663

Elbow/Sheep Area: Elbow Valley Visitor Information Centre: (403) 949-4261

Tourism Canmore: (403) 678-1295 Web: www.tourismcanmore.com

Canmore/Kananaskis Chamber of Commerce: (403) 678-4094. They can provide general information on tourism in the Canmore/Kananaskis area.

### Accommodation

Delta Lodge at Kananaskis and Signature Club: (403) 591-7711 Web: www.deltahotels.com

Kananaskis Mountain Lodge: (403) 591-7500 Web: www.kananaskismountain-lodge.com

Mount Engadine Lodge: (403) 678-4080

Rafter Six Ranch Resort: (403) 673-3622

Kananaskis Guest Ranch: (403) 673-3737 Web: www.brewsteradventures.com/kgrhome2%20.html

Ribbon Creek Hostel: (403) 591-7333 Web: www.hostellingintl.ca/Alberta/Hostels/Ribbon.html

Canmore Bed & Breakfast Association Summer Hotline: (403)609-3399

Tourism Canmore: (403) 678-1295 Web: www.tourismcanmore.com

### Camping

see page 41

### Golfing

see pages 42 and 70

### Horse Rides/Pack Trips/Hunting

Boundary Ranch (Guinn Outfitters): (403) 591-7171

Rafter Six Ranch Resort: (403) 673-3622

M & M Ranch (Bragg Creek): (403) 949-3272 Web: www.mm-ranch.com

Anchor D Guiding & Outfitters (Black Diamond): (403) 933-2867 Web: www.anchord.com

### Rafting

Canadian Rockies Rafting: (403) 678-6535 Toll Free: 1-877-226-7625 Web: www.telus planet.net/public/canrock

Mirage Adventure Tours: (403) 678-4919 Toll Free: 1-888-312-7238 Web: www.mirage-tours.com

Rainbow Riders: (403) 850-3686 Toll Free: 1-877-717-RAFT (7238) Web: www.rainbowriders.com

Chinook River Sports: 1-800-482-4899

### Cross–country Skiing

Canmore Nordic Centre: (403) 678-2400 (page 73)

### Dog Sledding

see page 84

## Recommended Reading

Cameron, Ward. *Mountain Bike! The Canadian Rockies*, Birmingham, Alabama, Menasha Ridge Press, 2000.

Daffern, Gillean. *Kananaskis Country Trail Guide Volumes I and II*. Calgary, Alberta: Rocky Mountain Books, 1997.

Eastcott, Doug. *Backcountry Biking in the Canadian Rockies*. Calgary, Alberta: Rocky Mountain Books, 1999.

Fisher, Chris. *Birds of the Rocky Mountains*. Edmonton, Alberta: Lone Pine Publishing, 1997.

Gadd, Ben. *Handbook of the Canadian Rockies*. Jasper, Alberta: Corax Press, 1995.

Godfrey, Earl W. *The Birds of Canada*. Ottawa, Ontario: Supply and Services Canada, 1976.

Hallworth, Beryl and Chinnappa, C.C.. *Plants of Kananaskis Country in the Rocky Mountains of Alberta*. Calgary, Alberta, The University of Calgary Press, 1997.

Herrero, Stephen. *Bear Attacks—Their Causes and Avoidance*. New York, New York: Winchester Press, 1985.

Kananaskis Country. *The Kananaskis Country Environmental Education Library*. Canmore, Alberta: Kananaskis Country, c. 1988.

Karamitsanis, Aphrodite. *Place Names of Alberta—Volume 1…Mountains, Mountain Parks and Foothills*. Calgary, Alberta: University of Calgary Press, 1991.

Kershaw, Linda, MacKinnon, Andy and Pojar, Jim, *Plants of the Rocky Mountains*. Edmonton, Alberta, Lone Pine Publishing, 1998.

McGillivray, W Bruce and Semenchuk, Glen P. *The Federation of Alberta Naturalists Field Guide to Alberta Birds.* Edmonton, Alberta: Federation of Alberta Naturalists, 1998.

Oltmann, C. Ruth. *The Valley of Rumours...the Kananaskis.* Seebe, Alberta: Ribbon Creek Publishing Co., 1976.

Scoter, George W. and Flygare, Hälle, *Wildflowers of the Canadian Rockies.* Edmonton, Alberta: Hurtig Publishers, 1986.

Sheep River Historical Society. *In The Light of the Flares.* Turner Valley, Alberta: Friesen Printers, 1979.

## Acknowledgements

Special thanks to Susan Cameron, who gave the author the strength and encouragement to keep going. Many thanks to the following people for their invaluable assistance in the completion of this book: Ian Waugh, Eric Kuhn, Ron Chamney, and Scott Maier of Kananaskis Country, The Staff of the Kananaskis Visitor Centre, The Whyte Museum of the Canadian Rockies, The Glenbow Museum Archives, The Canmore Centennial Museum, Mike Mitrovic of Mirage Sports, Jules Leboeuf of the Alberta Forest Service, Laurieanne Lynne of Shell Canada,

## Photographic Credits

All photographs are taken by the author except:

**Canmore Centennial Museum**
65, 66 (top & bottom)
**Glenbow Archives, Calgary, Alberta**
34 (NA-2736-1), 35 (NA-4139-3), 36 (NA-4002-16), 37 (NA-5124-22), 95 (NA-4824-2), 107 (NA-695-32), 114 (NA-695-1), 115 (NA-695-39), 145 (NA-2468-36), 146 (NA-695-29), 147 (NA-152-1), 152 (NA-4386-1)
**Don Harmon**
15
**Kananaskis Country Photo Collection**
50, 55, 57
**Donna Jo Massie Collection**
74 (left & right)
**Dennis Schmidt**
front cover (inset left), 19, 22 (top right), 24 (top middle), 25 (top right, middle right), 26 (top right, top middle, middle left), 27 (left & right), 28 (left & middle), 94 (bottom), 130, 131, 135, 157, 202
**Esther Schmidt**
24 (top left), 25 (top left, top middle, bottom right), 26 (top left, bottom left), 27 (middle), 28 (right), 29 (middle), 123, 141 (bottom), 208
**Stone Creek Properties**
70 (left)
**TGS Properties**
70 (right)
**Whyte Museum of the Canadian Rockies**
72

## About the Author

*Ward Cameron*

**Ward Cameron** has spent many years in the Kananaskis. In 1983, he was hired as an Interpretive Naturalist. In 1986, he began helping in the management of the various information Centres within the boundaries of Kananaskis Country. He left the public service in 1989 to work as a freelance naturalist and historian, and since that time has spent an increasing amount of time showing groups the riches of the Kananaskis.

His photographs routinely appear in Kananaskis Country brochures and posters. He has done extensive work as a photographer and author for Travel Alberta. In order to sell his photographs, Ward began writing magazine articles. This has now expanded into a growing writing business. For five years, he wrote a weekly natural and human history column for the Canmore Leader newspaper, and currently writes feature articles for a variety of magazines. He is the author of two other guidebooks on the Canadian west entitled: "Mountain Bike! The Canadian Rockies" and "Mountain Bike! Southwestern British Columbia". Ward has expanded his writing to the internet, and his web site: www.mountainnature.com is an online guide to the nature of the Rocky Mountains.

Another focus falls in the area of storytelling. The history of the west is filled with adventure, and Ward uses these stories to excite and motivate visitors to the Rockies. As Ward puts it: "The history may be short, but there's no shortage of history!"